D1083055

Psychoanalysis
&
American
Literary
Criticism

PSYCHOANALYSIS

AMERICAN

LITERARY

CRITICISM

Louis Fraiberg

OCTAGON BOOKS

A DIVISION OF FARRAR, STRAUS AND GIROUX

New York   1974

Reprinted 1974
by special arrangement with Wayne State University Press

OCTAGON BOOKS
A DIVISION OF FARRAR, STRAUS & GIROUX, INC.
19 Union Square West
New York, N. Y. 10003

Library of Congress Cataloging in Publication Data

Fraiberg, Louis Benjamin, 1913-
    Psychoanalysis & American literary criticism.

    Reprint of the ed. published by Wayne State University Press,
    Detroit.

    1. American literature—20th century—History and criticism.
    2. Criticism—United States.   3. Psychoanalysis and literature.
    4. Psychoanalysis.   I. Title.
[PS78.F7   1974]   810'.9'3   74-12171
ISBN 0-374-92837-1

Printed in USA by
Thomson-Shore, Inc.
Dexter, Michigan

To Selma

ACKNOWLEDGMENTS

To Beacon Press for permission to quote from Lionel Trilling, Freud and the Crisis of our Culture *(2nd printing, 1955).*

To Dodd, Mead and Co., Inc. for permission to quote from Sigmund Freud, Delusion and Dream, *originally published by Moffat, Yard & Co. (1917).*

To E. P. Dutton and Co., Inc. for permission to quote from Van Wyck Brooks, The Ordeal of Mark Twain *(1920).*

To George Allen & Unwin, Ltd. for permission to quote from Sigmund Freud, The Interpretation of Dreams *(1st Modern Library edition, 1950).*

To Hogarth Press and Basic Books for permission to quote from Sigmund Freud, Collected Papers *(1946).*

To the Macmillan Company and the Hogarth Press for permission to quote from Sigmund Freud, "Group Psychology and the Analysis of the Ego," in the Standard Edition of the Complete Psychological Works of Sigmund Freud *(1955).*

To Imago Publishing Co., Ltd. and Hogarth Press for permission to translate from Sigmund Freud, Aus den Anfängen der Psychoanalyse *(1950).*

To International Universities Press, Inc. for permission to quote from Ernst Kris, Psychoanalytic Explorations in Art *(1952).*

To Joseph Wood Krutch for permission to quote from his book, Edgar Allan Poe, *published by Alfred A. Knopf, Inc. (1926).*

To Liveright Publishing Corporation for permission to quote from Sigmund Freud, A General Introduction to Psychoanalysis *(1943).*

To Louisiana State University Press for quotations from Kenneth Burke, The Philosophy of Literary Form *(1941).*

To W. W. Norton and Co., Inc. for permission to quote from Ernest Jones, Hamlet and Oedipus *(1949).*

To Oxford University Press for quotations from Edmund Wilson, The Wound and the Bow *(1947).*

To Mrs. Louise Lewisohn for permission to quote from Ludwig Lewisohn, The Story of American Literature *(1st Modern Library edition, 1939), published by Random House, Inc.*

To Random House for permission to quote from Sigmund Freud, Leonardo da Vinci *(1947).*

To Sci-Art Publishers for permission to quote from Hanns Sachs, The Creative Unconscious *(1942).*

To Viking Press, Inc. for permission to quote from Lionel Trilling, The Liberal Imagination *(1950) and* The Opposing Self *(1955).*

ERRATUM

Page 44, lines 21 and 32 have been incorrectly transposed in printing.

Line 21 should read: "The emotional life moves in the direction of normality and . . ."

Line 32 should read: "The artist seeks primarily his own inner tranquillity. In this . . ."

PREFACE

I have been able to combine two interests in writing this book. My study of psychoanalysis had led me to look for ways in which it could contribute to my understanding of literature, and I began to read the work of men who had been described to me as "psychoanalytic" critics. It soon became evident that the term covered a variety of attitudes toward psychoanalysis, a diversity of uses and even disagreement as to what it was. As I read further I found statements attributed to Freud that, to my knowledge, he had never made, statements, moreover, that contradicted the teachings of psychoanalysis as I understood it. In addition there were juxtapositions and interconnected uses of the ideas of Freud and other psychologists (e.g., Jung) who had taken paths so divergent that their concepts were actually incompatible. These discrepancies called for an explanation. Therefore, when the opportunity arose to devote considerable time to an investigation of the problem, I welcomed it.

It was clear that the key to its solution lay in a detailed examination of critical writings which had made use of Freud's ideas, but in view of the disagreements I had found, it seemed necessary first to set forth what those ideas were. This did not prove to be simple. No comprehensive statement of his views on literature had ever been made by Freud, and the only way to remedy this deficiency was to read the whole of his published work. While engaged in this demanding and rewarding task I saw that a fairly large number of his books and papers—not only those in which he addressed himself specifically to matters of art—were relevant to my purpose. Accordingly, I have incorporated into the first chapter everything which seemed to bear on the subject even when it was originally written with something else in mind. This has incidentally resulted in an exposition of psychoanalysis as Freud conceived it, although it is by no means a complete account because large tracts of clinical and theoretical material have had to be neglected or subordinated to my immediate needs. The purpose of the chapter, of course, is not to describe all the ramifications of psychoanalysis but merely to report and explain the meaning of Freud's ideas for art.

Since Freud's writings are not the whole of psychoanalysis, I also read the relevant works of his chief colleagues and made appropriate selections from them. These, together with the chapter on Freud, constitute a summary of the concern of classical psychoanalysis with art from the beginning up to the present day and make up the first part of the book. Its function is to provide the scientific background for the critical studies which follow.

I chose Freudian psychoanalysis as promulgated by its founder and as further developed by men who shared his conception of it—what I have called classical psychoanalysis—for several reasons. It is the original and, I believe, the most important form taken by this seminal idea, incomplete though it is. It is the source of a number of psychological schools, some psychoanalytic and some not, which have had influence on literature and criticism and which are not always sufficiently distinguished from it. It is the psychology, especially in the form of Freud's published books, which was most used by the critics I have studied. Finally, there is a distinct advantage in adhering to a consistent body of scientific fact and theory: It helps to maintain clarity in the discussion by providing a standard definition of psychoanalysis against which the critics' understanding of it may be measured.

Having established as best I could the classical psychoanalytic views of the psyche and of art, I next examined the writings of six prominent critics who used these or related ideas. I chose American critics partly because Freudian ideas received such a warm reception in this country and partly because the American frame of reference helps lend unity to the book. To have ranged into European criticism—which I was tempted to do—would have made this undertaking far more difficult than it was. Perhaps such a study will be undertaken some day. I hope it will, but I have already seen enough to suspect that it will confirm my findings, with allowances for local and individual differences.

To enhance the validity of the study I selected critics who had considerable standing and who had used Freudian ideas in more than just a casual way. I looked particularly for any attempt to utilize them in a systematic formulation of critical theory. The six whom I picked represent critical practice in America during the two important phases of public awareness of psychoanalysis, the periods of emphasis on the id and the ego, respectively.

I wish to acknowledge my indebtedness to a number of people who have been of material assistance in the planning, writing and producing of this book: To Professor Norman Nelson, University of Michigan, who, by taking nothing for granted, compelled me to defend my convictions about psychoanalysis and thus enabled me to reaffirm them on an even more solid basis. He was instrumental in arranging conditions that made it possible for me to write on the subject of my choice, and he offered not only stimulating challenge but encouragement all the way. To Associate Professors Morris Greenhut and Allan Seager, University of Michigan, especially for their painstaking scrutiny of the chapters on criticism and their suggestions for improvements. To Dr. Frederick Wyatt, Chief of the Bureau of Psychological Services, and Dr. Herbert Schmale, Chief, Department of Neuropsychiatry, University Hospital, both of the University of Michigan, for their assistance in insuring the accuracy of the psychoanalytic material. To Dr. Harold A. Basilius, Director of the Wayne State University Press, for his scholarly interest and his friendly reception of the book. To Mrs. Esther Ellen Jacoby, editor, for her understanding and capable editing. My thanks to all of them would be ambiguous indeed if I did not at the same time absolve them of responsibility for any shortcomings this book may have.

Besides these there are others who influenced the book indirectly: Dr. Richard Sterba and Dr. Editha Sterba whose psychoanalytic seminars I was privileged for some years to attend; Dr.

Alexander Grinstein who gave me bibliographical assistance; the late Robert Wayne who checked my translation; and Dr. Mildred Peters who accompanied my wife and me in profitable and enjoyable studies of the development of psychoanalytic ego psychology.

Finally, I wish to record my thanks and appreciation to my wife, Selma.

L. F.

CONTENTS

I. Freud's Writings on Art

1

II. Ernest Jones and the Psychoanalytic Interpretation of Hamlet

47

III. Hanns Sachs: The Creative Act

64

IV. Ernst Kris: Ego Psychology and Art

90

V. Van Wyck Brooks versus Mark Twain versus Samuel Clemens

120

VI. Joseph Wood Krutch:
Poe's Art as an Abnormal Condition of the Nerves

134

VII. Ludwig Lewisohn
and the Puritan Inhibition of American Literature

145

VIII. Edmund Wilson and Psychoanalysis in Historical Criticism

161

IX. Kenneth Burke's Terminological Medium of Exchange

183

X. Lionel Trilling's Creative Extension of Freudian Concepts

202

XI. Summary

225

Notes

241

Index

259

I

Freud's Writings on Art *

OF ALL the scientific disciplines psychoanalysis has most in common with art. Both seek an understanding of the human spirit by directly observing man's actions and words as manifestations of his innermost needs conditioned by the exigencies of his body and of the world he lives in. Art, of course, is wider-ranging than any branch of science, for it explores not only the secrets of personality but the moral significance of the universe. Psychoanalysis, not so ambitious, restricts itself to what man perceives, imagines and feels. It does not attempt the problem of the cosmos but merely that of man's conception of the cosmos. Its concern with art is not with the nature of the beautiful but with what man considers beautiful and with why he so considers it. There is no fully developed psychoanalytic theory of aesthetics, although there are psychoanalytic studies of some of the constituent elements of aesthetic experiences. Psychoanalysis is aware of its limitations as a branch of biology whose special province is the scientific study of mental functioning. Any theories which it offers to explain phenomena, especially outside these limits, are intended to be taken as proposals subject to clinical verification and not as dogmatic assertions of revealed truth.

* This chapter, in shortened form, was originally printed in the *International Journal of Psycho-Analysis*, XXXVII, Part I (January–February 1956). A later adaptation appeared in *Literature and Psychology* VI, No. 4 (November 1956).

Without invading the territory of the philosophers by judging the intrinsic worth or weakness of the moral law, psychoanalysis exercises the right to investigate it as something which man has produced and which therefore can, when properly comprehended, throw light upon his mental life. From this standpoint it is similarly interested in law, politics, education, religion— and even in itself. The evaluation of man's life and works in philosophical, social, economic or anthropological terms it leaves to the appropriate disciplines. It wishes to know only out of what psychic needs they arose, what psychic materials they use, how they use these and what psychic purpose they fulfill. Every human thought or action is made to serve as a lens which, when correctly focused, will make visible its psychic origins and the paths of its development. Art, too, is accessible to such study.

Looked at in this way it discloses a great deal about those experiences of the artist which have achieved artistic expression and about their communication, by the medium of art, to others. Art is a record of the gifted; it translates events and the artist's reflections upon them into forms by which they can be transmitted symbolically. But it is not simply a message in code. It preserves (in modified form) and creates again and again on demand an experience, or rather the aesthetic equivalent of an experience, which has brought satisfaction to its author and is capable of bringing a corresponding pleasure to its audience. Literature, whose medium, like that of psychoanalysis, is language, lends itself readily to scientific investigation without the necessity of constructing a new symbolic foundation; while Freud was interested in other arts, notably painting and sculpture,[1] it is not surprising that he freely and familiarly used literature and its auxiliaries, biography and criticism, to support and illustrate his psychology.

Although Freud never produced a complete exposition on the subject of art, contenting himself with occasional passing references to it and with a few considerations of specific works and artists, the scattered fragments gathered together here display complete consistency with the principles of psychoanalysis as it developed during his lifetime. A proper understanding of his writings on art, therefore, requires a grasp of nothing less than the whole of psychoanalysis. This is true not only because what he wrote specifically about art requires a background in psychoanalysis but also because many of the psychoanalytic concepts which he never applied to artistic problems himself nevertheless have such applicability.

From the earliest days of psychoanalysis to the end of his career Freud turned frequently to literary art and to the lives of literary men for elucidation and example. The small number of workers in the new field—for a number of years Freud was the only psychoanalyst—meant that the quantity of clinical information was small; additions from non-clinical but reliable sources were welcome. But more important than that was the growing isolation in which Freud found himself after the violent initial rejection—without benefit of scientific checking—of his discovery that the psychoneuroses had a sexual origin. Whether he intended it so or not, there is no doubt that literary corroboration of certain psychoanalytic observations lent some of the prestige of established art to the embryonic science which was undergoing the painful but apparently inevitable process of being first unreasoningly attacked and thereafter consigned to limbo. The world did not thank him for disturbing its sleep; he withdrew from the struggle and consoled himself with advancing his work, at first alone, later with a few followers. To this consolation literature also contributed.

Breuer, Freud's collaborator in *Studies in Hysteria,* was actually the first to mention a literary figure in published psychoanalytic writing.[2] In a discussion of the tendency of affects to seek discharge when the feeling of tension became sufficiently strong, he wrote: "Goethe was never through with an experience until he settled it in some poetic activity; to him this was the preformed reflex of an affect, and as long as it was not accomplished, he suffered from a painful enhancement of excitement."[3] Breuer's use here of a literary figure was similar to Freud's. It illustrated, almost casually, a scientific point and was obviously regarded as an example which would be familiar to its readers.

Freud, too, found apt parallels in literature. One of the earliest was Othello's outburst of rage at Desdemona's loss of the handkerchief. He used this to illustrate the process of displacement of affect in which "ideas of feeble potential, by taking over the charge from ideas which have a stronger initial potential, reach a degree of intensity which enables them to force their way into consciousness." [4] Art, of course, was not Freud's sole reliance for illustrative material; he gave several other, non-literary, examples in the same passage. He often employed it, however, to supplement extra-clinical observations as well as the direct products of psychoanalytic research.

The appearance of an ambitious wish and the accompanying fantasy of its fulfillment during one of his dream interpretations gives him occasion to remark in passing that, "Shakespeare's Prince Hal cannot rid himself of the temptation to see how the crown fits, even at the bedside of his sick father." [5] He seeks support for his view of the nature of daydreams, which is not wholly in agreement with that of the psychiatrists of his day, by reminding his readers that "the significance of the daydream has not escaped the unerring insight of the poets," and cites an example from Alphonse Daudet's *Nabob*.[6]

The high regard Freud felt for the psychological acuity of artists often appears in his works. Not only does he praise them for their accurate observations but he also frequently gives them credit for discovering certain phenomena before these became evident to scientists, himself included. When such intuition had anticipated his own findings he acknowledged its priority. His "disconcerting discovery" that the very earliest experiences have a strong influence upon later life, for instance, was also to be found in E. T. A. Hoffmann who

> used to explain the wealth of imaginative figures that offered themselves to him for his stories by the quickly changing pictures and impressions he had received during a journey in a post-chaise, lasting for several weeks, while he was still a babe at his mother's breast.[7]

Freud was not jealous of priority, and was not only fair but extremely generous in his acknowledgement of the work of others.[8]

The psychological observations of the artist, however, are not the direct equivalent of those of the psychologist. The differences in the situation and the intent of the two are great. We shall see that Freud did not take every such report at face value. His psychoanalytic experiences had taught him caution and given him remarkable skill in estimating the objective reliability of such data.

When properly evaluated, however, they were often useful. Freud used a letter of Schiller's, which explained the necessity of removing the constraining effect of the intellect in order to permit the unhampered functioning of poetic imagination, to elucidate his description of the relative ease with which both he and his patients attained an uncritical state of self-observation.[9] The technique of free associaton, like the literary method recommended by Schiller, consists essentially in first allowing ideas to rise to consciousness while all conscious judgment of them is deliberately suspended, and only afterward subjecting them to moral, aesthetic, or other scrutiny. It is necessary first to assemble the raw material; premature discrimination may prevent it from emerging at all.

Freud followed the practice of drawing upon literary sources throughout his life. In his last book he turns to literary biography for an illustration of the return of the repressed, with the remark that "even the great Goethe, who in his *Sturm und Drang* period certainly did not respect his pedantic and stiff father very highly, developed in old age traits that belonged to his father's character." [10]

These scattered specimens show the frequency and readiness with which literature and its auxiliaries occurred to Freud as illustrative matter for his often difficult expositions. Most of his examples were taken from dreams, jokes, myths, customs, or the mental phenomena of everyday life, but art, especially literature, supplied a natural abundance of materials.

Of greater significance than such casual allusions was the active enlistment of the psychological insights of artists in support of psychoanalytic findings. We have noted that Freud considered artists better able than ordinary mortals to see into human motivations and actions. The accuracy and keenness of their observations was so high that it frequently permitted him to use their creations in much the same way that he used clinical records. The two are, of course, not exactly equivalent, and Freud was careful to distinguish between fictional and "scientific" elements in the material he chose. Within limits, however, the practice was valid, and proved useful as long as confusion of the real with the contrived was avoided.

Slips of the tongue, although popularly regarded as accidental and meaningless, nevertheless had a meaning whose import had not escaped the poets, for, as Freud shows by examples from Schiller's *Wallenstein* and Shakespeare's *The Merchant of Venice,* they sometimes constructed such slips intentionally.[11] The character into whose mouth a slip was put was thus represented as blurting out something which he was consciously trying to conceal, precisely what happens in everyday life.

Freud went further. He wrote that even if slips did not have the significance which he attributed to them, "poets would still be entitled to refine them by infusing sense into them for their own purposes. However, it would not be surprising if more were to be learned from poets about slips of the tongue than from philologists and psychiatrists." [12] Even granting the artist's license to modify reality for aesthetic purposes, Freud found in literature a discernment and an honesty which were not always present in the work of the psychiatrists of his day. Many of them had closed their minds to the phenomena which artists and others had observed and which psychoanalysts were now beginning to study systematically. The reports of the poets, moreover, were frequently found to be in accord with what had been ascertained clinically, as in the matter of slips of the tongue.

Poetic insights could be much more complex than this and still retain their validity, as Freud was able to demonstrate strikingly in the work of Wilhelm Jensen, a minor romancer, whose *Gradiva: A Pompeiian Fancy* unwittingly corroborated the psychoanalytic view of dreams and delusions. Freud's masterpiece, *The Interpretation of Dreams,* had been completed in all its essentials in the early part of 1896, although it was not written down until 1899 and not published until the following year. *Gradiva* appeared in 1903. When Jung brought it to his attention Freud found its correspondence with his theories to be so close that he published a psychoanalytic study of its characters.[13] His main point, worked out in elaborate detail, is that dreams and other mental processes contrived by writers for literary purposes, when drawn as directly as possible from the inner springs of the creative imagination, present the same picture of psychic life that psychoanalysis does. Allowance must, of course, be made for mutations which the material undergoes in the aesthetic process. "I have made use of this agreement between my investigations and the creations of the poet," wrote Freud, "as a proof of the correctness of my method of dream-analysis." [14] From this point of view "Delusion and Dream" may be regarded as a supplement to *The Interpretation of Dreams*, but it also casts light upon certain artistic problems.

The first of these problems is whether fictional dreams have any real meaning at all. Freud's answer is that they do:

> For when [authors] cause the people created by their imagination to dream, they follow the common experience that people's thoughts and feelings continue into sleep, and they seek only to depict the psychic states of their heroes through the dreams of the latter. Story tellers are valuable allies, and their testimony is to be rated high, for they usually know many things between heaven and earth that our academic wisdom does not even dream of. In psychic knowledge, indeed, they are far ahead of us ordinary people because they draw from sources that we have not yet made accessible for science.[15]

Freud holds that writers possess a heightened sensitivity that enables them to apprehend their own psychic processes more readily than most people can. The dreams which they invent come from the same sources as real dreams and are therefore subject to the laws which govern the latter, with the single and important qualification that such invented dreams are at the same time subject to the laws of artistic necessity. In the analysis of a fictional dream these two aspects must be sharply distinguished and each set of laws applied only to its appropriate portions of the dream. Psychic reality and aesthetic reality may be mingled but should never be confused. It follows, then, that the dream devised by an author, if it is not distorted by extraneous forces, has validity not only for the imaginary character who "dreams" it but for science as well.

The same holds true for other mental processes—delusions, for instance:

> One could raise only one more question: why the author [Jensen] should introduce a dream for further development of the delusion. Well, I think that is very cleverly arranged and again keeps faith with reality. We have already heard that in actual illness the formation of a delusion is very often connected with a dream, but after our explanation of the nature of dreams we need find no new riddle in this fact. Dreams and delusions spring from the same source, the repressed; the dream is, so to speak, the physiological delusion of the normal human being.[16]

Even the method by which the clever heroine cures the hero of his delusion "shows a considerable resemblance, no, complete agreement, essentially, with [psychoanalysis]." [17] Such remarkable accord could not be dismissed as mere coincidence.

At this point there naturally arose the problem whether Jensen knew Freud's theories when he wrote *Gradiva*. The question was accordingly put to him and "our author answered, as was to be expected, in the negative, and rather testily." [18] Perhaps by that time he had heard of them. Freud later obtained much the same reply—minus the testiness—from Stephan Zweig, who was a personal friend of his. Zweig assured him that he was not aware of any scientific foundation for the psychic details in one of his stories although to Freud it seemed almost as if these details had been deliberately intended to provide clues to its interpretation.[19] Evidently the adherence of an author to the principles of mental functioning need not be conscious; his intuition is often enough. Even if he denies all knowledge of the rules, and protests that he did not have the intentions which are imputed to him, Freud holds that his good faith need not be questioned: "We are probably drawing from the same source, working over the same material, each of us with a different method, and agreement in results seems to vouch for the fact that both have worked correctly." [20] Instead of inhibiting his fantasies by the exercise of his critical faculties the author has permitted them to achieve artistic expression. The actions of his characters embody the laws of the mind's operation whether he has learned them consciously or otherwise, whether he is aware of knowing them or not.

With the final product before him the psychoanalyst is often able to traverse the same path from its end back to its beginning, thus arriving at the author's sources in the psyche. In this way the laws of mental functioning may be demonstrated from an examination of fiction just as they may be from an analysis of any human production which provides enough clues. There is nothing surprising in this. The writer has always searched for and described the inner story of man, and he has shown a high degree of accuracy in doing so. "The portrayal of the psychic life of human beings is, of course, his most especial domain; he was always the precursor of science and of scientific psychology." [21] The same theme, therefore, may legitimately be investigated by both author and psychologist. The aesthetic requirements of its treatment by the former sometimes results in changes from what has been observed or in departures from probability which either destroy or greatly minimize its clinical value, but the scientist must, like everyone else, freely grant the artist's license. It is possible, however, for a theme from psychology to be used unchanged in literature without detracting from its aesthetic effectiveness. In this respect science need not necessarily interfere with art. The ability of the psychologist to discriminate between artistic insights which may be used to supplement clinical observations and those which have been aesthetically altered is the prerequisite for a study such as Freud made of *Gradiva*.

The most famous instance of the psychological keenness of writers is the regular appearance in world literature of the dramatic theme whose psychoanalytic manifestation Freud named the Oedipus complex. Though he gradually came to see its ubiquity in human affairs he was puzzled by the poets' choice or invention of "such a terrible subject" and by its great effectiveness in dramatic form.

> But all of this became intelligible when one realized that a universal law of mental life had here been captured in all its emotional significance. Fate and the oracle were no more than materializations of an internal necessity; and the fact of the hero sinning without his knowledge and against his intentions was evidently a right expression of the *unconscious* nature of his criminal tendencies.[22]

The discovery of the Oedipus complex had arisen out of Freud's self-analysis and had been confirmed by his work with his patients; by 1897 he held it to be "a universal occurrence of early childhood."

> If this is so, then one can understand the moving power of King Oedipus in spite of all the objections which are raised against the destiny-hypothesis by our critical faculty. . . . The Greek saga fastens upon one compulsion with which everyone is familiar for he has felt its existence within himself. Each person in the audience was once potentially and in fantasy such an Oedipus, and before the distorted dream-fulfillment which is thus brought into reality everyone shudders back with the full force of the repression.
>
> The question has passed briefly through my mind whether the same thing may not be fundamentally true of Hamlet. I am not thinking of Shakespeare's conscious intention, but rather believe that an actual experience of the poet impelled him to the production in which the unconscious in him understood the unconscious in his hero. How does the hysteric, Hamlet, justify the remark, "Thus conscience does make cowards of us all," how does he, the same man who unconcernedly sends his courtiers to their deaths and actually impetuously murders Laertes [*Sic*. It is of course Polonius who is meant.], explain his delay in avenging the murder of his father by his uncle? [23]

Freud concludes that Hamlet's arm is held back by his unconscious sense that he is guilty of wishing for the very things that Claudius has achieved, the death of his father and the possession of his mother. He cannot punish Claudius; vengeance would be almost like suicide. Freud conjectured that the actual writing of *Hamlet* was motivated by an event in Shakespeare's life, namely the death of his father, which reactivated his dormant infantile feelings. Later he added to this the effect of the death of Shakespeare's son, Hamnet, with nearly the same name as the play's hero. There is no direct evidence for this, but clinical experience lends considerable weight to the guess since such a sequence has many parallels in psychoanalytic research.

*   *   *

Although the needed information from Shakespeare's life is not available to confirm this speculation, we are more fortunate regarding other writers. One of the most fascinating applications of psychoanalysis which suggested itself to Freud was the study of the lives of artists and the reconstruction by its aid of certain meagerly documented episodes from them. He had already shown in his analysis of *Gradiva* that dreams invented by writers are to be regarded psychoanalytically like real dreams.[24] He extended this kind of research further in the case of four important artists, Shakespeare, Goethe, Dostoevsky, and Leonardo da Vinci.

His essays toward the elucidation of Shakespeare's life and character are fragmentary and tentative, occurring only in scattered passages throughout his writings and nowhere systematically developed. Their gist has already been given. From the death of Hamnet the chain of association led naturally to the theme of childlessness which Freud saw as underlying *Macbeth*. He analyzed the play from this standpoint [25] but did not propose any further connections with the psychic life of the playwright. The only other surmise of this nature which Freud made was the remark that

> the sexual aversion which Hamlet expresses in conversation with Ophelia is perfectly consistent with this deduction [that Hamlet is a hysteric]—the same sexual aversion which during the next few years was increasingly to take possession of the poet's soul until it found its supreme utterance in *Timon of Athens*.[26]

Beyond these he does not go. He is careful to state that more than one level of interpretation is possible, and indeed necessary, before a work of art can be understood properly. Ideally, every one of the poet's motives should be comprehended, although practically this goal cannot be attained. Here he is attempting to deal with "only the deepest stratum of impulses" in Shakespeare's mind.

Next Freud investigated an incident which Goethe reported as having occurred when he was about three and a half years old.[27] This was solely an exercise in biography; no attempt was made to find any connection between it and Goethe's writings. It dealt with one facet of a child's reaction to the birth of a sibling. One day while playing in the garden-yard by himself he suddenly threw into the street a small earthenware toy dish, part of a set which had been given to him when the family had bought a supply of new ones for the household. He was delighted with the way it broke into bits, and threw all the others after it. Egged on by three neighbor boys, he ran into the house, fetched a load of dishes from the kitchen, and broke them in the same way. He continued this destruction until a grown-up arrived and stopped him. Freud interpreted the act as a symbolic aggression against the parents for having brought his little sister into the house as a rival for their affections and as a wish to rid himself of the intruder as well. In addition, it signified that the poet regarded himself as a child of fortune to whom such things had no right to happen, an attitude which had a favorable influence upon his subsequent success.

In studying the screen memory of the vulture fantasy from the diary of Leonardo da Vinci, Freud likewise disclaimed any intention of doing any more than simply explaining the psychological material before him. Though making some provocative suggestions concerning the relation of Leonardo's character to his art, he restricted his aim to demonstrating connections between the artist's outer experiences and the paths of his instinctual activity, as he had done with Goethe. But he could not resist the temptation to remark, in an allusion to Leonardo's "Two Mothers": "It does seem, however, as if only a man with Leonardo's childhood experiences could have painted Mona Lisa and Saint Anne. . . . It seems as if the key to all his attainments and failures was hidden in the childhood fantasy of the vulture." [28] And the essay does try to account for his alternation between art and science. Nevertheless, despite these nibblings at the psychology of aesthetics, its primary purpose was to explore the artist's character; the other was explicitly ruled out as unprovable, but "even if psychoanalysis does not explain to us the fact of Leonardo's artistic accomplishment, it still gives us an understanding of its expressions and limitations." [29] Though the subject was an artist, artistic considerations were here subordinated to biographical ones.

Dostoevsky, too, is studied from the same standpoint. Freud announces at the outset that "before the problem of the creative artist analysis must, alas, lay down its arms." [30] The essay is confined to the study of Dostoevsky's motivations as learned from his biographies and echoed in his choice of material in the novels, which is attributed to his "sympathy by identification." This goes far beyond ordinary sympathy or pity:

> A criminal is to him almost a Redeemer who has taken on himself the guilt which must else have been borne by others. There is no longer any need for one to murder, since *he* has already murdered; and one must be grateful to him for, except for him, one would have been obliged oneself to murder.[31]

After making its reluctant and disguised appearance in stories first of common, then of political, and later of religious crime, the impulse toward father-murder emerged near the end of Dostoevsky's life as the theme of *The Brothers Karamazov*, which was used by the novelist, says Freud, "for making his confession."

Freud's studies of these individual artists are primarily analyses of behavior and inner motivations. The focus is upon these and not upon problems of art, with the single major exception of the reasons why the artist elects to treat certain themes. In some places Freud is forced to rely solely upon an informed guess, that is, a conjecture which, his psychoanalytic experience tells him, has a high probability. In others the extra-psychoanalytic evidence is also very strong and the two reinforce each other. When the limits of likelihood appear to have been reached, as in the analysis of Lady Macbeth, Freud is careful to say so plainly and to disclaim any further speculation. But he obviously feels that he is on solid ground when he can adduce clinical records of his own or of other analysts to fill in gaps in the biographies of writers or to justify a synthesis of otherwise unconnected biographical material. This is wholly in accord with the conception that the psychic life of all individuals conforms to ascertainable principles, many of which had already been discovered by Freud. His method is sound where complete information exists or where it is fragmentary but can be rounded out from scientifically reliable sources. The results, as indicated, show that the artist is a gifted and sensitive person, sometimes neurotic and sometimes not, but governed by the same inner forces that rule the rest of mankind.

*   *   *

Besides the study of artists' lives Freud now and then occupied himself with the examination of certain works of art from the standpoint of their manifest content and what this revealed about the latent impulses which had in part motivated their creation. He was interested not only in the inner life of the artist but also in the artistic treatment of certain themes whose appearance in his patients he was studying psychoanalytically. He had found them also in legend and mythology and was intrigued by the fact that writers and plastic artists had often dealt with the same basic material. Since he valued the insight of their creators into motivation and behavior he scrutinized these works with a clinical eye, proceeding in a manner analogous to the technique of dream interpretation or the analysis of neurotic symptoms in order to find, if he could, what lay behind the finished product. The results further corroborated his psychoanalytic discoveries.

His methods were applicable equally to literature, painting and sculpture, studies in the latter two being of particular interest. Starting with a childhood memory recorded in the journal of Leonardo da Vinci and utilizing material from the artist's life, the writings of art critics, the history of Renaissance Italy, mythology and his own psychological data he reconstructed the probable basic pattern of Leonardo's psychic life and traced its influence upon his career as reflected in his works. Freud showed how the investigative impulse became unusually strong in the artist's childhood, how it entered the service of his art, how later it dominated and finally replaced it so that for a time Leonardo was a scientist and engineer rather than a painter, and how in the later years it subsided to permit painting once more.

He described the fascination of Mona Lisa's smile and suggested the possibility that it was a reminder to Leonardo of the smile of his own mother, which appeared again in the picture of Saint John and on the faces of both women in the painting of Saint Anne, Mary and the Holy Infant. Freud interpreted the latter as an unconsciously motivated representation of Leonardo's real mother, the peasant woman who had borne him illegitimately, and of his father's barren wife who had taken the boy from her and brought him up in her husband's home. The childhood group of two mothers and infant son was an idealization of Leonardo's own history, both real and fantasied—the father is conspicuously absent. No less significant was the portrait of the handsome youth, Saint John, with the same enigmatic conformation of the mouth. The power which enabled Leonardo to use his skill as artist and scientist in the way that he did was attributed by Freud to his legacy of love from his mother, the happiness of which remained always with him, although sometimes hidden or finding expression in strangely turned fashion. Childhood memories and fantasies, mythology, religion and the conventions of Renaissance portraiture are integrated effectively in these paintings. All can contribute their clues to our psychic understanding.

Sculpture yielded even more than painting in the case of Michelangelo's statue of Moses, even though here the biography of the artist was of less assistance. A close examination of the work itself, which Freud greatly admired, produced all the necessary information. The method used was an adaptation of one suggested by the art critic, Ivan Lermolieff, who had developed a technique for determining the genuineness of paintings by carefully scrutinizing details rather than by the overall conception. By comparing the treatment of ear lobes, fingernails, and such trivia he was able to find discrepancies and to establish identities which could not be detected by an examination of mere composition or color values. Such an approach suited psychoanalysis exactly; it too found meanings—often decisive ones—in unconsidered trifles. Using this method Freud set out to see if he could determine Michelangelo's artistic intent.

The problem had engaged critics for a long time, and each of them had evolved an opinion which differed in some respects from all the others. By a review of their writings and by his own repeated painstaking observations of the statue itself Freud concluded that Michelangelo had wished to represent a particular moment in the life of Moses, not as historically recorded but rather as imaginatively reconstituted by the artist. That moment was the one in which Moses was beginning to master the anger which he felt at seeing his people worshipping the golden calf when he came down from Sinai with the Tables of the Law. By analyzing the position of the hands, the beard and the Tables, Freud interpreted the statue as depicting the traces of passion left

as Moses began to recover his composure, "the remains of a movement that has already taken place." [32]

> In his first transport of fury, Moses desired to act, to spring
> up and take vengeance and forget the Tables; but he has
> overcome the temptation, and he will now remain seated and
> still in his frozen wrath and in his pain mingled with con-
> tempt. Nor will he throw away the Tables so that they will
> break on the stones, for it is on their especial account that
> he has controlled his anger; it was to preserve them that he
> kept his passion in check. In giving way to his rage and
> indignation he had to neglect the Tables, and the hand which
> upheld them was withdrawn. They began to slide down and
> were in danger of being broken. This brought him to him-
> self. He remembered his mission and renounced for its sake
> an indulgence of his feelings. His hand returned and saved the
> unsupported Tables before they had actually fallen to the
> ground. In this attitude he remained immobilized, and in
> this attitude Michelangelo has portrayed him as the guardian
> of the tomb.
> Viewed from above downwards, the figure exhibits three
> distinct emotional strata. The lines of the face reflect the
> feelings which have become predominant; the middle of the
> figure shows traces of suppressed movement; and the foot still
> retains the attitude of the projected action. It is as though the
> controlling influence had proceeded downwards from above.[33]

This is, of course, not in accord with Scripture nor even with the
enduring tradition of Moses the wrathful. Michelangelo, not being bound by the historian's obligation to documented fact, has
exercised his artist's prerogative of alteration for aesthetic purposes.

> He has modified the theme of the broken Tables; he does
> not let Moses break them in his wrath, but makes him be
> influenced by the danger that they will be broken and calm
> that wrath, or at any rate prevent it from becoming an act.
> In this way he has added something new and more than
> human to the figure of Moses; so that the giant frame with
> its tremendous physical power becomes only a concrete ex-
> pression of the highest mental achievement that is possible
> in a man, that of struggling successfully against an inward
> passion for the sake of a cause to which he has devoted
> himself.[34]

To such an end psychoanalysis itself is directed, its ultimate goal being to establish the dominance of our moral natures over the might of our instinctual energies. As Freud succinctly put it: "Where Id was, there shall Ego be," and something very like this must have been in the mind of the sculptor.

Only twice did Freud essay such detailed analyses of painting and sculpture; most of his application of psychoanalysis to art was in the field of literature. There the presentation of the themes which interested him was on the whole more explicit and lent itself more readily to study, being closer to the kind of material which he obtained from his patients. Very early in the history of psychoanalysis he had been impressed with the importance of the feelings clustering around the relationship of children and their parents. He soon found that a disturbance in the normal development of this relationship was at the root of the neuroses. Conversely, a successful surmounting of the problems of this difficult period was the prerequisite for a normal adult life. In fact, the key to an immense area of psychic behavior lay in this constellation of affects which he came to call the Oedipus complex. Thus the profound effect of the ancient legend of Oedipus lay in its ability to reawaken in us the persistent but hidden emotions which in their earliest form had accompanied our upbringing by our parents or their surrogates.

Freud pointed out that dreams of having sexual intercourse with the mother and of killing the father had been known from antiquity; such dreams were also reported by his patients "with indignation and astonishment," but attendant feelings of horror and revulsion did not prevent them from occurring. The continuing reappearance of themes which are so repugnant to our conscious selves indicates their power, and their power indicates their importance. They refer to "the painful disturbance of the child's relations to its parents caused by the first impulses of sexuality." [35] The naive wishes of the child for direct gratification are abruptly modified by reality and relegated to unconsciousness. In this state they lose none of their potential force and continually seek expression, compelling the psyche to expend large quantities of energy in order to prevent their emergence. In this it is not always successful. One of the ways in which these forbidden desires manage, at least partially, to circumvent the effort to keep them unconscious—that is, repressed—is through the agency of the dream, a more or less direct representation of psychic reality. The two typical dreams growing out of the fundamental relationship of the child to its father and mother, fortified and amended by suitable fantasies and thoughts, are believed by Freud to have furnished the raw material first for the legend and then for the drama which gave the phenomenon its modern name, the *Oedipus Rex* of Sophocles.

The Greek play is often regarded solely as a drama of fate, the conflict of the will of the gods with the puny and foredoomed efforts of humans to escape disaster, but Freud saw this view as "the result of an uncomprehending secondary elaboration of the material which sought to make it serve a theological intention." [36] The original psychic conflict took place between the child's desires and the necessity for it voluntarily to thwart them, a situation which contains the germ of all drama. Freud realized that Sophocles was compelled for dramatic reasons to show Oedipus as being unaware of doing wrong. This adds nothing to the original content of the legend and remains faithful to psychological truth. Therefore destiny in the philosophical or religious sense need not be assumed to be the motivating force of the drama. From the psychological point of view it serves as a screen behind and through which the real human quality of the tragedy is discernible. What the playwright has given us is

> a legitimate representation of the unconsciousness into which, for adults, the whole experience has fallen; and the doom of the oracle, which makes or should make the hero innocent, is a recognition of the inevitability of the fate which has condemned every son to live through the Oedipus complex. [37]

This accounts for its power to grip even modern minds. The use of destiny as a tragic force in other dramas is open to the objection that the supposed determinant of the action is not only arbitrary but oversimplified; the fate of Oedipus, however, is that of all sons, a fate from the realization of which they recoil. The failure of modern tragedies of destiny and the success of *Oedipus Rex* must be due not to "the conflict between fate and human will but to the peculiar nature of the material by which this conflict is revealed." [38] We are all, in a sense, victims of the same curse, and the recognition of its fulfillment in another arouses in us the same combination of revulsion and fascination from which the hero is suffering. We have tried to put away such thoughts since childhood, but they lurk in darkness awaiting only a chance to come forth. Through the skill of the playwright we are once more made to feel the delicious and horrifying reverberations of our incomplete struggle for self-mastery. The fate of Oedipus moves us "because it might have been our own."

The *Oedipus Rex* displays likewise, says Freud, the degree of repression presumably attained by Greek society at that time, which he thinks was not very great. The child's wish-fantasy is disclosed and stated in the play as baldly as it is in dreams, for the hero actually commits the crimes and only later realizes what he has done. There is little disguise beyond that afforded by dramatic conventions. Shakespeare's England accepted a more roundabout presentation of a similar theme in *Hamlet*. There the Oedipal fantasy is at one more remove. The hero is paralyzed by his unconscious guilt which arises not from the actual perform- ance of the deeds but from the unconscious wish to perform them. He dare not punish Oedipus-Claudius for having done what, after all, he himself wished to do. The recent movie performance of Sir Laurence Olivier as Hamlet, in which notable emphasis was given to the hero's incestuous ties to his mother as well as to his hatred of his father, implies that the star regards modern au- diences as capable of dispensing with Shakespearean concealment. In our time, when psychoanalytic ideas are a widespread if some- what debased currency, a less disguised representation is possible. But a presumed scientific sophistication on the part of the audi- ence will not affect the impact of the drama; it is conceivable that it might even become one of the conventions of Shakespearean production. The enduring attractiveness of *Hamlet* depends not upon the degree of repression of our society or its technical aware- ness but upon the ability of the play to make a human appeal, and this there is no sign of its losing.

Except for his elucidation of the mainspring of the drama, Freud did not further concern himself with *Hamlet,* leaving this to others, notably Ernest Jones. He touched again, incidentally, upon the theme of father-murder in *Macbeth* where, however, it was not the basic Oedipal pattern itself but its dramatic consequences which concerned him. In 1928 he returned to the theme in connection with *The Brothers Karamazov* which he ranked with *Oedipus Rex* and *Hamlet* as one of the "masterpieces of the literature of all time." [39] The point of this juxtaposition was that all three dealt with parricide, and all three revealed the motive as rivalry for sexual possession of a woman. However, Freud pointed out, the artist could not present it as openly as a case-history, for that would have been intolerable. Sophocles accomplishes "the indispensable toning-down" [40] by transforming the hero's unconscious motive into the compulsion of destiny imposed upon him by the irresistible gods. Once his crimes have been revealed to him, Oedipus accepts his own guilt and punishment without seeking exculpation on the seemingly reasonable ground that it was none of his conscious doing. While this violates our conception of justice it satisfies psychological requirements. The combination of his unconscious desires to commit the forbidden deeds and the proof that he had actually committed them made it inevitable that Oedipus would not try to evade the responsibility. He was overwhelmed with horror and remorse; punishment was absolutely essential.

In *Hamlet* the crime is committed by Claudius, for whom it is not parricide, except symbolically; the motive, therefore, can be shown more openly: he marries the Queen. Hamlet's turmoil is caused by the reactivation in him of the guilty desires for which he unconsciously wishes to be punished. He feels not only his own unworthiness to avenge his father but also his sharing of unworthiness with all men. "Use every man after his desert, and who should 'scape whipping?"

The Brothers Karamazov goes further in the same direction. The crime is committed not by the hero, Alyosha, but by an illegitimate son of the same father. All the brothers, however, share the guilt, for all more or less openly desire the same thing and, in a measure, overtly contrive to make it possible. Ivan prepares the way by persuading Smerdyakov that there is no God and therefore nothing to restrain or punish the murderer. Dmitri is an example to the others of violently expressed hatred of his father whom he openly threatens to kill. Freud exempts Alyosha from the collective guilt, but there seems to be ample evidence in the novel that he too has not only unconsciously desired his father's death but also found it expedient not to heed Father Zossima's insistence that he keep close watch on Dmitri in order to prevent the crime which Zossima foresees. Again and again Alyosha finds other things which he feels he must do before he can perform the duty laid on him by his beloved elder. One of these is a visit to a woman—to *the* woman.

Freud's interest in the literary treatment of the theme of father-murder is epitomized in his studies of *Oedipus Rex, Hamlet* and *The Brothers Karamazov.* He saw it first of all as support for his conception of the universality of the Oedipus complex. In this way it provided valuable assistance to psychoanalysis when aid from respectable sources was most needed. He showed the necessity for the presence of such material in literature and art and for its alteration into forms acceptable to audiences in different stages of emotional receptivity. Tentatively in the case of Shakespeare and with greater assurance in that of Dostoevsky he established connections between the artist and his work, between the psychic life of the writer and the characters or actions depicted in the play and the novel. Where biographical information was available he was able to draw psychological conclusions which supplemented the revelations in the work of art and helped our understanding of the character of its creator. Freud's concerns were with the central theme of normal human development and the dramatic values of the vicissitudes which it so often undergoes.

C. F. Meyer's *Die Richterin* was the first literary work analyzed by Freud from the psychoanalytic viewpoint.[41] The dominant psychological phenomenon which was fictionally represented there was the feminine counterpart of the Oedipus complex, the incest theme for women. In commenting upon the story Freud used as a parallel the common fantasy of servant girls that they would get rid of the mistress of the house and then take her place in the affections of the master. The same pattern, more intricately worked out, also underlay the story of Rebecca Gamvik in Ibsen's *Rosmersholm,* to the analysis of which Freud devoted a large portion of his essay on character types since, for reasons of discretion, he could not use the examples of his own patients. In accordance with his recognition of the psychological insights of writers he used two literary characters accurately representing people who are wrecked by success. In the play Rebecca has driven the pastor's wife to suicide and has been living in an intellectual and ideal relationship with Rosmer for over a year. He proposes marriage to her, upon which she refuses him and threatens suicide herself. What had been so desirable before is now unendurable. The reason for this astonishing rejection of the fruits of her ruthless campaign for Rosmer soon appears.

Using Rebecca's own words, into which Ibsen has skillfully incorporated hints of the psychic truth, Freud reconstructs the story of her past. Briefly, it is that she has committed incest unknowingly by succeeding her mother as mistress of Dr. West, whom she discovers to be her own father. Her actions in the Rosmer household are an unconscious attempt to repeat this situation. When the second, symbolic, incest approaches reality for Rebecca the unconscious wish comes so close to realization that her guilt becomes unbearable. She has been able to tolerate the partial success of getting rid of Rosmer's wife, but the full impact of the forbidden wishes emerging into the open is too much for her. The tragedy, remarks Freud, lies in the fact that her undefined guilt, by skillful dramatic revelation, is made specific. Her interview with Pastor Kroll brings the realization to her that Dr. West is her father; at that moment she is made aware of her incest as actual rather than wishful. This makes it impossible for her to accept Rosmer as a husband, for the original guilt is so reactivated and reinforced by the plight in which she finds herself that she is overwhelmed by what she has done and by the recognition that she is on the brink of repeating it.

The representation of the same theme in Lady Macbeth presents a more difficult problem. She too is a woman who achieves success, this time a criminal success, and soon thereafter suffers a disintegration of character. Freud says the difficulties here are so great that he is unable to explain why success is her downfall. However, he carries the analysis as far as he can and makes a tentative suggestion. He begins with a consideration of the motive for the murder of Duncan which he ascribes not merely to simple ambition but to ambition plus the desire to found a dynasty, to hand down the succession to Macbeth's children. Psychologically, the key to the actions of Macbeth and his lady is to be found in the father-and-children relationship.

> The murder of the kindly Duncan is little else than parricide; in Banquo's case, Macbeth kills the father while the son escapes him; and he kills Macduff's children because the father has fled from him.[42]

But the prophecy of the weird sisters comes true. Lady Macbeth, as if in response to her own plea, is indeed unsexed, not only in becoming temporarily a steely-hearted murderess but also in remaining barren. Thus the full profits of the crime are denied the unhappy King and Queen. As though by the law of the talion their "crimes against the sanctity of geniture" are punished by childlessness. It is as if

> Macbeth could not become a father because he had robbed children of their father and a father of his children, and as if Lady Macbeth had suffered the unsexing she had demanded of the spirits of murder. I believe one could without more ado explain the illness of Lady Macbeth, the transformation of her callousness into penitence, as a reaction to her childlessness, by which she is convinced of her impotence against the decrees of nature, and at the same time admonished that she has only herself to blame if her crime has been barren of the better part of its desired results.[43]

The chief difficulty in the way of this theory, Freud points out, is the brief time apparently allotted to the entire action of the play by Shakespeare. Only about a week seems to elapse before the tragedy has run its course, obviously not enough to bring about the changes in character which in Holinshed's chronicle, its historical source, took over ten years. "There is no time for a long-drawn disappointment of their hopes of offspring to enervate the woman and drive the man to an insane defiance. . . ."[44] The psychological requirement and Shakespeare's dramatic modification of the action remain irreconcilable.

Freud then begins a second attempt to approach the problem,

but only indicates the direction in which such an investigation might proceed without himself carrying it out. He cites the opinion of Ludwig Jekels that Shakespeare

> frequently splits up a character into two personages, each of whom then appears not altogether comprehensible until once more conjoined with the other. It might be thus with Macbeth and the Lady; and then it would of course be futile to regard her as an independent personage and seek to discover her motivation without considering the Macbeth who completes her.[45]

Freud notes that there is some supporting evidence for this in the play and remarks tentatively that "perhaps they are the divided images of a single prototype," but he leaves the matter there.

The Oedipal conflicts of the heroine of *Die Richterin,* of Lady Macbeth and of Rebecca Gamvik as presented by three different literary artists constitute the principal material used by Freud in exploring the question of the incest theme of women in literature. Each shows conformity to the true pattern of basic feminine behavior despite the fact that all three authors are men. Further, each has significant variations whose dramatic values are appropriately exploited.

Freud's chief concern in these studies is to show not merely that the Oedipus complex manifests itself even in literary representations of life—that is elementary and in any case has been abundantly demonstrated—but that it appears in varying forms each of which has its own specific significance. The form which it is made to assume in a particular case depends upon the intentions and capacity of the artist. As far as *Rosmersholm* and *Macbeth* are concerned, Freud points out that literature and clinical experience are in complete agreement. "Psychoanalytic work teaches that the forces of conscience which induce illness on attainment of success, as in other cases on a frustration, are closely connected with the Oedipus complex, the relation to father and mother, as perhaps, indeed, is all our sense of guilt in general." [46] In the course of his analyses he deals not only with the motivations and actions of the characters but also with the changes made by the authors for dramatic purposes. These are handled like the elaborations of a patient's dreams, and psychoanalytic techniques are used to unravel them, insofar as this can be done. By such a procedure the relation of the author to the thought of his time, to current literary conventions, and to the requirements of his medium are shown to be as intimate as that of the variations and conformities of his own life to the typical basic patterns of psychic life.

The final vicissitude of life which is shared by all men, the approach to death, was the third great problem whose literary treatment drew Freud's interest. "The Theme of the Three Caskets" [47] is a study of the way in which man's attitude toward death is manifested through his relations with women in literature and mythology as seen through psychoanalytic eyes. The starting point is the choice between the caskets of gold, silver and lead made by Portia's suitors in *The Merchant of Venice*. Bassanio's speech rejecting the gold and silver and choosing the leaden casket has a perfunctory and unconvincing air as though he were trying, neither very hard nor very successfully, to justify a choice which he had determined beforehand to make but for which he could not state the real reasons. "If in psychoanalytic practice we were confronted with such a speech, we should suspect concealed motives behind the unsatisfying argument." And the forced explanation is not the true one. The three caskets are traced back by Freud to an astral myth in which they stand for the sun, the moon and the star youth.

But this does not explain the meaning of the myth except in astral terms. Freud proceeds upon a different principle: "We are more inclined to judge . . . that [myths] were projected on to the heavens after having arisen quite otherwise under purely human conditions." By utilizing the psychoanalytic discovery that a casket is a female symbol he is able to show that the choice is really one between three women, like Lear's choice between his three daughters. Other examples of such a situation from mythology (Aphrodite, Cinderella, Psyche) lead Freud to a psychoanalytic interpretation which may be stated as follows. A man is required to choose between three women, the third being the youngest and fairest who is also endowed with the characteristic of silence; usually voluntarily and for compelling reasons she refuses to speak. Psychoanalytically this signifies death, and the third sister is therefore its Goddess. But if this is so, then "we know the sisters. They are the Fates, the Moerae, the Parcae or the Norns, the third of whom is called Atropos, the inexorable."

Does man, then, freely choose death? Here, too, psychoanalysis advances our understanding of the myth. The well-known tendency of the mental apparatus unconsciously to represent contraries "by one and the same element" has been at work.

> The Moera were created as a result of a recognition which warns man that he too is a part of nature and therefore subject to the immutable law of death. Against this subjection something in man was bound to struggle, for it is only with extreme unwillingness that he gives up his claim to an exceptional position. . . . So his imagination rebelled against the recognition of the truth embodied in the myth of the Moerae, and constructed instead the myth derived from it, in which the Goddess of Death was replaced by the Goddess of Love and by that which most resembles her in human shape. The third of the sisters is no longer Death, she is the fairest, best, most desirable and the most lovable among women.[48]

For this there is additional warrant in human ambivalence as expressed in the dual nature of dieties like the ancient Mother-goddesses of the Orient. The element of choice, too, is explicable on similar grounds: it is a denial of the truth. We must all die, but the myth offers the comforting wish-reassurance that we are free to choose. And, naturally, we choose not the horror of death but love and life.

This fundamental problem thus found a variety of mythological expressions which, by way of the *Gesta Romanorum* and perhaps other sources, reached Shakespeare. Freud states his impression that in the mind of the poet

> a reduction to the original idea of the myth is going on, so that we once more perceive the original meaning containing all the power to move us that had been weakened by the distortion of the myth. It is by means of this undoing of the distortion and partial return to the original that the poet achieves his profound effect upon us.[49]

In *Lear* the powerful impact of the play is due to more than the force of the "two prudent maxims" that one should retain one's possessions and privileges as long as one lives and that one should not succumb to flattery. To Freud it seems

> quite impossible to explain the effect of the play from the impression that such a train of thought would produce, or to assume that the poet's own creative instincts would not carry him further than the impulse to illustrate these maxims. Moreover, even though we are told that the poet's intention was to present the tragedy of ingratitude, the sting of which he probably felt in his own heart, and that the effect of the play depends on the purely formal element, its artistic trappings, it seems to me that this information cannot compete with the comprehension that dawns upon us after our study of the theme of a choice between the three sisters.[50]

While not denying the value of the spectator's reaction to the "purely formal element," Freud assigns the primacy to feelings of another order, to the unconscious echoes aroused in the audience by recreation of a human situation on the stage. It is conceivable that either could serve alone, but together they enhance and augment the dramatist's achievement.

The scene in which Lear enters with Cordelia dead in his arms thus represents symbolically the reverse of the apparent action. It is the Death Goddess bearing away the dead hero. "Eternal wisdom, in the garb of the primitive myth, bids the old man renounce love, choose death and make friends with the necessity of dying." The poet has shown us a man who is old and must soon die, a figure closer than Bassanio was to the original conception of the myth and so of greater force, since he carries with him more of the emotive connotations which we all dimly perceive below the surface. Both *Hamlet* and *Oedipus Rex,* as well as other great works, derive their power partly from the skill of the playwright and partly from the circumstance—not an accidental one—that the essential pattern of the action on the stage conforms to the Oedipal experiences which we have all undergone, each of us in his fashion. The dramatist's intuitive recognition of this helps to motivate his choice of subject which he then creatively adapts to meet both formal dramatic requirements and the expectations of the audience. But no matter what changes may have been wrought in the familiar fantasy by theatrical necessities, we can discern behind the changes and elaborations the ancient emotional constellations which even in less cunning hands evokes our deepest response.

*   *   *

In his application of the psychoanalytic method to the study of artistic works and their creators Freud was careful to point out its limitations. The aims of psychological science are much more modest than those of philosophy; many of the mysteries of aesthetics are beyond the reach of psychoanalysis. But even in the physical and psychic spheres its scope is restricted:

> The impulses and their transformations are the last things psychoanalysis can discern. Henceforth it leaves the stage to biological investigation. The tendency to repression, as well as the ability to sublimate, must be traced back to the organic bases of the character upon which alone the psychic structure arises. As artistic talent and productive ability are intimately connected with sublimation, we have to admit also that the nature of artistic attainment is psychoanalytically inaccessible to us. . . . Our aim remains to demonstrate the connection between outer experiences and reactions of the person over the path of the instinctual activity.[51]

The origin and nature of the constitutional capacities of the artist are matters properly belonging to other branches of science; psychoanalysis concerns itself only with their psychic manifestations. To this conception of its role Freud consistently adhered.

> The layman may perhaps expect too much from analysis in this respect, for it must be admitted that it throws no light upon the two problems which probably interest him most. It can do nothing towards elucidating the nature of the artistic gift, nor can it explain the means by which the artist works —artistic technique.[52]

By these modest disclaimers Freud did not intend a surrender of scientific responsibility but rather a recognition of the psychoanalytic frontier. Within its boundaries lay many unexplored areas, and to some of these he turned his attention.

As it had done with other mysterious and neglected human phenomena such as dreams, errors and delusions, psychoanalysis began to look at art without magical or aesthetic preconceptions and to consider it as a mental product subject to the same laws of psychic functioning that governed other, more familiar activities. Although art is extremely complex and lies in large part outside the compass of science, the available information about certain areas of mental life which can be described psychoanalytically is applicable to it. Creative activity has its roots in the earliest experiences of the individual, traces of which are to be found in even the most polished work of art. The passage of the child through the oral, anal and genital phases of development culminating in the Oedipal stage at about the fifth or sixth year is a process of continuous curtailment of instinctual satisfactions and of progressive control over them. In psychoanalytic terms it is the gradual but steady replacement of id by ego; in ordinary language it is growing up or education. It must not be supposed, however, that infantile impulses disappear; they merely seek channels for expression other than those which the ego closes to them. Since the world of real objects does not permit full gratification of the child's impulses, their energy must find some outlet through imagination. Among the chief means by which this necessary and normal adjustment is carried out are play and fantasy-making.

These activities are in the nature of compromises on the principle that half a loaf is better than none. The original impulses (notably the sexual ones, but not only these) are forbidden direct expression, but they can be appeased, for a time at least, in disguised form. For instance, the child's wish to incorporate orally the objects about him may take the harmless form of a dream in which he eats all the candy he wants, a quantity far greater than the capacity of his stomach. Or the wish to replace the father may emerge as the common daydream in which the little boy performs heroic deeds and wins the adulation of the populace. For the moment, the tension is alleviated, and the dreamer can go on to other things until it mounts again, whereupon he repeats a variant of the same process.

Play is the active performance of the fantasy, the acting-out of wishes. The spontaneous games of childhood serve the purposes of adjusting to the demands of the adults and mastering the fears and other psychic problems of that period. The same is true, at one remove, of those games which have become ritualized and which are repeated almost unchanged all over the child world. As a matter of fact, any physical activity may, in addition to its other functions, serve the same process. This is one of the important findings of psychoanalysis; the therapeutic method of Freud and Breuer depended on the fact that it "abrogated the efficacy of the original non-abreacted ideas by affording an outlet to their strangulated affects through speech." [53]

In adolescence the child may exhibit either rebellion against adult values or conformity to them in varying degrees. This constitutes the normal ambivalence of that difficult period. The bodily changes of the age bring with them a psychic turmoil in which the rapidly developing sexuality presents a formidable problem. Fantasy-life is especially active; this is the time when poets are made—and unmade. Fantasy is a refuge from painful reality. The world is remade nearer to the heart's desire, a pleasant occupation which nobody ever willingly relinquishes. The personal daydream in its pure form "abandons its dependence on real objects" [54] and remains subject only to the pleasure-principle. It is the admixture of portions of reality with such uninhibited reveries which provides much of the basis for poetic visions.

The normal adult, having passed through the typical experiences of growth, has learned at each stage to make the required adjustments. But every struggle, though successfully concluded, has left some residue in the personality, and his handling of the daily crises of life after reaching maturity echoes his past. The common heritage of all men is this store of memories, psychic and somatic, which responds to dozens of great and trivial stimuli between morning and evening of any day. This is the instrument upon which the artist plays, both in himself and in others:

> Some actual experience which made a strong impression on the writer had stirred up a memory of an earlier experience, generally belonging to childhood, which then arouses a wish that finds a fulfillment in the work in question, and in which elements of the recent event and the old memory should be discernible. [55]

Freud also made clear the relationship between ideas and emotions, pointing out that it is not the memory alone or the idea itself which has power to move.

> We remain on the surface so long as we treat only of memories and ideas. The only valuable things in psychic life are, rather, the emotions. All psychic powers are significant only through their fitness to awaken emotions. Ideas are repressed only because they are connected with liberations of emotions which are not to come to light; it would be more correct to say that repression deals with the emotions, but these are comprehensible to us only in connection with ideas.[56]

The psychic life, then, is the life of the emotions. From the point of view of psychoanalysis they are what is important; sensations and ideas of all kinds are merely their servants. It is concerned with the latter not for their own sakes but for their effects upon the psyche. Psychoanalysis is not indifferent to the truth or falsity of ideas—on the contrary, this is obviously of extreme importance in establishing the nature of external reality as well as in contributing to the understanding of the psyche itself—but its chief interest is in what the idea, whether true or false, will lead its holder to do. His conduct must then be evaluated in the light of the conformity of his frame of reference to the objective world or in its deviation from it.

In studying the writer, then, psychoanalysis sees him as a person who deals with the universal problems of emotional life in a very special way. Its contribution is in defining, describing, and, if possible, explaining this way. Leaving aside questions of aesthetic value or philosophical truth, of the relative merits of romanticism and realism, of the artistic functions of poetry, drama, and the novel, of style and form, it looks at the representation of persons in the story and at the representation of what happens to them primarily as reflections, however distorted, of the fantasy going on in the mind of the author at the time of composition.[57]

The writer is, naturally, subject to the same motivating forces as everyone else; he differs in his as yet unexplained ability to embody his fantasies in forms which are attractive to others. He is a story-teller, and his stories are about the psychic experiences of his readers as well as his own. The basic function of the psychic component in any activity is to facilitate the biological and social career of the organism. The writer has chosen the life-task which affords him, taking everything into account, the greatest degree of inner satisfaction. In psychoanalytic terms, it assists him in maintaining internal balance by controlling levels of psychic tension and preventing them from shifting too rapidly or too far.

Freud recognized this psychological function of artistic activity very early. He saw in Wilhelm Jensen's *Gradiva* that "our author . . . directs his attention to the unconscious in his own psyche, listens to its possibilities of development and grants them artistic expression, instead of suppressing them with conscious critique. Thus he learns from himself what we learn from others." [58] The working of creative imagination is ultimately an outgrowth, far removed, of the play of the child. "Perhaps we may say that every child at play behaves like an imaginative writer in that he creates a world of his own, or, more truly, he rearranges the things of his world and orders it in a new way that pleases him better." [59] There is a difference, however. The child, no matter how much he may become absorbed in the world of his play, distinguishes it clearly from reality. He borrows real situations and incorporates them in his temporary and voluntary delusion without changing them very much. Anyone who has observed children at play has noticed how easily they move from what is objectively real to what they imagine, that is, what is subjectively real. "Let's pretend" is a declaration that the distinction is clearly understood.

> Now the writer does the same as the child at play; he creates a world of phantasy which he takes very seriously; that is, he invests it with a great deal of affect, while separating it sharply from reality. . . . The unreality of this poetical world of imagination, however, has very important consequences for literary technique; for many things which if they happened in real life could produce no pleasure can nevertheless give enjoyment in a play—many emotions which are essentially painful may become a source of enjoyment to the spectators and hearers of a poet's work. [60]

The satisfying of instinctual wishes which is afforded the child through play is granted the writer by his work. By the same token it also serves to alleviate psychic discomfort. This is accomplished by "transferring the instinctual aims into such directions that they cannot be frustrated by the outer world." [61] The artist is a sensitive and introverted person who "has not far to go to become neurotic." [62] He is not necessarily a neurotic, however, but continually wavers on the threshold of neurosis, sometimes crossing it for a time and then being brought back to normality by the healing effect of his creations.

> The artist is originally a man who turns away from reality because he cannot come to terms with the demand for the renunciation of instinctual satisfaction as it is first made, and who then in fantasy life allows full play to his erotic and ambitious wishes. But he finds a way of return from this world of fantasy back to reality; with his special gifts he moulds his fantasies into a new kind of reality, and men concede them a justification as valuable reflections of actual life. [63]

The therapeutic effect resides in the acceptance of the fantasies by others and the granting of honor, respect and admiration to their creator. In this roundabout fashion he achieves, not the original psychic aims, to be sure, but another kind of satisfaction which is similar in that the wishes which were forbidden in their original form are permitted in art and that the person who expresses them in artistic form is not denounced but praised. This worldly success serves at least temporarily to return the artist to normality until the tensions build up again—for his basic problems have not been solved thereby—and the whole thing must be gone through once more.

How does it happen that the artist's open presentation of his personal desires and his self-magnification which, if he took them literally, could lead to neurosis, actually have the opposite effect of bringing him into a satisfactory relationship with reality, even temporarily? Why do his readers not only allow him to set forth in artistic form that which is forbidden to them and to him in any other form but also esteem him for doing so? The answer is not fully known, but Freud has advanced a tentative suggestion based upon his theory of the origin of society. He proposed the possibility that, after the killing of the primal father,

some individual, in the exigency of his longing, may have
been moved to free himself from the group and take over the
father's part. He who did this was the first epic poet; and the
advance was achieved in his imagination. This poet disguised
the truth with lies in accordance with his longing. He invented the heroic myth. The hero was a man who by himself
had slain the father—the father who still appeared in the
myth as a totemic monster. . . . The myth, then, is the step
by which the individual emerges from group psychology. The
first myth was certainly the psychological, the herd myth; the
explanatory nature myth must have followed much later. The
poet who had taken this step and had in this way set himself
free from the group in his imagination, is nevertheless able
. . . to find his way back to it in reality. For he goes and
relates to the group his hero's deeds which he has invented.
At bottom this hero is no one but himself. Thus he lowers
himself to the level of reality and raises his hearers to the
level of imagination. But his hearers understand the poet and,
in virtue of their having the same relation of longing towards
the primal father, they can identify themselves with the
hero.[64]

The artist cannot live by himself any more than can other men.
Solitary brooding leads only to morbidity, to the consumption
of one's own entrails. Participation in the life of humanity is
normal, and communication is a form of participation. The
telling of tales is thus healthful both for the narrator and for
his listeners.

What are the tales which have such importance? It is not
surprising that a large number of them are variants of the
Oedipal story. Writers, too, experience the struggles of emotional
adjustment to their parents and are left with impressions comparable to those of others. The significance of this fact for our
subject lies in the thesis of Freud that "the beginnings of religion,
ethics, society, and art meet in the Oedipus complex." [65] Its
influence has ramified throughout many important areas of
human activity and has profoundly affected man's view of the
world he lives in. Among its products is the "racial treasure-
house of myths, legends, and fairy-tales." [66] These, according
to Freud's view, are reactions to basic human experiences which
have, over long stretches of time, been given their distinctive
forms. For example, the Oedipus fable upon which so much

of our great literature is based is what fantasy has made of the two typical dreams depicting the death of the father and the possession of the mother, which we have already mentioned. This casts light upon the perennial fascination of artists with mythological themes and the seeming necessity for each generation to produce its own version of the age-old story, even if only in the form of a new translation of an older work. *The Silver Cord, Strange Interlude,* and *Death of a Salesman* are all part of this tradition and illustrate the wide latitude permitted the artist in his treatment of the underlying material. No rigid formula is imposed upon him; he may freely exercise his poetic judgment. In fact,

> incomplete and dim memories of the past, which we call tradition, are a great incentive to the artist, for he is free to fill in the gaps in the memories according to the behests of his imagination and to form after his own purpose the image of the time he has undertaken to reproduce. One might also say that the more shadowy tradition has become, the more meet is it for the poet's use.[67]

These contributions by the artists are not, however, destructive of the myth. Its character remains unchanged in essence no matter what details the current interpreter adds to it. Indeed, for the purposes of art the accessions—and omissions—are necessary. When the objection was raised, for example, that the legend of King Oedipus was not in accord with the psychoanalytic view of it because the hero was unaware that it was his father whom he had killed and his mother whom he had married, Freud replied that the myth-makers had nonetheless correctly presented the psychological facts. "What is overlooked . . . is that a distortion of this kind is unavoidable if an attempt is made at a poetic handling of the material, and that there is no addition of extraneous subject matter but merely a skillful employment of the factors present in the theme." [68] The ignorance of Oedipus in the legend corresponds to the fact that these desires and feelings are normally hidden from us; it constitutes a symbolic representation of that fact. The writer, then, may draw upon fantasy material which has already assumed artistic form, since this is based upon universal human experiences. His own life repeats the pattern, and so do the lives of his readers, in a way which may be regarded as analogous—if the analogy is not pressed too far—to the recapitulation of phylogeny by ontogeny in physical development. Thus there exists a common body of subject matter which is of enduring interest because nothing is so fascinating to ourselves as ourselves, whether directly observed or seen as the reflection of another person who is at the same time like us and yet different.

The particular has interest for us as well as the universal. In art, we find recorded not only the psychological heritage of the race but also the author's unique daydreams.

> They march with the times; and they receive as it were "date stamps" upon them which show the influence of new situations. They form the raw material of poetic production; for the writer by transforming, disguising, or curtailing them creates out of his daydreams the situations which he embodies in his stories, novels, and dramas. The hero of a daydream, is, however, always the subject himself, either directly imagined in the part or transparently identified with someone else.[69]

The writer, insofar as he is a daydreamer, is likewise his own hero. Freud observed that in psychological novels

> only one person—once again the hero—is described from within, the author dwells in his soul and looks upon the other people from outside. The psychological novel in general probably owes its peculiarities to the tendency of modern writers to split up their ego by self-observation into many component-egos, and in this way to personify the conflicting trends in their own mental life in many heroes.[70]

The use of material from mythology, that is, from established story patterns representing fundamental human experiences, need not be direct. As we have seen in "The Theme of the Three Caskets," it may be altered beyond immediate recognition and still retain its power to affect our feelings. Freud says that this is because the poet succeeds in bringing us back to the original idea of the myth and thereby arouses in us responses to it as well as to the others which have accrued to it in the course of its elaboration. The strongest of the responses is this basic one. It is independent of the dramatic values inherent in the "lessons" of King Lear's folly or of the poetic values residing in the lines themselves. Moral, aesthetic and other considerations all contribute to the total effect which a work of art has upon the reader, but in Freud's view the most important ingredient is the emotional one, the appeal to psychic fundamentals, to which all the others must be subsidiary.

> In my opinion, it can only be the artist's intention, insofar as he has succeeded in expressing it in his work and in conveying it to us, that grips us so powerfully. I realize that it cannot be merely a matter of intellectual comprehension; what he aims at is to awaken in us the same emotional attitude, the same mental constellation as that which in him produced the impetus to create.[71]

We must now examine the means by which the artist achieves his goal. The fusion of daydream and myth, of personal fantasy and universal illusion presents a problem and at the same time offers a partial solution. The problem is that each individual is interested primarily in his own daydreams and does not care particularly about those of anyone else. Since daydreaming is narcissistic ego gratification, the symbolic self-aggrandizement of another person is at best irrelevant, while at worst it may actually prevent one's enjoyment of this self-sufficient pleasure. Leaving aside mutual daydreams or those communicated by a child to its parents, we seldom take any interest in the self-centered reveries of another person. But when the daydream is presented with the skill of which an artist is capable, then we do. The pleasure we feel in it probably arises from many sources, but mainly it lies in the success with which the artist makes use of his means of bridging the gap between personal fantasy and the stories which he shares with everyone, the artistic medium. The partial solution is in the experiences which all of us have had. Art is, among other things, communication. As Freud put it, "the essential *Ars Poetica* lies in the technique by which our feeling of repulsion [that is, unwillingness to enter into another person's daydream] is overcome." [72] There are, of course, barriers as well as bridges between individuals.

As to how the barriers may be bridged, Freud offers this much of an explanation:

We can guess at two methods used in this technique. The writer softens the egotistical character of the daydream by changes and disguises, and he bribes us by the offer of a purely formal, that is, aesthetic, pleasure in the presentation of his fantasies. The increment of pleasure which is offered to us in order to release yet greater pleasure arising from deeper sources in the mind is called an "incitement premium" or technically, "fore-pleasure." I am of the opinion that all the aesthetic pleasure we gain from the works of imaginative writers is of the same type as this "fore-pleasure," and that the true enjoyment of literature proceeds from the release of tensions in our minds. Perhaps much that brings about this result consists in the writer's putting us into a position in which we can enjoy our own daydreams without reproach or shame.[73]

Of the endowment of the writer which enables him to perform this feat, Freud tells us only that

Writers, indeed, have certain qualities which fit them for such a task; more especially, a sensitiveness of perception in regard to the hidden feelings of others, and the courage to give voice to their own unconscious minds. . . . [They] are bound to certain conditions; they have to evoke intellectual and aesthetic pleasure as well as certain effects on the emotions. For this reason they cannot reproduce reality unchanged; they have to isolate portions of it, detach them from their connection with disturbing elements, fill up gaps and soften the whole. This is the privilege of what is called "poetic license." [74]

The writer treats a significant theme according to his personal psychic adjustment to the problem which it represents. His choice of setting serves the same end. He decides the relative degrees of reality and fantasy which are needed, and he attempts to make the synthesis in his work. An aspect of poetic license is the right which we freely grant him of "building up a thoroughly valid development on an improbable supposition, a right which Shakespeare, for example, has asserted in *King Lear*." [75] This gives him the power of producing in a literary setting an effect whose counterpart is impossible in real life, for the uncanny in literature, for example, "contains the whole of the latter and something more besides, something that cannot be found in real life." [76] The reason for this is that, by definition, the realm of fiction is less subject to reality-testing and therefore more directly under the domination of the emotions. The writer, by arbitrarily and artificially establishing the conditions under which his tale will take place, makes us more susceptible to the feelings which he intends to arouse in us. This is fairly close to Coleridge's "willing suspension of disbelief which constitutes poetic faith." We voluntarily assume an attitude of receptivity in which we stand prepared to let the author's words, characters, philosophy, even literary devices and conventions, evoke in us the appropriate emotional responses. Because of the fundamental sameness in our makeups we are often able to respond in a way that is equivalent to his, although this equivalence may be only approximate and general. No two readers can respond in precisely the same way since, of course, no two have had precisely the same combination of experiences.

The achieving of emotional effects in art is not, however, a simple matter of representing by means of the artistic medium some variants of the emotional experiences which all humans undergo. The medium itself imposes certain limitations and at the same time presents the artist with certain powers which help him to approach the limits of its potentiality for expressing and communicating mental states. Artistic work is a mysterious combination of intuitive choice and treatment of materials, as well as craftsmanship which is largely deliberate and conscious. In the case of literature the medium of the art is also the medium of everyday communication. Psychoanalysis has thereby learned a great deal about its use from analytic patients. In *The Interpretation of Dreams, The Psychopathology of Everyday Life, Wit and Its Relation to the Unconscious* and other publications Freud deals with language specifically as a medium for literature.

Among its limitations for this use is the fact that it can be inhibited by unconscious forces in the writer. Freud notes, for example, that when the writer is attempting to express something to which he has some unconscious opposition this may appear in the finished work as an obscure expression. The same principle which is used to explain a single speech blunder also applies to multiple and complex expressions.

A clear and unequivocal manner of writing shows us that here the author is in harmony with himself, but where we find a forced and involved expression aiming at more than one target, as appropriately expressed, we can thereby recognize the participation of an unfinished and complicated thought, or we can hear through it the stifled voice of the author's self-criticism.[77]

Multiplicity of meaning, a matter of great importance particularly in poetry, is a proper subject of psychoanalytic study in connection with the communication and concealment of emotional states as related to ideas. The symbol-system of dreams conforms to laws which can be more or less directly applied to certain aspects of language symbols. Words, of course, frequently appear in dreams, where they behave very much like the more numerous visual representations. The variety of meanings which may be legitimately assigned to a poem spring from the variety of impulses, feelings and ideas which have clustered around the poem's theme in the mind of the poet; before they can reach us they are, as it were, refracted through his poem.

Just as all neurotic symptoms, like dreams themselves, are capable of hyper-interpretation, and even require such hyper-interpretation before they become perfectly intelligible, so every genuine poetical creation must have proceeded from more than one motive, more than one impulse in the mind of the poet, and must admit of more than one interpretation.[78]

The dream seeks "to reduce the separate dream-thoughts to the tersest and most unified expression of the dream . . . by fitting paraphrases of the various thoughts." [79] This is accomplished by the processes of condensation and displacement, with due regard for representability by visual symbols. Freud likened this to what happens in the composition of poetry:

The one thought whose mode of expression has perhaps been determined by other factors will therewith exert a distributive and selective influence on the expressions available for the others, and it may even do this from the very start, just as it would in the creative activity of a poet. When a poem is to be written in rhymed couplets, the second rhyming line is bound by two conditions: it must express the meaning allotted to it, and its expression must permit of a rhyme with the first line. The best poems are, of course, those in which one does not detect the effort to find a rhyme, and in which both thoughts have as a matter of course, by mutual induction, selected the verbal expression which, with a little subsequent adjustment, will permit of the rhyme.[80]

In *Wit and Its Relation to the Unconscious* Freud examined the problem of the verbal medium in and through which witty ideas are expressed. As might be expected there is a close correspondence between the mental processes which produce the visual symbols of dreams and those which operate in wit and in the artistic use of language. The same mechanisms of condensation, displacement, and representation are present but applied here to words rather than visual images. Freud condenses the process into this formula: "A foreconscious thought is left for a moment to unconscious elaboration and the results are forthwith grasped by the conscious perception." [81] This shows a close similarity to the dreamwork, and he has accordingly given it the name "wit-work." The purpose and result of wit-work is pleasure, the pleasure of achieving a socially acceptable expression of what must otherwise be kept bottled up. In the psychic economy this is brought about by a decrease in tension, usually a rather abrupt one. The obscene or aggressive impulse cannot be directly acknowledged, but it may be expressed in disguised form. The hearer recognizes in the witty expression an allusion to the same kind of impulse which exists in himself and which he is also forbidden to express openly. The realization that the forbidden material is out in the open causes in him likewise a release of some of the repressed affect, usually in the form of a quick laugh. All this, of course, takes place unconsciously; the overt actions seem automatic, almost like reflexes. And they are attributed by the laugher to the unexpectedness of the wit or to some other plausible quality in it—provided that he thinks about it at all. Freud's view is that there is an aesthetic pleasure, to be sure, in the formal aspects of wit but that the listener is most strongly affected by the elements which remain below the surface. It is the hidden meaning of wit and not its overt form which provides the major part of the motive power for the laugh. This hidden meaning is most likely to be sexual or aggressive; it affords a brief lessening of the pressures built up by the holding back of sexual or aggressive impulses in the laugher. Psychically, the pleasure in wit originates from "an economy of expenditure in inhibition," [82] that is, pleasure arises from the simultaneous conscious appreciation of form and of the gratification of the unconscious need for expression of that which is forbidden.

This kind of economy is a commonplace in art. Every work of art has multiple motivations and must therefore have multiple meanings. Carried beyond mere language, for instance,

> It is . . . a subtle economy of art in the poet not to permit his hero to give complete expression to all his secret springs of action. By this means he obliges us to supplement, he engages our intellectual activity, diverts it from critical reflections, and keeps us closely identified with his hero. A bungler in his place would deliberately express all that he wishes to reveal to us, and would then find himself confronted by our cool, untrammeled intelligence, which would preclude any great degree of illusion. [83]

In Shakespeare's *Richard III* the unconscious feelings represented by the hero's actions satisfy us as long as we are not permitted by the playwright's technique to bring our critical reflection to bear upon them. If the illusion were once destroyed, our inhibitory mechanisms would be permitted to function again, and we might draw back in revulsion from the actions instead of vicariously taking part in them. This is further borne out by the fact that

> A witticism heard for the second time will almost fail of effect; a theatrical performance will never make the same impression the second time that it did on the first occasion; indeed it is hard to persuade the adult to read again at all soon a book he has enjoyed. Novelty is always the necessary condition of enjoyment. [84]

*   *   *

Freud saw art, then, as a normal psychic activity carried on by individuals with special aptitudes for this kind of expression. From the psychic standpoint these individuals use their aptitudes in the same way that others use whatever special abilities they possess; the psychic function of art is basically the same as the psychic function of teaching, politics or the practice of law. "The forces motivating the artist are the same conflicts which drive other individuals into neurosis and which have impelled society to establish its institutions." [85] Freud means here the art which has successfully fulfilled its psychic function for its creator. This may be defined as assuaging the pain of an unconscious conflict by providing a temporary—sometimes only a momentary —substitute gratification through the agency of a creatively elaborated fantasy with its accompanying aesthetic pleasures. The instinctual aims are thus diverted, with the help of sublimation, into channels where the outer world cannot frustrate them.[86]

The satisfaction gained thereby, however, cannot last. Its intensity is far less than that which can be obtained by "gratifying gross primitive instincts," for these inevitably renew their demands when the relatively brief effects of art-pleasure have worn off. Art can achieve its psychic results because of the survival in adults of the childhood pleasure in fantasy-making, which is closely related to play. The diversion of psychic energy from real objects to objects in the fantasy cannot be permanent: "Art affects us but as a mild narcotic and can provide no more than a temporary refuge for us from the hardships of life; its influence is not strong enough to make us forget real misery." [87] It has been suggested by Freud that the artist is probably more sensitive to psychic stimuli than most people. If he is so endowed constitutionally, this would help explain the accuracy of his insights into human nature. It also bears upon the well-known sexual activities of certain writers and other artists which give the impression of being more frequent and more intense than those of most ordinary people. Generalizations are risky here, but as Freud points out,

> The relation between possible sublimation and indispensable sexual activity naturally varies very much in different persons, and indeed with the various kinds of occupation. An abstinent artist is scarcely conceivable: an abstinent young intellectual is by no means a rarity. The young intellectual can by abstinence enhance his powers of concentration, whereas the production of the artist is probably powerfully stimulated by his sexual experience.[88]

This sensitivity is combined with a tendency to look within himself. The artist, as we have seen, has "an introverted disposition and has not far to go to become neurotic." [89] Neurosis is not a condition of artistic creativity, be it noted; if an artist is neurotic it may be for reasons not necessarily connected with his art. In Freud's view the artistic gift is as likely to be used for the purpose of averting neurosis as for augmenting it. In fact, both uses may occur simultaneously, the preventive function usually being the dominant one. For the artist, with his extraordinary psychic sensitivity, the regulatory devices which society furnishes (education, convention, certain socially approved activities like business, politics and war) are not enough. He achieves his best results in the transformation of his instinctual impulses through artistic activity. If this fails, as it sometimes does, he crosses the border into neurosis. This aspect of the artist's psychic life, then, assumes the form of a series of advances and retreats. As the instinctual pressure rises and a neurotic "solution" appears imminent, the unconscious defense against it manifests itself through a work of art whose psychic effect is to discharge some of the affect and reduce it to a tolerable level. The artist seeks primarily his own inner tranquillity. In this remains there until the limits of toleration are once more approached and another reduction in pressure becomes necessary.

> The mechanism of poetry is the same as that of hysterical fantasies. Goethe combined in *Werther* something experienced, his love for Lotte Kastner, and something heard, the fate of young Jerusalem who ended in suicide. He entertained seriously the plan of killing himself, found therein a point of contact and identified himself with Jerusalem, whose motive he borrowed from the love story. By means of this fantasy he defended himself against the effect of his experience.[90]

The emotional life moves in the direction of normality and he is not different from the scientist absorbed in his laboratory, the lawyer engrossed in the intricacies of his brief or indeed anyone who is immersed in his favorite pursuit.

Psychoanalysis as Freud conceived it stresses the value of the social function of art, its communication of mind with mind and psyche with psyche. This involves the transmission of the artist's ideas and psychic states by the use of symbols capable of carrying both conscious and unconscious stimuli which together evoke in the appreciator a combined intellectual and emotional response. Their power is enhanced by their patterns (artistic form), especially when these approximate the patterns of the basic human experiences which both artist and audience have as their common heritage. It must be remembered that this experience includes the response to similar material in mythological or other form, and so there has been established an almost universally favorable predisposition toward artistic representation of the same themes.

By his technique the artist presents the reader with a daydream which might have been his own, but which has become more than that. In its new form it is no longer a simple wish-fulfillment, and it is no longer private. The unadorned report of another's erotic or aggressive fantasy is merely a bit of case-history and as such has no aesthetic value. But the artist

is not the only one who has a life of fantasy; the intermediate world of fantasy is sanctioned by general human consent, and every hungry soul looks to it for comfort and consolation. But to those who are not artists the gratification that can be drawn from the springs of fantasy is very limited; their inexorable repressions prevent the enjoyment of all but the meager day-dreams which can become conscious. A true artist has more at his disposal. First of all he understands how to elaborate his daydreams so that they lose that personal note which grates upon strange ears and become enjoyable to others; he knows too how to modify them sufficiently so that their origin in prohibited sources is not easily detected. Further, he possesses the mysterious ability to mould his particular material until it expresses the ideas of his fantasy faithfully; and then he knows how to attach to this reflection of his fantasy life so strong a stream of pleasure that, for a time at least, the repressions are out-balanced and dispelled by it.[91]

This explains how an event which might produce the opposite of pleasure if it were to occur in real life may give enjoyment when it is represented in artistic form. Writer and reader make a tacit agreement temporarily to suspend objective criteria of judgment in order to share an aesthetic experience. For the writer this is primarily a matter of formulation and publication; for the reader reception and partial re-experiencing. The full meaning of the underlying wish-fantasies or their applicability to the reader are, for the time, hidden. The work represents them as fulfilled.

> They become a work of art through alteration which softens objections to them, disguises their personal origin and, by observance of the principles of aesthetics, offers the onlookers or hearers attractive pleasure-premiums.[92]

Freud's basic contribution to the understanding of art is the psychoanalytic insight that the pleasure which we consciously take in form, technique and style is our acknowledged reward for having fulfilled our part of the compact with the artist and that our unacknowledged gain is the emotional release and enrichment the work of art affords us, a result which would not be possible without the relaxation of inhibition by aesthetic means.

II
=

Ernest Jones
and the Psychoanalytic Interpretation of HAMLET

ERNEST JONES became interested in the problem of Hamlet when
he saw Freud's suggestion, in *The Interpretation of Dreams,*
that the key to the mystery lay in the Oedipus complex.[1] In 1910
he published an article in exposition of this idea and on several
subsequent occasions he revised and expanded it until now it
comprises a fair-sized monograph.[2] The original study of the
character of Hamlet, which still remains central, has been augmented by chapters on "Tragedy and the Mind of the Infant,"
"The Theme of Matricide," "The Hamlet in Shakespeare,"
"Hamlet's place in Mythology," and Shakespeare's transformation
of his hero from the figure he found in his sources. These sup-
plemental studies, all of which illuminate and enrich the
basic Freudian solution, have grown out of the researches of
psychoanalysis into the genetic and developmental psychology
of the individual as well as the psychology of groups and society.
By utilizing the scientific advances of almost fifty years Dr. Jones
has added new depth to our understanding of Hamlet's inner
struggle and to the psychology of aesthetic creation.

In approaching the mystery of Hamlet's irresolution, which he
calls "the Sphinx of modern literature," Dr. Jones places particular emphasis upon the connection between character and
author and the effect of the play upon its audience. He shares
the conviction of A. C. Bradley, Darrell Figgis and others that
Hamlet bears an extremely close relationship to Shakespeare.[3]

Critics of this persuasion feel that while all of a writer's creations are invested with a portion, however minute, of their author's personality, Hamlet seems to embody most fully "the core of Shakespeare's philosophy and outlook on life." [4] If this is granted then it follows that, if we succeed in finding the inner meaning of the tragedy, we will be in possession of valuable clues to Shakespeare's inmost mind and can know some things about him which were hidden even from himself. There is ample justification for this kind of reconstruction in the psychoanalytic experience upon which Dr. Jones bases his study and from which he quotes in support of his exposition. The long-established hold of the play upon its spectators testifies to the presence in its theme of elements which command an almost universal human response. These are to be found, Dr. Jones feels, in certain aspects of the personality of its hero. He follows Freud in maintaining that a writer inevitably reveals something of himself in his creations and that when the work is skillfully wrought the audience may enter vicariously into the experiences represented on the stage which, in reality or fantasy, they have all shared with him. He sees the play, then, from the psychologist's point of view (although he also seems to be more appreciative of purely literary values than most psychologists who have so analyzed literary works) as a vehicle for certain of Shakespeare's emotional reactions to some fundamental human experiences which have been incorporated into a form having a powerful appeal to audiences. The greater part of this appeal lies not in the beauty of the language or other attractions of which the onlookers are aware but in hidden responses to the situation depicted on the stage, responses which were unconscious (or nearly so) in the playwright and remain unconscious in them.

Dr. Jones reviews the most important attempts which have been made to explain the mystery of Hamlet, and concludes that nearly all of them are untenable.[5] Some account for only a portion of the facts and conveniently ignore those which do not fit the theory; some are not in accord with what is actually known, whether psychologically or textually. He takes the work of J. Dover Wilson as the authority for matters "on the literary and historical plane, where it becomes the mere psychologist to be silent." Since the Hamlet enigma is a question of human nature, he insists that scientific criteria also be applied to it. He holds particularly that the inherent qualities and overt behavior of the characters in the play should be subjected to the test of consistency with psychoanalytic findings. What takes place upon the stage and what the author evidently intended us to imagine as taking place within the minds of his characters must conform, in dramatic terms, to human reality as we know it. One of the measures of the validity of a character such as Hamlet must be not only what our eyes, our hearts and our minds tell us as we watch him, not only the reflections which the perception and experience of generations of dramatic critics have made available to us, but also those insights which have been won from nature by the patient labors of the psychoanalysts. Far from destroying the beauty of Hamlet, as some fear it will, this actually adds to its luster as a work of art, for the play "passes this test however stringently it be applied." [6] Furthermore, it does not threaten any critical interpretation on its own ground, remaining scrupulously outside the sphere of philosophical, historical or aesthetic studies. What it accomplishes is to add one more point of view to the existing ones and so to make visible yet another facet of the whole.

The psychoanalytic solution begins with the recognition that what prevents Hamlet from acting is an internal and not an external force. Indeed, the effect of the social code by which he is governed is to compel active revenge, even despite the fact that violence must thereby be done the sacred person of the monarch. Hamlet openly acknowledges his duty, but for reasons unknown to him he cannot bring himself to perform it. What these reasons are and why they so effectively stay his hand constitute the mystery.

Medically speaking, Hamlet is suffering from an aboulia, an inability to exercise his will power and come to decisions. Moreover, it occurs in a clearly defined set of circumstances and takes its shape from them, being in many respects like no other.

> Instances of such specific aboulias in real life invariably prove, when analysed, to be due to unconscious repulsion against the act that cannot be performed (or else against something closely

associated with the act, so that the idea of the act becomes also involved in the repulsion). In other words, whenever a person cannot bring himself to do something that every conscious consideration tells him he should do—and which he may have the strongest conscious desire to do—it is always because there is some hidden reason why a part of him doesn't want to do it; this reason he will not own to himself and is only dimly if at all aware of. This is exactly the case with Hamlet.[7]

Clinical findings thus prove to be directly applicable to the dramatic situation devised by Shakespeare some three hundred years before the discovery of psychoanalysis.

Dr. Jones is struck by the fact that Hamlet, while appropriately outraged by Claudius' murder of his father, is even more deeply moved by the loathing he feels for his mother's incest. The two events, seemingly unconnected, are related by the Ghost's announcement.

> They represented ideas which in Hamlet's unconscious fantasy had always been closely associated. These ideas now in a moment forced their way to conscious recognition in spite of all "repressing forces," and found immediate expression in his almost reflex cry: "O my prophetic soul! My uncle!" The frightful truth his unconscious had already intuitively divined, his consciousness had now to assimilate as best it could. For the rest of the interview Hamlet is stunned by the effect of the internal conflict thus re-awakened, which from now on never ceases, and into the essential nature of which he never penetrates.[8]

Nevertheless, the greatest intensity of Hamlet's feeling is directed not at the murderer and usurper but at the queen. Such an attachment of emotion to what appears superficially to be a secondary object (the murderer being the more obvious one) arouses the psychoanalyst's suspicions. The mere fact that Queen Gertrude has married again is not by itself sufficient to account for the strength of the reaction.

> In real life speedy second marriages occur commonly enough without leading to any such result as is here depicted, and when we see them followed by this result we invariably find, if the opportunity for an analysis of the subject's mind presents itself, that there is some other and more hidden reason why

the event is followed by this inordinately great effect. The reason always is that the event has awakened to increased activity mental processes that have been "repressed" from the subject's consciousness. His mind has been specially prepared for the catastrophe by previous mental processes with which those directly resulting from the event have entered into association.[9]

Claudius' crime, then, has awakened in Hamlet reverberations of the Oedipal period, the time of childhood during which feelings of love for his mother and hatred toward his father were uppermost. He had, in the fashion of boys, "bitterly resented having had to share his mother's affections even with his own father, had regarded him as a rival, and had secretly wished him out of the way so that he might enjoy undisputed and undisturbed the monopoly of that affection." [10] The gratification of these desires being strictly forbidden, he had relegated them to unconsciousness. There they remained making their presence felt in what ways we know not until the (unconsciously) hated father was slain by a jealous rival. With that event the entire turmoil was once more stirred up. The wish still remained unconscious, but it had now received reinforcement, and it clamored for expression with an unprecedented power. As an adult, Hamlet could not permit it to emerge into the open, for his conscious self, actuated by love for his father and by a high sense of duty, would have found it intolerable. In this impossible situation, with the strength of his personality taxed to its limit, the psychic defense was compelled to yield somewhat. The upwelling from within achieved utterance, but it could be neither complete nor direct; in order to escape at all it had to do so in disguise. In psychoanalytic terms, the recathected (reinforced with psychic energy) instinctual drives became strong enough to force their way past the resistance of the unconscious ego. That agency, however, fortified by the unconscious superego, permitted the energy to be discharged only in association with a symbolic form which was acceptable to it. The result was a compromise—a symptom. The partial gratification of the forbidden wishes coupled with the moral revulsion against them brought about in Hamlet a feeling of depression which found a conscious reason for being in his ideas of his own unworthiness, and it lent them such strength that he soon extended them until they encompassed the unworthiness of all men. It is this internal struggle, unwittingly and unerringly portrayed by Shakespeare, which furnishes the stuff of the drama.[11]

Although the objection has been made that Hamlet cannot be studied like a human being because he is after all only an imaginary figure in a play, Dr. Jones points out that there are nevertheless very good reasons why this can be done. To begin with, there is a well-established convention which permits the spectators of a play to speak of the characters on the stage as if they were human; at least, he notes, they have been observed to exercise this right in theater lobbies. One of the measures of a play's effectiveness is the ability of the author to bring about an absorption of the audience's attention so that they participate vicariously in the action. This need not abruptly cease at the final curtain; the recollection of it, at least, may persist long after the actual performance. Shakespeare, of course, possessed this skill in the highest degree. If this is one of the desiderata of dramatic appreciation for the audience, then there is no reason why critics should not have leave to adopt such an obviously useful device. They may regard Hamlet as a symbol possessing whatever human characteristics may be relevant to the drama in which he exists; this need not cause them to forget that he was invented by Shakespeare. It is even more than a mere convenience, thinks Dr. Jones, for he goes so far as to say that "no dramatic criticism of the personae in a play is possible except under the pretence that they are living people, and surely one is well aware of this pretence." [12] But if we grant Hamlet humanity in this sense, then in order to be consistent we must also be allowed to postulate a similar "existence" off the stage. No one is born an adult. Every human action—and consequently every dramatic action—presupposes certain antecedents. We therefore have a right to imagine that dramatic characters also had a "life" before they appeared on the stage just as we speculate on the motives for their actions or on what may be "happening" between the acts. This right is subject to two rigid conditions. First, our imaginative reconstruction must be in accord with the artistic reality created by the author, that is, with his intention as realized in the drama; and second, as we have already noted, it must conform to the realities of life. There can be no departures from probability in either if the whole is to have validity. We find further justification for this in the fact that the author does not make everything manifest to us, for his art requires that he enlist our imagination in the service of the drama so that we may be the more intimately affected by it. Much that is unsaid is left for us to supply, and this material is derived, in part, from our intellectual understanding of the real world which provides the pattern for our temporary but whole-hearted participation in the world of the dramatist. For the fullest appreciation of a work of art some undefinable "aesthetic sense" is not enough; all of our resources are needed. Dr. Jones does not fear the intrusion of the real into art because he does not consider beauty so fragile that it cannot withstand scrutiny. On the contrary, he believes that "intellectual appreciation comprises an important part of the higher forms of aesthetic appreciation," [13] and that it inevitably enhances the latter.

A part of what we know—as nearly as anything can be known —is that the play was written by Shakespeare. To isolate the work from its author is arbitrarily to set up restrictions and limitations on the possibility of our fully understanding it. Not only can we learn more about the work from a study of the author's character and his artistic development than we can perceive without it, but, reciprocally, the work can enrich our biographical information as well. Specifically, we can thereby increase our comprehension of both "the inner nature of the composition . . . and the creative impulse of its author." [14] Dr. Jones maintains here that the unconscious elements in the author's creativity find expression in his works and may sometimes be identified by discerning eyes. Hamlet, then, may be seen as a symbolic embodiment of certain emotional experiences undergone by Shakespeare at the time the play was conceived and written.

Dr. Jones adopts the view that Shakespeare wrote *Hamlet* first in 1591–2. This was essentially a revision of Kyd's earlier play. In 1603 the first printed version (Q₁) appeared, apparently pirated and based on the actor's copy which had been circulating since 1593. Going back to this, Shakespeare then rewrote it, issuing what was practically a new play (Q₂) in 1604–5, presumably to counter the pirated version. This chronology lends weight to Freud's original suggestion that the play was rewritten at a time when Shakespeare was under the influence of the strong feelings which had been aroused by his father's death in 1601.

However, Dr. Jones does not wish to imply that this event was the only begetter of the drama. Such an explanation would be far too simple to account for the many levels of meaning in *Hamlet*. It is a well-known psychoanalytic principle that significant actions are overdetermined, that is, they are stimulated by —and therefore express—more than one instigating force. Conversely, when such an action is analyzed, connecting threads will be found leading in a number of directions. When it is possible to trace them to their sources (this cannot always be done, for various technical reasons) a complete set of psychic determinants can be obtained and the causal sequence reconstructed. This has been established in the analysis of dreams, neurotic symptoms, errors and slips of the tongue, and is true generally of the psychic components of any behavior, normal as well as pathological. Dr. Jones has applied it to the problem of the playwright and the prince in his chapter entitled, "The Hamlet in Shakespeare," which might well have been subtitled, "The Shakespeare in Hamlet."

The evidence leads him to believe that Shakespeare emerged from the Oedipal situation in childhood with a greater accentuation of his feminine tendencies than might ordinarily be expected. Perhaps his mother was a more forceful person than his father; we have no way of knowing, but it seems that, whatever the cause, the young Shakespeare acquired an unconscious identification with his mother, the strength of which complicated his psychic development. It should be stated at once that there is no evidence that Shakespeare was an overt homosexual, but it seems clear that he had a strong latent homosexuality which apparently caused him great suffering without his ever being aware of the cause. When Dr. Jones refers to him as bisexual

it is with the knowledge that his femininity remained unconscious and manifested itself only in such disguised and roundabout ways that it could not be recognized by him. To put it
another way, the great amount of internal effort necessary to
keep it hidden from his conscious self caused Shakespeare to over-
react when faced with any situation that stirred it up again. Dr.
Jones speculates, for example, that the hasty marriage to Ann
Hathaway may have been against Shakespeare's will and that
his resentment at this act of domination by a woman might
well have contributed to his mysogyny.

Be that as it may, we know that Shakespeare's little son was
born in 1585 and christened Hamnet, a variant of Hamlet, a not
uncommon name, the two forms of which were apparently used
interchangeably even for the same person. Some of the sources of
the Hamlet story must have been available to him although it
is impossible to establish precisely which ones he consulted or
even when he did so. Kyd's lost *Hamlet* had been acted by 1588
if not before, and it was upon this that Shakespeare's first version
appears largely to have been based in 1591 or the year after.
In 1596 Hamnet died. In 1601 the Earl of Essex was executed
and the Earl of Southampton, Shakespeare's earlier patron,
imprisoned on a charge of treason and consequently in danger
of his life. In the same year Shakespeare's father died. As
Freud has noted, the death of a man's father is the turning point
of his life, the time when he becomes the head of the family
in actuality or fantasy. The psychic effect of this event is to arouse
once more the feelings toward him which have been developed
during the Oedipal struggle and which may have from time
to time been agitated by other happenings. As the sequence
presented here shows, Shakespeare had had abundant opportunity to undergo re-activation of the inner storm in relation to
the powerful figures of Essex and Southampton as well as his
own father, to suffer some of these feelings in reverse in relation
to his own son, and to associate many of them with the drama
of Hamlet. We have already seen how the killing of the king
mirrors the feeling of hatred toward the father.

The other side, the boy's love and admiration for his father's
manly qualities, is displaced in the play upon the ghost of

Hamlet's father. This, of course, involves no psychic conflict since the feeling is honorable and may be openly expressed. The ghost and Claudius, taken together, probably represent these two aspects of Shakespeare's ambivalence toward his own father. But the balance is not perfect: for most of the play Hamlet disobeys his father's command to kill the king. The inner guilt which paralyzes him is reinforced by his over-identification with the queen and the consequent terrible combination of desire and loathing of her sexual submission to his father-surrogate. He can neither endure nor relinquish it, although his desire is unconscious. Dr. Jones thinks it likely that Shakespeare expressed in the play an almost identical conflict of his own. Hamlet's brutal rejection of Ophelia and his aversion to all women are behind the despairing cry that the uses of this world are weary, stale, flat and unprofitable. In this "almost physical disgust at sex" which is so prominent in the drama, Dr. Jones sees the signs of "some overwhelming passion that ended in a betrayal in such circumstances that murderous impulses . . . were stirred but could not be admitted to consciousness." [15]

The requirements for this are fulfilled by the situation set forth in the Sonnets written, as nearly as we know, between 1593 and 1603, the "Hamlet period" of Shakespeare's life. The poet introduces his friend to his mistress and is betrayed by both. It is noteworthy that in depicting his sufferings he is much more severe with the lady than with his friend and eventually becomes reconciled with him. We are left to conclude that he valued the (latent) homosexual attachment more than the (overt) heterosexual one. Whether Shakespeare actually underwent the experience described here we do not know. Dr. Jones, while rejecting the hypothesis that Mary Fitton was the lady in question, nevertheless feels as a psychologist that the poet must have passed through something closely akin to it and that the evidence for this is in the Sonnets and the great tragedies. It may be that "behind Queen Gertrude stands someone like Mary Fitton, but behind that lady certainly stands Shakespeare's mother." [16]

The unstable resolution of his Oedipus complex left him with an imbalance between the masculine and feminine elements in his personality in which the latter threatened constantly to erupt into consciousness and were kept down only with great difficulty. They made their appearance disguised as a close friendship with the original of the man of the Sonnets and as the choice for a love object of a woman with somewhat masculine traits. When the betrayal occurred it is significant that, though it was painful for him to relinquish either, he decided in favor of the man, not the woman. But, says Dr. Jones, "The theme of homosexuality itself does not surprise us in Shakespeare. In a more or less veiled form a pronounced femininity and a readiness to interchange the sexes are prominent characteristics of his plays, and doubtless of his personality also." [17] The double faithlessness aroused such an inner storm that the stirred up feelings clamored for release. One of the ways in which this was achieved was through the writing of *Hamlet,* which may thus be said to have been precipitated by a disappointment in love.

But the poet's psychic situation at the time also included the feelings we have reviewed in relation to his father and mother, his wife and son, and other people who meant to him at least a portion of what these did. Among these feelings must be included a resentment amounting to hatred against his betrayers, but a resentment which he could not afford to express lest he lose them both. Dr. Jones speculates that in real life he "apparently smothered his resentment and became reconciled to both betrayers. Artistically his response was privately to write the Sonnets . . . and publicly to compose *Hamlet* not long afterwards—a play gory enough to satisfy all varieties of revenge." [18] The emotional intensity of Shakespeare's feelings which so animate these masterpieces derived not simply from the precipitating situation nor even from the recent past, during both of which they were reinforced, but ultimately from early childhood and finally from the cumulative effect of all these events. Those which occurred late reawoke the memory of the earlier ones and reinvested them with such quantities of psychic energy that it was no longer possible to keep them repressed. But the strength of Shakespeare's ego was sufficient to control the manner of their expression, and he directed their power into his writing. The internal struggle which in a lesser man might have dissipated itself to no lasting effect here contributed to the production of works of genius.

* * *

Some of the foregoing, of course, repeats what Freud had been the first to say about *Hamlet* and Shakespeare. Dr. Jones retraced this ground and made a number of notable additions besides enriching the whole with many details. In his original essay (1911) he had written a somewhat expanded exposition of Freud's suggestion that Hamlet's conflict was largely a result of repressed parricidal impulses. In the ensuing forty years the advance of psychoanalysis and his own continuing interest in the problem enabled him to extend the depth of his insight so that in *Hamlet and Oedipus* (1949) there was added the understanding of the dangerous homosexual attachment to an idealized father. The ordinary Oedipal pattern was seen to be varied by this new complexity, and a new dimension was added to our understanding of Hamlet—and therefore of his creator.

An enlarged conception of the relationship to the mother also emerged. Freud had said that Hamlet was reacting in typical Oedipal fashion in that he repressed his incestuous longings. In order to strengthen the inner forces which kept them in check he developed a "disinclination toward women in general." [19] Dr. Jones's close and continued study revealed still another facet of this behavior, Hamlet's unconscious playing off Ophelia against his mother like a disappointed lover attempting to arouse jealousy in his beloved by paying attention to another woman.[20] This serves to accentuate the sexual nature of the inner turmoil.

One of the crucial points in the play is the relationship of Hamlet to Claudius. Freud had pointed out the basic psychoanalytic truth that Hamlet saw in the king the man who had committed the acts that he himself wished unconsciously to commit and whom he therefore dared not kill. Dr. Jones shows that the combination of incest and parricide, committed moreover by a member of Hamlet's own family, is too much to be borne.

The uncle has not merely committed *each* crime, he has committed *both* crimes, a distinction of considerable importance, since the *combination* of crimes allows the admittance of a new factor, produced by the possible interrelation of the two, which may prevent the result from being simply one of summation. . . . The possible interrelationship of the crimes, and the fact that the author of them is an actual member of the family, give scope for a confusion in their influence on Hamlet's mind which may be the cause of the very obscurity we are seeking to clarify.[21]

The childhood conflict which had been more or less successfully controlled was thus revived in a most painful manner, and Hamlet's lacerated feelings exacerbated by a daily reopening of the wounds. Since to kill Claudius (who represents in living form the deepest part of his own personality) is the equivalent of suicide, Hamlet drifts into a course of alternate action and inaction which, together with the provocations he gives the suspicious king, can lead only to his ruin. But it is a ruin which is at the same time a satisfaction, for it is also an expiation of his unconsciously desired crimes. He is able to accomplish it at the end of the play when he has at last given up his hold on life and reached the point of self-punishment. "Only when he has made [this] final sacrifice and brought himself to the door of death is he free to fulfill his duty, to avenge his father, and to slay his other self—his uncle." [22]

*   *   *

Of particular interest to literary scholars is the development of a work from its sources, and to this Dr. Jones also devotes some attention. Consistently adhering to his conception that Shakespeare was fulfilling his need to create "a drama with inner, tragic meaning . . . rather than merely a play with a plot," [23] he examines the plot changes, so far as we can reconstruct them, in the evolution of *Hamlet*. He is careful to make explicit at the outset that, while the personal needs of the artist may be discerned in the finished work and may be extrapolated from it by those who are equipped to do so, it is necessary to recognize in dealing with the production of any great artist "the subordination of either current or tendentious interests to the inspiration of the work as an artistic whole." [24] He sees the work not simply as the embodiment of Shakespeare's neurosis but as an artistic entity with an integrity of its own. It can in no way be divorced from its constitutents but rather exists through them. But they serve its purposes at least as much as it serves theirs, perhaps more.[25]

Shakespeare effected two major changes from the existing versions of the Hamlet plot. In the old Amleth saga [26] the king had slain his brother publicly on the pretext that he was thus defending the queen from the threats of her husband. The avenging hero then had to contend with the purely external difficulties of protecting his own life until he could reach and slay the murderer. There is reason to believe that Kyd had made the original crime into a secret murder; however this may be, Shakespeare's use of this change, even if he did not originate it, is clearly intended to show that Hamlet was troubled solely by difficulties from within, since the physical obstacles to the killing of Claudius are removed. Having thus prepared the way, the playwright introduced vacillation and hesitancy into Hamlet's attitude towards his task, transforming the hero from a man hot for vengeance, though prudent for his own safety, as Amleth had been, to the tortured and immobilized prince. The play thus became in his hands not simply a bloody revenge tragedy but a drama based on an internal conflict of character.

The manner in which the hero's father meets his death is one of the keys to the play, for it reflects the hero's—and the author's—relationship to him. The "coarse Northern butchery [of the saga is] replaced by a surreptitious Italianate form of murder." [27] Dr. Jones analyzes the three versions of the latter—Claudius', the ghost's, and the Gonzago story presented by the players at Hamlet's request [28]—and emerges with the conclusion that psychoanalytic considerations justify calling Claudius' attack on his brother "both a murderous aggression and a homosexual assault." [29] Furthermore, it was Shakespeare who introduced the latter. So our examination of the manipulation of plot elements leads us once more to the intimate relationship between the author and his work, and casts new light on one of the problems of artistic form. The invention, selection or alteration of a plot must, like all other mental processes, serve psychic ends, but at the same time it places these in a position of subordination to the formal requirements of the work. Seen from an artistic or critical, rather than a psychoanalytic, viewpoint, this emphasizes. the inseparability of the artist's intention, unconscious as well as conscious, to produce a particular kind of work from the shape which it finally takes. Its form helps to express various ideas of the author—philosophical, social, moral, political—each of them bearing a relationship to the whole, analogous to that of some of the unconscious ones we have seen. The final product may have any combination of these, but if the intention of the artist has been successfully realized, the most important will carry the main artistic weight. This is the case with *Hamlet,* for Shakespeare's

> own Oedipus complex was too strong for him to be able to repudiate it as readily as Amleth and Laertes had done, and he could only create a hero who was unable to escape from its toils. Shakespeare had failed in early life to find a solution to the problem of the "eternal triangle" with which every child is faced. For years he had been familiar with the legendary story of Hamlet, the meaning of which his unconscious was gradually divining. Then when the double betrayal by his friend and his mistress broke over him like a thundercloud he was unable to deal with it by any action, but it aroused the slumbering associations in his mind, and he responded by creating Hamlet, who expressed for him what he could not express for himself—his sense of horror and failure.[30]

There is one more matter which belongs here: the problem of artistic creativity, a problem which has never been solved but to the understanding of which psychoanalysis has made some contributions. Dr. Jones reiterates Freud's discovery that the mental mechanisms by means of which artistic creativity proceeds have much in common with those of other mental processes and that all bear "an intimate relation to fantasy, to the realization of non-conscious wishes, to psychological 'repression,' to the revival of childhood memories, and to the psycho-sexual life of the individual."[31] His study of *Hamlet* is based upon this conception, and he believes that the more deeply the artist goes into his unconscious for inspiration—that is, in the direction of the sources of emotional experience—the more profound the result is likely to be.[32] Psychoanalysis has shown that the aggressive and erotic impulses of infancy and childhood are extremely violent and that as we grow we are compelled to temper or suppress them in order to be accepted into the family and society. That this process is not always successful is obvious from a glance at the daily newspaper, but it is nonetheless one of the cornerstones of civilization. Technically, it involves sublimation, which means the detaching of energy from one or more of the dangerous impulses, and its use to carry out some activity which is socially acceptable. The tension is thus relieved, and the satisfaction obtained from the substitute activity must suffice in place of that which might have come from the forbidden one, the whole process being, of course, unconscious. The individual is aware only of the urge to do what society—and his own ego—approves. (To this must be added any other conscious values of the activity which are not related directly to its psychic origins but have accrued to it later, such as the appreciation of dramatic form, for instance.) One of the means by which this is accomplished is the attaching of an unconscious feeling of guilt to the forbidden act. Dr. Jones suggests that genius, which he defines as "the capacity to apply unusual gifts with intense, even if only temporary, concentration," depends upon "a special capacity for discovering conditions under which the unconscious guilt can be held in complete abeyance." [33] When this is done the artist may function according to the rigorous demands of his artistic conscience. Sublimation assists him by reducing the power of the dangerous impulse with its accompaniment of guilt, thus not only protecting the integrity of his ego but also strengthening it by the positive effects of the artistic achievement in the outer world. In this way restitution is made to the unconscious portion of the ego for the guilt which it feels at harboring such sinful wishes. *Hamlet* itself is an illustration of the way in which a criminal impulse can be turned into such an honorific accomplishment as a drama. The infant's jealousy and hate are the crude and raw forms of tragedy, for they occupy its whole universe while they last, and its response to them is total, if temporary. As we grow older we reduce some of their intensity, but they still retain sufficient force to move us, "and all the tragedies of poets are ultimately derived from them." [34]

Dr. Jones's analysis of *Hamlet* is based not only on Freud's suggestion concerning the play's psychological significance but, more fundamentally, on the whole Freudian view of artistic activity. It adheres closely to the findings and precepts of classical psychoanalysis and nowhere wanders from the paths which Freud originally charted. What it accomplishes is to extend those paths so that in the successive revisions of the *Hamlet* study the accumulated insights of advancing psychoanalysis are made available for increased understanding of the play. Dr. Jones, as he himself reminds us, is a psychoanalyst, not a literary scholar or critic, and his heavy reliance upon the Shakespearean views of J. Dover Wilson, author of *What Happens In Hamlet*,[35] may be objected to by those who disagree with Wilson. To the extent that such controversy affects the scholarly data with which Dr. Jones works, this may be a valid criticism. But until all Shakespearean questions are resolved to everyone's satisfaction, there appears to be no alternative for the layman to adopting, at least tentatively, the views which seem to him most reasonable. It is clear from *Hamlet and Oedipus* that Dr. Jones has acquired a fair degree of competence in those phases of *Hamlet* scholarship and criticism which concern his thesis and that, while we might ideally wish for more, what he has done seems enough for his purpose. From the psychoanalytic standpoint, at least, his work is unassailable.

III

Hanns Sachs: The Creative Act

HANNS SACHS has studied art from the standpoint of its origin in the hidden part of our lives, holding that "every creative possibility is contained in the 'stuff dreams are made of.'"[1] He emphasizes particularly the variety of psychic achievements having their roots in the Unconscious[2] and examines closely three mental phenomena having enough in common so that they may be arranged in a rough scale of ascending complexity, culminating in the creations of the poet.[3] The simplest of these is the daydream.

Its psychic purpose is to give pleasure directly and easily by the conscious devising of fantasies in which the daydreamer's acknowledged desires are gratified. These range from the longing of the hungry man for food to the wish that his ambitions may be achieved, his enemies humiliated or destroyed, and his love attained. For the moment, he lives in a world where no obstacles stand in his path; power, fame, wealth and adulation are his; there is no end to his self-aggrandizement. From this nearly uncontrolled inflation of the daydreamer's importance there follow several results. The daydream relegates other people to subordinate, passive and inglorious roles. Hardly anyone would be pleased with his part in another's fantasy. Together with this the contents of the daydream are frequently aggressive or erotic in a way that would not be tolerated or approved if they were made known to others. Daydreams therefore tend to be private;

their secrets are nearly always kept. On the one hand this makes it possible for the daydreamer to indulge himself and imagine whatever he wishes, no matter how impractical or immoral. On the other hand it means that daydreams are typically withheld from communication.

When the daydream concerns itself with erotic or aggressive fantasies rather than the "harmless" kind, a special problem is introduced, for this material is associated with feelings of guilt and shame. The fact that only the dreamer knows about it relieves him from facing the disapprobation of his fellows, but this does not eliminate the feelings. He may not be aware of them or he may summarily dismiss them from his thoughts in an attempt to receive unalloyed the gratification from the daydream, and in this he may succeed in so far as his conscious perception is concerned. But this only means that the feelings become unconscious, in which state they continue an active existence. The penalty for indulgence in such forbidden thoughts is a burden of guilt which one must bear alone.

Since there is no need to communicate with anyone else the daydreamer is free to manipulate the contents to please himself. Form is of little importance; for all practical purposes the daydream may be said to be formless:

> In most cases it clings to certain scenes which are repeated over and over again and elaborated with loving care. The rest of the story, the details of the plot, the necessary antecedents and consequences, the characterization and interrelation of events are neglected. It does not matter that the daydream consists of two unequal parts, the one in the spotlight being distinct and perfected in every detail, the other left in a jumble, without order and continuity. Even the most coherent daydreams . . . do not achieve the right balance between those bits which are the daydreamer's delight and the rest which is treated more or less as deadweight.[4]

This constitutes one of the most significant differences between literature and the daydream; another is the latter's treatment of language. The writer has both a special affinity for words and great skill in handling them so as to heighten their power to inform and to move. "For him, the sound, the music, and cadence, the rhythmical possibilities of a word are no less an

intrinsic part of it than its meaning." [5] In daydreams the identity
of author and audience makes care superfluous. There is no
danger that the daydream will become incomprehensible. Not
only are the ordinary forms ignored or misused but "the disintegration of language may go even farther—about halfway to
the dream." Fragmentary expressions may be supplemented by
or actually give way to pictures which may then carry the story
more or less unaided. All this is in the interest of facilitating
the fulfillment of wishes and is about as far removed from the
composition of serious artistic works as it is possible for a mental
process to be. The daydream appears to share with art only this:
that reality is imaginatively manipulated for other purposes. And
the kind of fantasy typical of daydreams is related only to the
kind of popular sub-literature which provides repetitive examples
of a few basic plots, nearly all with happy endings. Sachs points
out that some of them "would be indistinguishable from the
common or garden variety of daydreams if it were not for one
decisive factor: they retain their social function. They give
pleasure not only to their author . . . but to an indeterminate
number of people." He contrasts them with the works of
literature that we can properly call great. The latter need not
end happily, of course. Indeed, those which are tragic take as
their theme the hero's guilt and its expiation by death. A happy
ending satisfies only for the moment. Stories of this kind are
consumed in vast quantities since a fresh supply is always needed.
"On the other hand the great works of art, those that are not
afraid of admitting the Unconscious as a collaborator, are
'social' in the most magnificent sense. When they have once made
an impression, it will last, and even deepen with time."

But a problem arises here. In the making of personal fantasies
the unconscious wish is disguised very slightly, if at all, and the
result is that the daydreams are not readily communicable to
others because their contents are so distasteful. In great art the
material may be presented just as openly, yet it exercises the
most profound and lasting attraction not only upon the immediate audience but upon future generations as well. This
apparent contradiction may be resolved by a consideration of the
social role of fantasy. In the private kind this role simply does

not exist except in the rare instances where a person confides his daydream to another, perhaps—even more rarely—receiving a similar confidence in exchange. This is not likely to happen after childhood, and even there it indicates an unusually strong feeling of intimacy. However, there is another kind of daydream which is the joint product of two persons who enter wholeheartedly into its making. Here we have a kind of communication which is germane to our study, "an intermediate form of daydreams which has ceased to be entirely asocial, without becoming art." [6] Sachs cites two cases [7] illustrating these mutual daydreams whose characteristics may be described with reference to both private daydreams and to night dreams.

The basic feature differentiating them from the kind we have just described is that they link the imaginations of two individuals and thus represent a reaching out to at least a part of the outside world. The daydreamer no longer dreams in isolation, but the partners do not let anyone else in on their secret, either. Thus, while shielding themselves from the censure of society they are still enabled to share the experience with a sympathetic soul. In fact, it is an indispensable condition that mutual daydreams may be formed "only when two individuals are for a time brought together by a strong, suppressed, preferably unconscious wish which they have in common." The strength of the wish supplies the motive power for two significant results. Material which is so unacceptable that it might have to be repressed, or which has actually been repressed, might produce anxiety. This is the classical formula for the formation of certain psychoneurotic symptoms. But this may be averted if the fantasy which embodies the feelings is shared, because in this way the feelings, too, are shared and thus diluted so that each person has a smaller quantity of guilt to cope with. Since the quantity of energy is thus reduced to the level of toleration, the wish that would otherwise be forbidden may be partially acknowledged by the conscious part of the mind. Mutual daydreams thus afford emotional relief which the dreamers experience as pleasure in the intimacy of the collaboration as well as in the embroidering of the joint production. But it should be emphasized that the recognition of the underlying drives is only partial. They are not thrust naked into the light but disguised ingeniously after the manner of dream symbols so that their ultimate significance can be arrived at only through further interpretation. This, needless to say, the partners are not interested in at all; they are satisfied with being only one step closer to the unpalatable truth since it is not truth they are after but pleasure.

As far as they are aware, the pleasure comes from the fantasy even though they make no attempt to analyze it, or perhaps just because they do not. It tells them that they are not alone in their forbidden wishes, that at least one other person has exactly the same feelings. Neither one then faces the danger of excommunication with the resultant loss of comfort, love and protection by society. Though the Unconscious is asocial, the need of dealing with it here gives rise to "the formation of the smallest social unit—a community of two." [8] All this is possible if the right partner turns up. But what if he does not?

* * *

For those individuals who possess the artistic gift another avenue out of isolation is open. It is less direct and more difficult than either private or mutual daydreams but in the end more satisfying and lasting. This consists in the control and manipulation of fantasy life and its public expression in such a manner that not merely an uncritical partner but any number of others may be induced to share it. The artist works alone; the entire burden of the task is his. And this time it is not reverie which he produces but a finished elaborated whole which merely had its starting point in reverie. The daydream, his free-flowing, crude, repetitious and uninhibited self-indulgence, is transformed so that its origin is hidden from the awareness of both creator and audience. This concealment is an essential feature of the work of art. It is what makes palatable the acceptance of ideas that would otherwise be unpleasant, or even forbidden, and the vicarious participation of others in a fantasy that they would reject if it were offered to them openly. If it is successful in attracting an audience, then the artist has performed a remarkable feat of communication, for he has made his fantasy "the daydream of every individual—a 'mutual' daydream with an unlimited number of partners." [9]

The area in which Sachs made his greatest contribution to the psychoanalytic understanding of art lies precisely here, in the study of artistic form beyond the mere translation of its symbols into their universal unconscious equivalents. Up to this point such a study—all too common in "psychological" literary criticism—merely shows that one fact is equivalent to another without casting much light on the significance of either. Sachs goes beyond this necessary but elementary step. His concept of form is more complex than that:

> We understand by *form* everything that makes the poem (or story or play) pleasing and attractive to the audience. This is done by different techniques; some of them are what we may call "external," i.e., symmetry, rhythm, rhyme, alliteration, the euphony and clarity of language, the prosody of a poem, the manner of presentation on the stage, or the progression of an epic. Other form-elements are woven into the texture of the composition and less easily traced. Among these belong the atmosphere in which the whole or each separate part is steeped, the style in which it moves, the structure of the plot and its relation to the characters, the retardations and accelerations, the subsequent grades of intensity and expectation; and most of all, the way in which all these various techniques are concealed from the conscious attention. *Ars est celare artem*—the audience should feel their effect without being aware of them and should be surprised by what it was unwittingly led to expect. [10]

All of this has its impact upon the reader, and conceals the important dynamic interplay which we have described as the writer's role. For the reader, form may be a façade, but if it is artificially attached without an organic relationship to the contents, then it fails to perform its function of attracting and holding him. The importance of the attracting function of form arises from the social nature of art; the writer must have readers. But how can he induce people to enter his private fantasy-world?

Form is the means by which this is accomplished. It attracts the reader's attention and then leads him into a "daydream" which he need not even trouble to construct for himself but only to receive. So far it is not different from the method of many popular sub-literary television "dramas." The first difference between entertainment on that level and art lies in the nature of their respective contents. Art does not offer immediate and easy gratifications but only a partial access to those powerful unconscious feelings which so often shake us. According to Sachs, aesthetic enjoyment does not reside solely in either the conscious pleasure we take in the form of a work of art or the unconscious pleasure we derive from the gratification of unconscious desires. It is compounded of both of these, to be sure, but the essential ingredient is a psychological one, namely, "the ease with which the transition from the apparent façade to the invisible interior proceeds." The role of the artist here is, by means of his skill in the manipulation of his medium, to facilitate the inward journey of the reader. This is the way mere words, bits of paint, and musical notes having no particular significance in themselves acquire the special values which we designate aesthetic.

Artistic skill is a mystery to which we have only a few clues. Science knows very little, for instance, about the role played by inborn abilities. Sachs is able to point out at least one of the psychological mechanisms involved. Expressed in terms of psychoanalytic theory it is a shift in cathexis from the artist's ego to the artistic medium and thence to the ultimate product, the work of art. The writer, according to this conception, is endowed with a certain capacity for self-esteem which is perhaps greater than that of most people. He is also endowed exceptionally with a feeling for his potential medium, language. In the course of his career he develops not only his manipulative skill with words but also the associated pleasures which he derives from it. As we have seen, he relinquishes the direct gratification of the daydream for the highly evolved fantasy which others can share, a condition for this being his retirement from the center of the stage or even his withdrawal into the wings. But his narcissism will not be denied its satisfaction, and since it cannot obtain this in the usual way, it devises another. The psychic energy which invests the ego and so gives force to the self-esteem is now diverted to the product. This is easy because of the artist's special attachment to his medium, his high emotional valuation of words, which has already established a channel through which the energy can flow and to which it can cling. It is this energy, of course, which gives rise to the feelings of which he is aware or half aware when he works (or plays) with words. The raw self-love is thus relegated to the background and rendered relatively powerless while the energy which has been taken from it now gives strength to the fantasy.

One of the principles of mental functioning is that the shifting of quantities of psychic energy affords pleasure to the degree that obstacles to its free flow are eliminated. The most gratifying results are obtained emotionally when the greatest economy of expenditure is achieved. The form of a work of art facilitates this process. It provides a means by which previously unconscious feelings may be acknowledged by consciousness since they are connected, so far as the artist and his audience are aware, not to the hidden, forbidden impulses but to the bright and attractive artistic edifice. They are thus at the same time highly pleasurable and socially valuable. Sachs concludes that "aesthetic effect seems to be the result of the more or less masterly manner in which things that under all other circumstances would be trivial and indifferent—a certain rhythm, the arrangement of words—are made to be the bearers of a soul-stirring message." [11] The reader is aware of pleasure; real emotions are aroused. But he is not aware of the way the symbols, imagery and form of the art work have impressed them upon him as independent elements, unrelated to his own unconscious psychic life. Since this connection is concealed from him, he is free to enjoy the feelings as though he had no direct responsibility for them, and the burden of guilt is eased, sometimes almost to the vanishing point.

In the artist the equivalent of this process has taken place, the major difference being that he has created the edifice which the spectator passively or actively enjoys. The act of creation involves a number of steps, each of such complexity that no one has ever completely analyzed them—or perhaps ever will. Beginning with a drive which is the resultant of impulses and the psychic conditions of the moment, he is impelled to select the words, style, imagery and form which best express his inner psychic needs in a manner palatable to others. He is aware only of "indirect signals of it, in the form of heightened tension, restlessness, absent-mindedness, depression and the like." [12] When all his powers are functioning in the best relationship to each other, he is at the peak of creativity, and by solving the artistic problem he has achieved a discharge of the pent-up tensions. The outcome is a satisfaction which he attributes wholly to the finished work before him but which owes a large part of its happy results to what is hidden even from himself.

From a narrowly psychological point of view, then, form in a work of art is chiefly a means to a psychic end. The inner conflict of the writer is projected onto the screen of his work in symbolic fashion and assumes a shape which corresponds to the psychic reality from which it sprang. The plot of the elaborated fantasy is the restatement of the problem in terms of words, but it may not be done too openly, for such treatment would arouse too much of the original guilt, fear or anxiety. Consequently, a disguise is necessary, although not a complete one. It must hide the real intensity of the original affect as well as its real source, but it must at the same time reveal enough of it so that a partial outpouring of the feeling may take place and the tension be reduced to a level which can be tolerated once more. To bring this about it is necessary to satisfy the critical intelligence of the waking mind that the actions in which author and readers imaginatively participate are not precisely those which in reality awaken feelings which are perhaps pleasurable but also dangerous or forbidden. A nice balance is needed between the degree of revelation of the underlying truth and concealment of it. This is accomplished with the help of one of the oldest, most transparent but nevertheless continually effective bits of self-delusion, the pretense that one is looking in another direction altogether.

The musical and rhythmic qualities of words, the striking expression of ideas, the organization of the plot and all the rest of that which is properly within the domain of the critic combine to draw nearly all of the conscious and at least a part of the unconscious attention to the aesthetic values of the work itself—and no psychoanalyst considers these nonexistent or irrelevant—

thus diverting the reader from the area of emotional pitfalls. This should not be taken as a denial of the aesthetic value of form or even as an intimation that it is somehow of less importance than that which it embodies. Such evaluations have traditionally been regarded as outside the scope of psychoanalysis which has, for the most part, concerned itself with the unraveling of form chiefly in order to reveal the original psychic content. Sachs was one of the first psychoanalysts to consider it in connection with artistic content as well. He has been able to see that it grows out of the reluctance to admit discreditable motives, and that it results in the attachment of high psychic value to things already having high social value. This is not simple concealment, as some naive "psychoanalytic" critics would have us believe, but a complex, reciprocating arrangement. Form helps us attain pleasure from the psyche, and this pleasure heightens our appreciation of form.

*   *   *

Although there is no fully developed psychoanalytic theory of aesthetics it was inevitable that attempts should have been made to construct one. There are several now in existence, of varying degrees of completeness and tentativeness. The one with which a consideration of the subject should begin is that of Hanns Sachs because its author was the beneficiary of a happy combination of circumstances which fitted him especially for the task. His formal academic training was in law, but his inclination was toward literature; this engaged him, sometimes at the expense of his legal studies, to a greater extent than it did—or does—most psychoanalysts. Not only did he study literature but he also produced small quantities of it, some original and some in the form of translations, notably his rendering into German of Kipling's *Barrack Room Ballads*.[13] Despite his remark that this book "was the farewell, or rather the tombstone, for my purely literary interests," the subject held its fascination for him throughout his life, but from this time forward as critic and theorist rather than as creator. On the scientific side he had the fortune to be closely associated with Freud almost from the

organization of the Vienna Psychoanalytic Society. Together
with Otto Rank he founded *Imago,* a journal for applied
psychoanalysis in many fields, including literature.[14] He was
a member of the inner circle, "the Seven Rings," which dedicated
itself to the maintenance of the highest scientific standards in
the development of psychoanalysis.[15] With Abraham and
Eitingon, he was entrusted with the responsibility of conducting
the Berlin Psychoanalytic (Training) Institute. He thus had
extraordinary qualifications stemming from his literary interest,
his scientific training, his fruitful relationship with Freud, his
eminence as a psychoanalyst in his own right, and his contributions to the main stream of psychoanalysis.

It is not surprising, therefore, that his consideration of the
problem of beauty should be based upon Freud's ultimate
psychological concept of life:

> Starting with the conflict between certain psychic tendencies,
> Freud finally saw in every manifestation of organic life the
> result of the unending conflict between the life-instinct, with
> its spectacular triumphs, and the death-instinct, with its
> silent and invisible, yet irrestible force—the struggle between
> Eros and Thanatos.[16]

It should be noted here that this dualism of Freud's is not
universally accepted, even by psychoanalysts. No conclusive
clinical proof of it has ever been offered; perhaps none ever
can be. However, as one prominent analyst [17] remarked, whether
one can believe in the death instinct or not, it must be given
careful consideration as the conception of a very great psychologist, many of whose other difficult formulations have eventually
established themselves. To Sachs it was evidently a completely
satisfying idea for he used it as the foundation of the last third
of *The Creative Unconscious,* which he entitled, "Beauty, Life
and Death."

Although rejecting the approach of the philosophers to the
problems of aesthetic experience, Sachs retained some things
from their work, the most important being the "idea" of beauty.
He did this because it indicated that such a phenomenon actually
existed and that the possibility of experiencing it was not

restricted to a few talented individuals but common to all mankind. Such universality was necessary to the development of his psychological conception. A further value to be derived from treating it as an independent entity (but a psychological rather than a logical one) was that this enabled him to differentiate it from such emotional states as pleasure, relief, and gratification. However difficult the problems of definition, this was essential not only to avoid confusion but also to anticipate the criticism that psychoanalysis had nothing new to offer in this field. Beauty, he felt, "has a special quality which we cannot describe, since the special qualities of our sensations nearly always defy description, but which we acknowledge as something characteristic and unique whenever we meet it." And in embarking upon the analysis of beauty he warned that, even if it were complete, it would not furnish a full answer to the problem "since the phenomenon or experience of beauty is an entity, something different from the mere summation of its parts." [18]

As a psychologist he asked two questions at the outset:

> First, by what psychic process, or in which peculiar psychic situation, or under what specific emotional influence does the sensation which is recognized as that of beauty emerge in the mind of an individual? Second, when this has been ascertained for a sufficient number of cases (individually and collectively), is there enough regularity in the process to consider it as a manifestation of a general rule? [19]

He defended this subjective point of view on the ground that an external object—"beautiful" or not—is not needed to elicit or arouse the sensation of beauty, as can be seen in the experiences of saints in ecstasy or writers in moments of creative inspiration. This position is further bolstered by the variety of ways in which objects are regarded in different eras by different people, in short, by fluctuations in taste.

However, the objectivists' case also has some merit. Objects which have been regarded as beautiful in past times or other places (e.g., primitive art) exhibit characteristics which afford valuable clues to the psychologist. Despite the tremendous variety to be found in our collections of these artifacts there are also discernible certain tendencies toward similarity, such as the endeavor to produce harmony by the recurring patterns of lines, curves and contrasting colors, or to reproduce living things and preserve as much of their vitality in the reproduction, as the paleolithic cave dwellers did in their miraculous carvings and paintings. The similarities are still greater with the primitive forms of music and poetry which consist mostly of rhythmical repetitions.[20]

The object, insofar as it demonstrates the attempt to satisfy what might be called the aesthetic urge, deserves our attention. From it we may make useful deductions about the nature of that urge.

Beauty may be produced also by objects which occur in nature, uninfluenced by human minds. Sachs notes two classes here. The first is the kind of object in which "beauty is the consequence of a development of which we can trace the direction and tendency," like wild flowers, or butterflies' wings. The second includes those which seem to be without plan, accidental, often ephemeral, like a fortuitous combination of wind and waves or the fleeting combination of colors in a rain puddle. He thinks that human perception of these as beautiful, particularly the second class, probably came as a result of the leadership of a few sensitive individuals which others then followed. Originally, the primitive reaction to the world was a fearful one (which accounts for the growth of magic as a means of "controlling" it). Consequently, the sights and sounds of every day aroused anxiety, a condition which is fatal to beauty. The strong minds which were able bit by bit to overcome this anxiety were thereby enabled to perceive beauty where there had formerly been only fear. In a sense, says Sachs, "beauty of this sort is rather a work of art, reprojected into nature." [21] Therefore, the object which produces beauty need not be in itself beautiful, as witness *The Brothers Karamazov,* a novel of father-murder.

*   *   *

But if beauty is as indefinable in words as color, for instance, then how can the idea of it be conveyed to others? Are we limited to describing only the overt manifestations which accompany it, after the fashion of the behaviorists, and missing the point altogether?

When asked: What is this beauty you are talking about? we have no better answer than to quote the naive country girl in one of Johann Nestroy's comedies, *"Ja, wenn das schön ist, das ist freilich schön."* (Well, if beautiful is like this, all I can say is it is beautiful indeed.) [22]

Sachs does not think we are so badly off as that. We need only remember that beauty is an experience we have all had; it may therefore be examined from the social standpoint. The kinds of people it affects most strongly, its influence upon their view of the world, whether it binds people closer together or drives them farther apart—all these are relevant to the psychological approach.

Art, of course, brings people together and in a very special way. Even if they are not in physical proximity, like the scattered readers of a book, they are "knit together by the brotherhood of common emotional reaction." In inquiring whether this is brought about by the beauty generated by art, a key question, Sachs is led to consider the relation of beauty to sexuality.

In literature two components are essential, the transformation by the author of his repressed impulses into fantasies by which a kind of communion is achieved between him and his audience, and the beauty with which he invests his work to compensate him for the loss of self-glorification that would have come from presenting the fantasies as undisguised daydreams with himself as the central character. It is the transformation which makes art socially possible; the beauty, on the other hand, enables him to regain the lost self-importance, and thus leads in the other direction, back toward isolation once more. If mere identification of artist and audience were sought, the crudest melodrama would accomplish it and lead to the sharing of guilt just as effectively as the most beautiful literary work. Beauty in its "pure" form is asocial because it fills the consciousness and makes other humans superfluous. "In its highest manifestation . . . it gives a feeling of expansion—not, however, toward other people, but toward a miraculous isolation." Its social effect varies inversely with its strength. We have thus left the realm of philosophical absolutes and find ourselves dealing with psychological quantities. The nature of beauty does not change, but the amount of it which happens to be present makes a difference.

Sachs now addresses himself to the question why sex-attraction may be felt for a person who is not beautiful. He cites Freud's remark that "even when the human body is considered as the chief revelation of beauty, the genitalia, the center of sexual attraction, 'have not participated in this development,'" and advances the hypothesis that if they ever were regarded as beautiful something must have happened to change this. Perhaps the guilt-feeling or anxiety which attends our sexual affairs tried to push them out of consciousness altogether but was not strong enough, and succeeded only in implanting a distaste for them. It is too much to say, as Schopenhauer does, that beauty "is made possible only by the absolute absence of desire," but Sachs maintains that there is a measure of truth in this, for it is "a form of self-abdication of the will, of which the libido . . . is the foremost representative." Beauty in a woman, after all, will hardly cause a lover's ardor for her to abate. A further difficulty arises when we remember that beauty may also cause overvaluation of the sexual object, so that the lover sees "Helen's beauty in Egypt's brow." But since overvaluation is due to anxiety also, we are left with a seeming contradiction. Sachs resolves this by applying quantitative considerations.

> [In the overvaluation] the repression is partial or temporary, which means that the struggle is not too embittered. The sex-drive is, after some hesitation, re-admitted when it has been idealized or ennobled by the beauty of the object which thus becomes a necessary condition for falling in love. . . . In the first case, the repression is much stronger and more insistent. . . . The sex-drive remains, but loses its psychic value and capability for progressive development; it is henceforth kept in a dark and dirty corner, something closely akin to its anal degradation. The sublimation is kept far apart from it and in this way escapes conflict with anxiety. This coincides with the fact mentioned above that beauty and anxiety are absolutely irreconcilable.[23]

Though most people primarily require interest and action in their entertainment, an element of beauty is present in even the most popular diversions, like movies and television soap operas.

In the nature of things, this can occur only to a minute degree; nevertheless it is not only there but, says Sachs, "indispensable for everyone." In small quantities it stimulates gaiety, sociability and friendliness. In too-large doses it drives the recipients in upon themselves. "It supersedes all their other interests, isolates them and makes them feel sad. The badge of true beauty is sadness." Everyone can discern beauty and appreciate it according to his capacity. Those whose capacity is greatest run the danger of experiencing too much of it at one time, which arouses anxiety and destroys beauty.

* * *

In his Chapter VIII, called "Digression into Movie-land," Sachs points out the close relationship of animated cartoons to the world of the id, in which our primary impulses are (wishfully) gratified without regard to outer reality. Mickey Mouse may be cut in half by a runaway locomotive, but the two parts reunite immediately and he functions unharmed as before. We are granted all our wishes in fantasy and never need pay the penalty which would be exacted in the real world. The spontaneous applause which frequently bursts from an otherwise lethargic movie audience when a cartoon is shown attests to the pleasure afforded by the promised excursion into the imaginary world of irresponsible childhood. The same thing is true of Punch and Judy, marionettes, clowns and "a hundred similar venerable institutions which have delighted children and put adults in a childish mood at all times and places." But however pleasurable it may be, none of these brings to us the feeling of beauty in its pure form.

The tremendous and amorphous vitality of the id is almost the negation of the condition in which beauty can exist. "Instead of boisterous gayety and surreptitious, unregulated motion, the elements of beauty are harmony and sweet sadness." It is not the direct expression of life but something which has grown out of these elemental forces and through discipline has achieved a new form. Here Sachs takes issue with psychologists, both lay and professional, who see in any work of art only the embodiment of the sexual and aggressive impulses, only psychic mechanisms, without paying the least attention to the process by which these have been transformed and without seeing that the final product owes something to the course by which it developed as well as to its origin. The road is as important as the starting point, and both help determine the destination.

We must not make the mistake, either, of assuming that since beauty does not arise out of pure activity, it must be derived from pure immobility. A mere listing of the arts—dance, poetry, music—is enough to refute this. Nevertheless, stasis is important to Sachs's thesis. His conception of it is, as might be expected, oriented to Freudian psychoanalysis. The first consideration is that the human mind conceives of moving objects as sharing at least one of the characteristics of life, motion; on a primitive level—and it should never be forgotten that civilized, sophisticated man still retains much of his primitive heritage—that which moves is regarded as alive. On the other hand, that which does not move is dead, or recalls death or represents it.

> Now, there are only two of our senses which convey to us what we consider as beauty in objects—seeing and hearing, with the addition of the kinaesthetic sense as a later discovery. The other three are not far enough advanced to permit a sufficiently sharp distinction between "beautiful" and "pleasant." [24]

It is the kinaesthetic sense which enables us to explain how a work of art may be "static" (in the narrow sense) and yet seem "mobile" to the beholder. In short, Sachs approaches the question of beauty from the point of view of the dynamic activity of the mind, the ebb and flow of psychic energy.

He sees the extremes of artistic effect in two contrasting examples. Egyptian statuary art incorporates the principle of immutability. The effect of Shelley's *Ozymandias* is enhanced by the image of the colossal fragment of the king's statue whose boast of power and implied boast of eternal life is reduced to mockery by the silent evidence of the barren sands which surround it. The spectator is brought to contemplate stillness by such works; symbolically they are death. Certain Greek sculptures, on the other hand, seem to be in motion, though fixed in stone or bronze. We ourselves supply the sensory and imaginative complement to the artist's work, for in statues like the Nike of Samothrace or the sitting Hermes at Naples the movement is not so much arrested as projected. The same principle was developed at length by Freud in "The *Moses* of Michelangelo." Such art is action and therefore life. "If we accept these two extreme types as really characteristic and confine our attention for the moment to art, we can envisage beauty as the opening of two alternative doors—one leading to death and the other to life."

The two prime antagonists, life and death, continue their struggle in every phase of man's existence. In the one which concerns us here, art can bring about a compromise between them, or rather their symbolic representatives, motion and immobility. As there is no end to the struggle so there is no permanence in the compromise, but it lasts long enough to provide a respite for the creator and results in the creation of an object which can perform the same office for the appreciator almost at his will. This is possible because the medium of the artist is also the medium of those who enjoy his art. The appreciator may be thought of as also a creator, or perhaps better, a re-creator. From the work of the artist, who was stimulated by his inner experience to construct an artifact expressing through "rhythm, gradation, harmony . . . the emotional effect of such a compromise," he is able to traverse the path of creation to its origins in himself. His work differs from that of the artist in that the immediate stimulus is not his own but one which he takes from another and in that he does not produce another work of art but re-creates an emotional state which is presumably very close to, if not identical with, the one that the artist symbolized in his work. The rest of humanity responds not only to the artist's hieroglyphics but to the same psychic forces that move him.

"The special qualities of the object and the individual reaction of the subject" interact to produce a sharing of emotional experience which is not yet a feeling of beauty, although it may eventually become one. In the object, form and content are inseparable. The words of a poem cannot be changed, as in translation, without altering the whole in some degree; Sachs says that the change is absolute. The whole as it comes from the hands of the artist expresses something unique. Any change in rhythm, sound, pattern or words destroys the integrity of the artist's conception. What is left in its place may have merit of its own, as certain translations do, but it is not an exact rendition of the original, no matter how closely construed. The object in its final form evokes a response which no other form can. Each artistic experience is *sui generis.* Furthermore, each is impossible for us to attain unaided. Although we have the potential ability, this cannot be utilized without the key provided by the specific work of art. Thus, we are "indebted to the poem. . . . We may add that the poem is also indebted to us." It is we who re-create merely by looking at the printed page the particular combination of responses from the immense "store of emotional possibilities which is our id."

We must do this actively and with a will if we are to produce an aesthetic response. Mere passive acceptance leaves only a pattern of lines on the page, a tinkling jingle or a mass of incomprehensible verbiage. The poet has given it shape, but we must reconstitute the shape for ourselves and order our responses in accordance with it. The appeal to the id is there, of course, but it is not enough, being formless and generalized. The work of art directs us to a "singular and definite [emotional reaction] . . . like a statue cut out of the shapeless block." This requires not only that we call up the appropriate id-impulses but also that we follow to the letter the directions which the poet has given us. To reach such a specific result the chaos of the id must be brought under control. This is accomplished through the agency of the ego, whose role here is far more than merely that of keeper of the peace. In the act of re-creation it is itself enriched, as any person who appreciates art will attest.

In regard to the role of the id it is necessary to add that, while it is instrumental in producing pleasure when it succeeds in slipping some of its contents into the open with little or no opposition from the ego or the superego, it is not needed at all in the production of beauty. Some beauty is distilled out of id-impulses; some comes from other sources. That which has been repressed is an important part of our lives whether we know it or not, but it should not be forgotten that what need not be repressed is important also. One of the values of the latter is the possibility that it, too, can be utilized in the creation of beauty. What poetry and the other arts do is more than to release emotion; they also embody it. The poem is not simply a cathartic device but "the emergence of an emotional experience, which was hitherto only vaguely known, into full comprehension and intuitive understanding; the formation of indistinct psychic material into a unique awareness or, to put it more forcefully, a new emotional reality which is safe from being spoiled or distorted or sidetracked, as happens so often to those in actual life."

This is different from ordinary emotional experiences. In them we seek release; the impulse comes as close as it can to direct expression. The mounting pressure must be discharged— at once. "The characteristic of emotional expressions is their explosiveness; they . . . want to spend themselves as fast as possible." Poetry retards this motion. "The rhythm, being based on repetitions, stems the flow while seeming to yield to it." All the devices of art, all the skill of the artist tends to the same effect. The rush is not merely slowed down; it is held to the exact rate desired by the artist, now faster, now slower. The underlying intention of the artist is not only to produce works of art but also to cause his audience to feel through experiencing these works something similar to what he felt in their creation. How he controls the motion is still largely a mystery. Few of the ways are known, and our understanding of these is meager. But they are the forces which serve stasis, for they place obstacles in the path of the free flow of emotion. Such immutability as is present is not as obvious as in the case of Egyptian statuary, but even in this compromise form it represents exactly the same tendency.[25]

* * *

The road that leads Sachs to his theory of beauty is the one traversed by the human race in certain aspects of its psychic development. As far as we can trace back the story, men appear to have been of two minds about their relation to the world they inhabit. On the one hand they have adjusted themselves to the conditions imposed upon them by nature, accepting the vicissitudes of life on earth, even taking pleasure in a good many of them. On the other hand the outer reality frequently prevented an inner urgency from attaining satisfaction and led to frustration. On this basic pattern the human mind was formed, part of it accepting reality and dealing with it as perceived by the senses, the other part driven or drifting into behaving as though the wish were actuality, even when this was plainly contradicted by the facts. Men have tried many ways to reconcile reason and appetite; one of these is the way of art that sometimes leads to beauty.

It begins with frustration. When direct gratification is impossible, then another route is sought, either through bodily activity or fantasy. These are not, of course, completely separable even for academic purposes; both occur simultaneously. What matters is which is in the ascendant at any given time. Fantasy can be kept private, but a physical action, no matter how slight, can be observed—and interpreted. It is social whether it is so intended or not. Presumably in primitive times a religious activity like the dance, for instance, was the spontaneous bodily expression (accompanied by appropriate fantasies) of the whole group. Each dancer was essentially concerned with his own feelings and paid a minimum of attention to his fellow-performers. Gradually, however, the influence of the others made itself felt. The dancers began more and more to follow expected patterns, the expected became established and a ritual grew. Thus not only the dancers but also spectators could witness it. The presumption is that those who looked on could identify with the actors and experience in fantasy what the others were doing physically. In some present-day primitive dances people dance for a time, drop out, and then return as active participants. But they always take their place in the established ritual and do not spontaneously devise new dances. The wish-fantasy which is acted out in these "collectivized and formalized movements . . . becomes the seed of art and religion." Those who do not bound into the moving circle but remain on the side as on-lookers play a role analogous to that of the appreciator of art, a receiver of signals which enable a re-creation of the common emotional experience. Sachs calls all such performances "play," so as to emphasize the fact that they must be distinguished from "real" activities, e.g., hunting and fishing.

Play, however, consists partly of bodily movements, which are actions in the real world. Actors as well as spectators therefore need to avoid confusing them with their practical counterparts. One of the most effective means for accomplishing this is standardization or stylization, such as we have just mentioned in the case of the dance. Not only does it make such collective action possible but its obvious difference from ordinary reality helps to keep its magical or artistic effects distinguishable from the effects of other actions in the physical world, the eating of food, for instance. This "insistence on the unreality of the act . . . helps to transform it from an irregular emotional response into a collective and standardized action. . . ."

Together with this there is another characteristic of play which is of importance for Sachs's thesis, its role in the service of the repetition compulsion. (This is the name given to the tendency to re-enact, either symbolically or literally, an un-pleasant experience in order by so doing to gain mastery over the painful emotional state in which it left one.) Having been forced in reality to suffer pain or frustration, one can reverse the role in play and become active rather than passive, the controller of circumstances rather than their victim. When the original emotion has been very strong many repetitions of the little drama may be necessary to overcome its effects. The infant playing peek-a-boo learns that though his mother seems to vanish she always comes back; by playing the action himself he actively brings her back. But the fear of loss of the mother is so fundamental that similar games persist into later childhood. Witness the popularity of hide-and-go-seek and the perennial fascination for adults of stories about missing persons. As this example indicates, the effects of the original discomfort are not completely obliterated, but enough can be accomplished so that the feeling is brought under control.

All this is on the surface, as it were. Within the psyche the explanation can be made along classical psychoanalytic lines. The frustrating of an impulse dams up the energy which seeks to flow outward. Kept within, it beats against the defenses of the ego and constitutes a threat to the latter's hard-won stability. One of the best remedies available to normal people is the attrition of these forces by fragmentary discharges along paths which they choose and in quantities which they permit. The position of relative weakness in which the ego finds itself at such a time is made palatable to it by the apparent control which it has over the actions of the body. It is usually willing to accept this at face value, conveniently ignoring the fact that the whole was instigated by the id and that it (the ego) is conducting a defensive action, not a voluntary one. This offers one clue to the high valuation placed upon such maneuvers, which include a wide range of human activities, among them artistic creation and appreciation.

To Freud's principle that "an economy of effort (*Aufwands-Ersparnis*) is achieved when, in place of the new and unknown, an entity with which we are already well acquainted reappears and fits so well in its new place that the expected effort becomes superfluous," Sachs adds "the usefulness of repetition in the service of the tendency to make any pursuit unreal without depriving it of activity." A practical action like the accomplishment of a task carrying some emotional value (routine and indifferent everyday chores are not in question here) cannot be repeated unaltered because the conditions under which it must be performed vary and require greater or lesser adjustments. When not constrained to make adaptations of this kind, an action may be repeated unchanged. It follows that such an action, which may assume the character of a ritual, takes on an unreal quality; it is not of this demanding world. It also fosters "the illusion of free activity," for it can be repeated at the will of the doer. This is a great comfort. The activity which formerly one was compelled to undergo and whose unpleasantness one was forced to endure can now be performed as frequently as one wishes and with the conviction that one is free to repeat it or not to repeat it. Nevertheless, one repeats it. The need to believe in one's power exists, and the exercise of this imaginary power eventually makes it real.

In the lifelong conflict between impulse and inhibition the best weapons of the superego are anxiety and guilt-feeling. By these warning signs it apprises the ego of danger so that it can mobilize its defenses against being overwhelmed by the instincts. Psychoanalysis has also shown "that this conflict, when fought out in the realm of fantasies and within a limited psychic area, can be made attractive and interesting, like a tourney or sham battle." Much of the appeal of fiction derives from the skillful use of anxiety to increase the reader's apprehension of frustration and to enhance the final release in a happy ending. It can do this because for the moment the fantasy takes the place of ordinary outer reality and because the imaginary situations can be contrived by the author so as to evoke genuine emotional reactions. But a pure fantasy, since it is by definition private, can never produce art; for that communication is needed. And communication requires acts in the real world outside the imagination. "A bit of playing—at least the playing with words" —is needed here.[26]

*   *   *

Having described the roles of the id and the ego in aesthetic experience, Sachs now turns his attention to that of the superego. Since "an indispensable condition [for beauty is] the absence of anxiety," this means that it is not offended by the moral contents of the art object. For the moment, a state of equilibrium appears between the normally rather severe demands of the superego and the imperfect approximation to its standards which is the best the ego can generally accomplish. Some id-drives are even permitted to come farther out in the open than before. This is not the result of simple sublimation because such a process would separate the intermingled erotic and aggressive drives, transforming the former into something acceptable to the superego but making the latter available to the superego and giving it greater severity against the ego. The resulting anxiety makes the superego still more severe and destroys the essential condition for beauty. Nor is it enough that presenting the whole thing in the guise of play relaxes the vigilance of the superego. All this may be true, but we still do not have a satisfactory explanation. One more factor which contributes toward the establishing of conditions favorable to beauty is the gratification afforded the superego by the knitting together of the strands of the personality by the experience of beauty. The id, the ego and the superego are, in a sense, at war with one another, and they pull the personality in three directions. The best that can be accomplished in normal living is to effect a compromise between their demands so that the individual may continue to function. This is necessarily a matter of improvisation with a constantly shifting, dynamic balance of forces. It is not surprising, therefore, that when the ego does part of the work of restraint, and when the usually high degree of severity has been relaxed by the special aesthetic situation the superego should feel a release of tension, as though its reason for being, "the narcissistic ideal of a complete, fully organized, and freely functioning personality," is close to realization. Thus the superego seems to abandon its role of strict moral judgment and actually to participate in the activity leading to this unusual but highly desirable result.

As Sachs restates Freud's theory, the aggressive drive

> is originally a part of the death-instinct, which urges each organic substance toward the shortest way of returning to the inorganic state, and would bring about instantaneous extinction if it were not counterbalanced by the eros. In order to get rid of the self-destructive tendencies, they are—with the help and under the guidance of the libido—turned against the outside world; they are changed into aggression. By sublimation the erotic and aggressive drives become separated, the libido disappears, and the aggression turns back against the Ego in the form of the greater severity of the Superego.

Since, as we have seen, the feeling of beauty can exist only where there is no anxiety or guilt-feeling, such a condition is brought about by "bribing" the superego not merely to relax its vigilance but actively to participate in the process. The narcissistic satisfaction described previously is the bait.

This means that the superego cannot at such times exercise its usual function of censure and control over the ego. The way is then open for the appearance of beauty.

Under these peculiar circumstances, the death-instinct cannot be converted into aggression, since an aggression which has no object, neither outside nor—as the guilty ego—inside the personality, is plainly nothing else but a self-contradiction. The death-instinct, therefore, cut off from any outlet by way of permutation or modification, continues in its original form or returns to it.

In this fashion the influence of the death-instinct is always to be found in beauty, although its intensity varies tremendously, as might be expected. Sachs remarks that when the intensity is relatively low, then the id-qualities of the work of art are correspondingly more prominent and the spectator is consequently more susceptible to the naked power of the fantasy. In other words, the less beauty the more direct gratification of the basic impulses. The "happy ending" type of popular fiction which offers such satisfactions is seldom regarded as beautiful. This kind of "art" is likely to be little more than a prefabricated daydream. An extreme example is the ubiquitous comic book with its crude variations on erotic and aggressive themes. By its constant stirring up of the id-impulses it produces the kind of motion unregulated by artistic skill, which cannot possibly be beautiful. However, when this "attenuated form" of the death-instinct is operating fully, "the result is a feeling of restfulness and bliss, of having found, at least momentarily, a haven of peace where the eternal necessity to choose between sensual gratification and peace of mind is abolished." The constant struggle between the instinct to live and the instinct to die has one of its battlefields here too, and the victories won by either side are neither lasting nor decisive until the final one. There is no discharge in this war, though beauty gives us the illusion that the irreconcilable have been reconciled and so spares us the pain of contemplating the inevitable outcome.[27]

IV
=

Ernst Kris:
Ego Psychology
and Art

MOST OF THE misunderstanding of psychoanalysis by laymen arises out of an ignorance of its investigations into the ego. It is therefore pertinent to our study to present certain of its findings in this area. This may best be done through the work of Ernst Kris who was not only one of the leaders in recent psychoanalytic ego psychology but was also very much interested in its applications to artistic problems. In his book, *Psychoanalytic Explorations in Art,* he has surveyed the accomplishments of psychoanalysis from its earliest days to the present and traced its attempts to see art from the standpoint of the scientific study of human behavior. He has carried the account to the very frontiers of psychoanalytic research and has pointed out the directions in which further investigation seems to promise the most fruitful results.

In his review of the work that has already been done he has been struck by the diversity of the approaches which have been made in the name of psychoanalysis and by the use of Freud's writings in ways that suggest the user's misunderstanding of their nature. It is not the diversity, of course, that Kris objects to but the arbitrary rejection of some portions of psychoanalysis and the just as arbitrary retention of others, the whole of which, with the addition of different matter, is then given the name of psychoanalysis. He holds, for example, that the work of Jung and Rank, after they left psychoanalysis, is invalidated for the scientific approach to art by their arbitrary exclusion of certain clinical data, their oversimplification of the conceptual framework and their elevation of a single psychic element to the status of sole determinant of behavior. The residue is then erected by them into a closed system to which no fundamental additions may ever be made. Their urge for certainty has blinded them to the complexity of the subject and allowed them to remain satisfied with the explanation of the whole by a part. Even those who cite Freud's writings verbatim in support of their ideas have often unwittingly presented an inaccurate picture of psychoanalysis through their use of "representative quotations." [1] By giving Freud's words without indicating the historical and theoretical context in which they were written, these unintentional non-Freudians imply that psychoanalysis was fixed by its founder in a rigid position; they do not show that he added to and emended earlier concepts in the light of later clinical findings. The character of psychoanalysis as an "open system," explaining only that for which it has thus far gathered data and ready to amend its explanations when new, and even contradictory, information is found, is thus misrepresented.

While this "tendency to simplify or to abbreviate psychoanalytic thinking" is common, says Kris, it is found particularly in writings on the relation of psychoanalysis to art. On the one hand these frequently present a narrow view of literature, as though all of it could be comprehended from the psychological standpoint alone; on the other they select certain psychoanalytic concepts for application to literary study and ignore the rest, leaving the reader to infer that somehow he needs less knowledge of psychoanalysis to understand art than the analyst needs to understand a patient. Especially noticeable have been the neglect of the artistic milieu in which the artist creates, the influences of tradition, of new movements and of the attempts to solve new artistic problems. The widespread fascination with the id—which is after all easy to understand—has hidden from these enthusiasts the newer work in the relation of the ego, artistic or otherwise, to its environment, a problem upon which the attention of psychoanalysts has been focused since Freud's publication in 1923 of *The Ego and The Id*. What is of most

importance is how we deal with our world and not simply what
is hidden in the depths of the psyche.

The psychoanalytic treatment of artistic problems falls historically into three stages, corresponding to the major advances
in the science itself. During the earliest days of psychoanalysis,
when the fundamental drives that govern the psyche were being
identified and studied, Freud and other analysts recognized in
mythology and literature the same themes which appeared in
the analyses of their patients. It was obvious that the experiences
of infancy and childhood retained their influence throughout
life and exerted it in the fantasy, the dreams, the work and the
creative activities of the individual, whether as an expression of
the past-in-present or as a defense against it. The ubiquity both
historically and geographically in our culture of such themes as
"the struggle against incestuous impulses, dependency, guilt and
aggression [is reflected in our literature] from Sophocles to
Proust." [2] It was natural that the young science should see this as
corroboration of some of its findings and should, in turn, use its
new insights to achieve an initial penetration of the ancient
mystery of art. Freud once remarked that his case histories read
like novels, and he attributed this to the nature of the material
rather than to any literary predilection on his part. In a review
of *Studies in Hysteria* in 1895 the theory was called "in fact
nothing but a kind of psychology used by poets." [3] There has
always been a free use of literary examples and instances by
psychoanalysts. Edward Glover even suggested that the reading
of great literary works be made a part of psychoanalytic training.

This recognition of universal psychic themes in whatever aspect
of human activity they appeared was a natural outcome of the
early psychoanalytic discoveries. But while the identification of the
Oedipus complex in a literary work told us something new about
literature, it did not advance psychoanalysis. It is with the growth
of ego psychology that the opportunity and the need have arisen
to study the appearance of the specific within the general. Kris
puts the problems this way:

> Under specific cultural and socioeconomic conditions, during
> any given period of history or in the work of any one of the
> great creators within each period, how have the traditional

themes been varied? What aspects of the themes are more and which less frequent, and how are they modified? [4]

It is a curious and unexplained fact that the challenge has been taken up by only a small number of investigators, not all of them psychoanalysts. One of the most promising areas for the psychoanalytic study of artistic problems thus remains relatively untouched.

There has also been but little work in another area of psychoanalytic interest, the relationship between the psychic life history of the artist and his work. A few notable achievements have been recorded here, such as Jones's study of Shakespeare in relation to *Hamlet* and Freud's analysis of Dostoevsky in his novels and of Leonardo da Vinci in his paintings, but it has remained impossible to solve the problem of the ultimate nature of genius. Kris suggests two of the reasons for this. Our understanding is limited not by paucity of psychic information—which is abundant in psychoanalyses of contemporary artists, for instance—but by our ignorance of the role played by constitutional endowment in vocational choice and success. In matters of art the problem further is why one artist becomes great and others remain mediocre.[5] More study is needed of the ways in which the artist's innate equipment facilitates or hinders the psychic processes entering into creative activity. The other reason is that, except for the work of Sachs,[6] little has been done psychoanalytically with the problems of artistic style, the historical setting for art, the effect of conformity with or revolt against tradition, the relationship of artistic material to the form which the artist chooses to give it, in short, to the media and techniques of art. But form and content should not be regarded as separate; as Kris cautiously puts it, "psychoanalytic orientation suggests the value of establishing their interrelation," perhaps after the pattern set by Freud in his analysis of dreams. The difficulties of this approach are apparent in Kris's remark about Leonardo's painting of the Madonna and Child with St. Anne:

> Our understanding of his achievement would gain if, in addition to being able to demonstrate that the desire to unite the Christ with two mothers is rooted in childhood experiences, we were able to find a similar root for the specific type of

merging—for instance, for the construction of a pyramidal unit into which the figures are made to fit.[7]

The third important way in which psychoanalysis studied art was in examining the relationship between the imagination of the artist and the mental processes observed in clinical work. Freud noted very early that artists exhibited particularly acute insight into psychological problems, and he envied them the apparent ease with which they achieved this as contrasted with the laborious and painstaking methods he had been compelled to develop. However, even the extraordinary intuition of the artist does not afford him an awareness of repressed material; for this it is still necessary to rely on psychoanalysis. The interaction between unconscious, preconscious and conscious elements is best approached by a method analogous to the one employed by Freud in "The Dream Work." [8] Kris, like Jones, suggests that this complex of processes be called the art work.[9] He has himself demonstrated many of the similarities and differences between what takes place mentally in caricature and artistic creativity and what occurs in dreams. His studies deal with the influence of the ego and the id upon each other, with the operation of the primary and secondary processes, with the artist's "flexibility of repression," [10] and particularly with "the role endowment may play in facilitating the detachment of certain ego functions from conflict, in establishing autonomy in certain activities." [11] The last problem, to the solution of which Kris has made notable contributions, concerns the transformation of universal instinctual impulses and universal psychic ways of handling them into specific creative activities whose connection with their sources is not easily apparent. This leads us closer than ever to the nature of art, since it encompasses not only the psychic impulses from which art springs but also the artistic medium and the role of the finished work of art in the social and artistic environment.

*   *   *

Human responses to significant experiences are the consequence of the interplay of a great many stimuli, and the end-product tends to be a massive action, their resultant, which accomplishes a

number of things simultaneously. Psychoanalytic clinical experience has demonstrated that every neurotic symptom is overdetermined, that is, that there is always more than one cause for
every action. Whatever the immediate occasion may be for a
mental act, it has either already formed or has the latent capacity
for forming surprisingly long trains of associations with other
elements in the psyche, some of them seemingly far removed from
the precipitating stimulus. Not only do intricate clusters of ideas,
feelings, images and sensations exist around meaningful events in
our private histories, but these constellations are continually add-
ing new units and seeking a way of expression.

The strength and duration of the bonds thus formed vary
greatly. Some last a lifetime; others are fleeting. When an action
occurs which permits at least a temporary association of the
waiting psychic elements, as many of them as possible link themselves to the outward movement and are carried along with it.
What then appears in the open sometimes seems irrelevant, if not
actually discordant, and we may find ourselves asking, "Now, why
did I do that?" The answer found by psychoanalysis is that there
is indeed a purposeful connection but one which we cannot
understand at the time. When such seemingly inappropriate
portions of otherwise perfectly coherent acts are traced to their
unconscious origins they are seen to provide some satisfaction
below the threshold of awareness and to be unconsciously related
to what we consciously know. Along the entire path the points at
which the connections have been made can often be determined
psychoanalytically, but just as often the complexity of the process
is too great for our present abilities to unravel.

All of this applies to artistic activity as well as to other kinds.
We do not know enough to construct a thoroughgoing exposition
of creative mental activity in general, let alone that particular
variety of it which is practiced by artists. But ego psychology has
already made some useful contributions to our understanding of
certain aspects of artistic creativity and promises to extend our
horizons further still. Early id psychology showed that art was
one form of response to instinctual strivings. As psychoanalysis
developed, it studied some of the ways in which art serves as
adaptation to the environment. These studies continue, but now it

is beginning to take up questions of greater difficulty which were previously left to aestheticians and critics. What is the relationship of art to its medium? To artistic traditions? To new artistic and intellectual movements? To society? To the individual capacities of the artist as a gifted human? Kris follows sound psychoanalytic practice when he begins his discussion of the subject with a description of play and daydreams for these represent some of the foundation stones upon which the vast and intricate superstructure is built.

It has long been recognized by psychoanalysis that the play of children is not the random and incomprehensible activity that many adults think it is. It has meaning and purpose, that purpose being nothing less than mastery of the techniques needed for living in the world as the child knows it. Play is therefore of the greatest importance for normal development both physically and psychically. The child's growing body demands the learning and constant refinement of physical skills, of increasingly complex feats of muscular power, sensory discrimination and thinking, both plastic and conceptual. These are accompanied by attempts to control the setting in which the child finds himself, as well as the objects, living and inanimate, which populate it. Symbolization and abstraction are parts of this process, for playthings, whether they are toys or "real" objects, may be regarded either literally or figuratively.

If the first attempt at mastery of a skill or overcoming of a fear is not successful, the child then repeats either the original action or some variation of it until the immediate problem is solved. Not only is such mastery through repetition a necessary part of growing up, it also continues to affect adult behavior in complex and subtle ways. For the child, play is the usual method of acquiring not only physical skills but also appropriate emotional behavior. A model given by Kris will illustrate:

> A huge Alsatian dog comes yelping at a little boy playing outdoors. The child is frightened by the creature's size and bark, and turns away, screaming for help. He may later elaborate this scene in many ways. In his play with his toys, roles will be reversed; the boy will conquer the threatening enemy and tame the animal, which may become his special friend and protector. The scene may occupy the boy's thoughts

at night in bed before he goes to sleep. The dog may grow in size and shape. Dangers that he had experienced before and other thoughts, common to all little boys, may merge with the latest encounter. When these thoughts recur during the day, the boy relives the pleasurable experience of the conquest of danger in his daydreams. The delight of the triumph explains why play and daydreams can be repeated again and again.

The influence of the traumatic experience . . . may be more or less lasting; play or daydreams may continue for a long time. They may change their content and still bear the imprint of flight from, or conquest of, danger, and when the boy comes of age he may translate fantasy into action. . . . Or else the specific matter of play and daydream may persist and cause him to become a fancier of pets or a scientific student of animal nature. . . . Clinical observation indicates . . . that the chosen solution serves many purposes at the same time and is, as it were, the resultant of many forces.[12]

The inciting event need not, of course, be traumatic. Any of the normal problems of getting along in the world would suffice, but they might not exhibit such easily recognizable results.

The bodily activities which are engaged in during play do not occur in a psychic vacuum. They are accompanied by fantasies, conscious and unconscious. These are the prototypes and the raw materials of art, crude and far removed from the finished productions which command our admiration but related to them all the same. This imaginative modification of reality for the easing of inner tension may be directed outward by the child. He may communicate some version of it to his mother or his playmates. What began as a personal problem thus acquires a social aspect, one of the requisites of art. Even at this early stage it is more than the mere transmission of a message. Frequently the hearers respond in such a way that it becomes a shared experience to be enjoyed passively or embellished and expanded by both parties. On the surface they are involved in the fantasy itself, taking pleasure in the unfolding of the plot, the twists and turns of language, the narrative skill of the teller. Underneath, they are reacting to their own need to air problems which are similar to, if not identical with, those of their colleague. By conscious participation they are alleviating unconscious tensions and gaining open satisfaction in the product without wholly realizing that it acquires most of its intensity from forces of which they are not even aware. This twofold response is closely analogous to that of the reader of fiction, the playgoer, the listener to music or the viewer of paintings and sculpture.

Religious practices characteristic of early stages of culture led to several forms of specialization of function which, Kris speculates, played a part in the evolution of certain modern arts. Magic rituals designed to influence or control the forces of nature or to appease the gods were probably performed by the entire tribe or at least by all the men together. Gradually some portions of the ceremony were by common consent allotted to small groups or to individuals who demonstrated special aptitudes for dancing, singing and the like. Such talents were probably assumed to be the gift of the gods, and it was therefore appropriate that their possessors devote them to religious service. It is probable also that a special aptitude entitled its possessor to modify his portion of the ritual as the spirit moved him so that successive generations of priests, shamans and medicine men introduced many variations within the general framework which supplied the continuity. In somewhat similar fashion the primitive religious rituals of ancient Greek civilization gradually evolved into the forms in which Greek drama has come down to us. By the time the plays were written they were far removed from their religious origin and retained only vestigial reminders of it, like the chorus which had itself undergone important changes in function. The players were also different from the primitive dancers around the ceremonial fire. They were no longer conducting a ritual, the larger value of which lay in its repetition of actions and sounds in almost unvarying sequence year after year. Now they stood ready to play one part after another at the direction of the dramatist. He perhaps partook of divine inspiration, but this was a far cry from the chant of the priest or medicine man; the drama no longer retained the force of religion. A great change had taken place in the role of the populace, too. From direct or vicarious participators in a ceremonial they had become spectators at a play, and their responses took forms ranging from naive "acting in one's seat" to full acceptance of the aesthetic illusion, the tacit assumption that the dramatist's world was, for the moment, real, although clearly different from the world outside the theater. Distance from artistic action while participating in it is a measure of aesthetic response, and this depends not only on phases in civilization but on growth in sophistication which enables the child to transfer values from one activity to another without confusing them.

From the standpoint of ego psychology this phenomenon is seen to have a relationship to the gratification afforded by the mastery of outer reality. It is also augmented by other gratifications. As indicated in Kris's model, some of the feelings may be transferred to the subject of a related train of thought or to an intellectual field having a consistency of its own and wholly independent of personal involvement, e.g., zoology. The psychic energy which formerly gave strength to the fear would, in such a case, be diverted toward the interest outside the self, and the new study invested with nearly all of the emotional power that the original affect carried. Thus the child gains in two ways: negatively, by removing the sting from the unpleasant experience, and positively, by acquiring an equivalent pleasure from the new interest. By this means a largely instinctual reaction may be transformed into a largely cerebral process.

This is accompanied by the functional pleasure which is the result of the reduction of tension between the agencies within the psyche. The ego, id and superego can now maintain their interrelationships with the expenditure of less effort than before, and this relative ease of operation, though not apprehended consciously, has a gratifying effect. Creative thinking, then, may provide pleasure over and above that which comes from external creative success. Even the frustration resulting from failure is mitigated by the harmonious operation of the psychic apparatus, for unsuccessful activity, too, results in the discharge of psychic energy no matter what the social outcome of its efforts may be.

These forms of gratification are related to preconscious mental activity and require a technical explanation. This is to be found in most essentials in Kris's paper, "On Preconscious Mental Processes," [13] a subject of great importance for the understanding of the psychoanalytic contribution to the psychology of aesthetics.

The current emphasis on ego psychology is turning the attention of more and more psychoanalysts to its study, and the needs of their patients will undoubtedly stimulate further research into matters having a bearing on aesthetic problems. We should begin here with a brief restatement of the anatomy of the mental personality.[14]

That portion of the psyche which is most intimately related to bodily functions and may be regarded as their psychic counterpart is the id, an accumulation of instinctual (that is, physically based) desires seeking only direct satisfaction. They are closely analogous to the stimulus-response mechanisms of the nervous system, both following the "all-or-none law." When the stimulus is applied, a total discharge is attempted, and this may be inhibited only with considerable difficulty. Both are unconscious; in effect they work automatically and are independent of our conscious will, although it is possible to learn a measure of control, as for instance, the inhibition of blinking when the eye is threatened by a dangerous object. The lines are by no means hard and fast; some id-impulses enter the sphere of the ego or that of the superego under special conditions, as we have already seen, but usually they remain in their own domain. Of this class of feelings we are not conscious; we can know them only indirectly, as depression or anxiety, for instance. Also unconscious are those thoughts and feelings which have for various reasons become too painful to be acknowledged and have consequently been banished from awareness (repressed) by the ego.

The ego itself is partly unconscious—this portion of it maintains the repression of unpleasant elements—and partly conscious. It therefore has access both to the inner life of the individual and to the outer world. This is the clue to its function, which is to regulate the psychic equilibrium, to temper the demands of the id to the requirements of outer reality, and to modify that reality, in so far as this is possible, to the needs of psychic life. This makes it the most important of the three agencies for our study. The function of the superego is to influence—to control if it can—our social behavior according to standards of conduct received from parents or society and incorporated by it into the personality so that their operation takes place without our being aware of it except in case of conflict. One of its commonly recognized functions is to be our moral guide (conscience). The demands of ego, id and superego cause a balance of forces to be struck which is relatively stable but always dynamic. A constant fluctuation goes on between the three with now one, now another momentarily attaining dominance, but most of the upsets in the equilibrium are transitory, and the shifting takes place within safe limits. In normal people the ego is in the most influential position most of the time, and it is this which, with the help of the superego, channels our animal nature into human directions.

One of the basic tenets of psychoanalysis is the concept of this flux in our unconscious mental life. But ideas, feelings and sensations may be either conscious or unconscious, that is, perceived or not perceived. Some, unconscious in origin, have made their way to awareness. Others were once conscious but are so no longer; unless brought to perception either by a breakdown of psychic controls or by psychotherapy they will forever remain hidden. There is also a third class which is not presently conscious but "is capable of becoming conscious easily and under conditions which frequently arise." [15] These are called preconscious. It is important to note that preconscious is an adjective for which there is no corresponding noun; there is no such thing as "the Preconscious." Either we are aware of an idea or we are not. Preconscious refers only to the fact that certain ideas can emerge into awareness without any particular resistance from the psychic apparatus. It is not the intrinsic nature of the ideas which matters so much as the quantity of psychic energy with which they are invested. Preconscious ideas which have relatively little energy remain in the latent, i.e., unconscious, state. Among these are ideas having no special significance, ideas relating to situations which occur infrequently (if needed, they can be recalled to consciousness by simply focusing attention on them), and ideas which may be unpleasant but not to the degree that they threaten our hard-won equilibrium (these may require a determined effort to bring back and to keep consciously in mind). Their ability to become conscious depends upon their power at a given psychic moment.

This ability is greatly affected by the modes of operation characteristic of unconscious and conscious mental processes, respectively. Unconscious processes utilize energy which is mobile, that is, it is not attached (bound) to only one activity but may range about the psyche, activating now one dormant chain of responses, now another. But this movement is not haphazard. Psychoanalysis insists that there are no accidents in psychic life; everything has meaning and purpose, if only we can discover what these are. The particular direction in which a quantity of psychic energy seeks to flow is governed ultimately by somatic requirements and by the degree of difficulty experienced in satisfying them. But there are so many possible channels that when one outlet is blocked it is easy for the energy to shift toward another, the one offering the least resistance to its passage at the moment. These can be understood as the operation of the primary process and the secondary process, respectively.

The former refers to the strong instinctual drives of the id which seek immediate and total discharge; this is the only action of which they are capable. They make use of the abundant "free" energy in this primitive part of the psyche to strive for such discharge, and in the effort they condense, displace and combine unconscious material according to the principle of least resistance stated above. It is not the nature of the mental act which matters to the id, but the amount of psychic energy which temporarily invests it.

The ego's role in this is to inhibit. Leaving aside the material which is totally repressed and never reaches consciousness, the ego permits partial discharge of psychic energy which it governs by the qualitative character of the mental acts which accompany and to some extent disguise it. This is the famous censorship which results in the modes of thought familiar to our waking minds after passing through intermediate stages. The ego aids the id in meeting its need to reduce psychic pressures, but it sets limits. Like a parent admonishing a child that too much candy is not good for it, it knows how much of the total appetite to satisfy and when to call a halt. The ego is aware of conditions outside the skin—which the id is not—and it is in position to avoid potentially dangerous or uncomfortable situations either by curbing the inner appetites or by taking external action. Psychically, it is able most of the time to channel the mobile energy of the id into desirable directions, granting as much discharge of excess quantities as is compatible with the safety and well-being of the individual. On the one hand it acts as a safety valve preventing the accumulation of too much force within. On the other it attempts to control the impulses so that they will not upset the psychic equilibrium. It can do this because it "binds" the energy, attaching it to an acceptable train of mental actions like an engineer directing electrical current from a dynamo into a circuit where it will do useful, controlled work. Such bound energy is thereby committed to one channel and cannot easily resume the mobility it had under the free-flowing conditions of the id. The success of the ego in this depends upon its ability to keep the energy where it wants it, i.e., bound. When the ego's ability to do this breaks down, the id invades its territory and controls mental activity according to its own rules. Energy which was bound becomes mobile again and the impulses run riot with their new power. The result is neurosis, criminality or worse, since the individual then acts not with regard to the necessities of the world but solely to gratify his inner needs. The normal ego's mastery of psychic energy makes it the agency which adapts the organism to its environment and obtains from the environment that which is necessary for the welfare of the organism.

In the operation of the secondary process we have the core of creative thinking. Here begin those manipulations of ideas and symbols which take cognizance of the need for at least a partial correspondence with outer reality. Not merely the superficial resemblances of sound and appearance but aspects of meaning in the conscious sense now exert their influence. This is still fragmentary; the dream which has a more or less fully developed dramatic structure occurs now and then, but it is a rarity. Most of the time the secondary process is carried out on only a few elements in a fantasy at a time without regard to the ones that precede or follow. It provides connectives and a degree of coherence sufficient to satisfy the casual scrutiny of the ego without attempting to organize the whole. Successive scenes in a dream, for example, may seem to make sense individually but to have no connection with one another. The secondary process is, like the primary process, unconscious, but it seems to be on the threshold of consciousness, since in it the requirements of our waking view of the world begin, although hazily and incompletely, to make themselves felt. The embryonic elements of artistic productions are to be found in id-impulses which have been subjected to the primary process, but this accounts only for what is universal in human nature as it makes its appearance in art. It tells us little about the ways in which one finished work differs from another. The tremendous variety of art arises from the (unconscious) secondary revision which softens objections, supplies transitions, finds points of similarity, and in general provides at least a patchwork of temporarily acceptable organization of the fantasy. The way is thus prepared for the artist's deliberate manipulation of the fantasy according to the requirements of his basic idea, his medium and his audience, all of which constitute the conscious exercise of his craft. But before it is ready for his hand, the raw material has first come from unconscious sources—the whole sequence may have been initiated by some conscious idea which then associated itself with suitable unconscious material—and it has been processed by unconscious forces.

The original psychoanalytic view of the manner in which forbidden ideas become transformed into acceptable ones has been somewhat modified by Kris and his co-workers.[16] They point out that while an idea needs psychic energy to overcome obstacles on the way to consciousness, mere quantity is not enough. They therefore suggest that when an idea acquires additional energy it takes on some of the emotional significance of the sexual or aggressive source from which the energy came. That is, energy which has activated a sexual idea lends a sexual quality to any other idea which it cathects (invests), and the same is true of energy which has previously activated an aggressive mental act. In order for ideas to pass the borders between areas under the control, respectively, of the id, ego and superego it is often necessary for them to divest themselves of such unacceptable flavoring. This is accomplished by a process which Kris calls "neutralization," which means that not only the idea but the aim as well are perceived as uncontaminated by the objectionable aura, and that the energy may therefore be used to bring to consciousness a thought that carries the id-expression along with it in concealment, like contraband being smuggled past customs. The modification proposed by Kris and his colleagues does not require any alteration of the original energic hypothesis. Psychic energy does not change its nature but merely fluctuates in quantity. What changes is the perception of it by the individual psyche, and this is all that the new view deals with. Underlying it is the assumption that there is a limit to the fineness of our discrimination. We can never wholly separate our awareness of energy from the flavor of the psychic material which it activates, although under certain conditions the sexual or aggressive residue may be barely perceptible.

> Sublimation . . . designates two processes so clearly related to each other that one might be tempted to speak of one and the same process: it refers to the displacement of energy discharge from a socially inacceptable goal to an acceptable one and to a transformation of the energy discharged; for this second process we here adopt the word "neutralization." The usefulness of the distinction between the two meanings becomes apparent when we realize that goal substitution and energy transformation need not be synchronous; the more acceptable, i.e., "higher," activity can be executed with energy that has retained or regained its original instinctual quality. We speak then of sexualization or aggressivization.[17]

The wording of this paragraph seems to refer to a change in the nature of the energy itself, but the context makes it clear that Kris is referring to the response and not to the stimulus. We may properly say, then, that the productions of creative thought are not necessarily sexual or aggressive in nature, even though they may have derived much of their psychic strength from sexual or aggressive sources. Not only may the work of the artist be psychically autonomous but it must be evaluated according to criteria having little or no connection with id-impulses.

But this does not mean, says Kris, that the final product is completely divorced from the sexual or aggressive nature of the original impulse which it expresses at many removes. It is able to retain at least a portion of this nature because a new variable has been introduced into the equation: the degree of neutralization that may be required by an activity. Although this may be low, "yet we may be dealing with secondary processes; while fully under

the control of the ego, fully bound, the energy may still have retained the hallmark of libido or aggression."

A further problem is the possibility that once the energy has
invested the artistic activity the flow may not be reversed, that is,
the work of art assumes an "independent" existence with its own
psychic reason for being and no further connection with its source.
(This is called "secondary autonomy in ego functions" and applies to a great range of activities besides artistic ones.) Theoretically, "sublimation in creative activity might conceivably prove
to be distinguished by two characteristics: the fusion in the discharge of instinctual energy and the shift in pyschic levels." [18]
Fusion here refers to the merging of libidinal and aggressive
energy, which helps disguise the nature of that which is being
discharged and so eases the path for it. Hartmann, Kris and
Loewenstein add "the special assumption that a certain degree of
energy neutralization provides favorable conditions for fusion
and hence for the mastery of even particularly intense instinctual
demands." [19] Whatever the theoretical validity of these new concepts may turn out to be, they offer the possibility that the problem
of the relation which a writer's work bears to his instinctual life
may be scientifically examined.

Kris's exploration and formulation of the ways in which ego
psychology tells us more about art has provided scientific understanding, some of it clinical and some hypothetical, about many
important aesthetic questions. By reminding us of the functional
pleasure derived from the mere operation of the psychic apparatus
he has given us one clue to the fascination of the creative process
for artists, even when it is artistically unsuccessful. By offering the
hypothesis of neutralized energy he and his co-workers provide a
new possibility for following in detail the transformation of psychic ideas into aesthetic products. By emphasizing the flexibility
of boundary lines between ego, id and superego he helps us see how
mental material may pass from the control of one to that of another and how each may make use of the others for its own purposes. This is a step toward the destruction of the over-simplified
image of the artist as the prisoner of his erotic and aggressive impulses. It gives comfort to those who respect and admire the artist
and who think of him as the master of his aesthetic fate. This view

is further enhanced by the concept of the autonomous functions of the ego, which produce works that assume independent existence, so that out of the basic physical realities of life grow the creations of artists leading to the highest spiritual achievements. The concepts of repression and sublimation are also of use in understanding and following the vicissitudes of ideas to their final embodiment in art. The shifting of psychic energy from place to place and from one kind of material to another within the mind, together with many of the laws governing this flux, permits the systematic understanding of the difference between the inspirational and elaborational phases of creative activity.

By focusing on the role of the ego, Kris emphasizes the higher mental nature of creativity. Art is a function not of our animal nature—although it may be said to grow out of this—but of that which makes us human; it does not come from our isolated selves but from that part of us which reaches out to the rest of humanity. It expresses not only our relationship to the world as it is but also to the world as we wish it to be, and it thus opens the way to limitless human aspirations.

* * *

Psychoanalysis can tell us little as yet about the reasons why a man chooses to become an artist, but that there is some quality which distinguishes artists from other persons is a matter of common belief, and there is truth in it. Members of certain vocations do share certain kinds of general characteristics which distinguish them from others as a group and which do affect their personal lives, considered apart from their professional careers. All this is recognized by the psychoanalyst who takes it into account in his clinical work:

> Our expectations are significantly limited when we hear that a certain patient is an actor, a dancer, a cartoonist, or a dress designer. They are less limited but still significant when we hear that he is a writer, painter, architect, or poet. In all these cases . . . we expect that certain typical conflict constellations will more likely occur than others. The problem of rapidly changing identification may be crucial in the actor, that of coping with exhibition in the dancer, the wish

to distort others in the cartoonist, and to adorn them in the dress designer; but each of these dominant wishes . . . is clearly merged with innumerable other tendencies in the individual, and each of them is rooted in his history.[20]

What ego psychology has shown us is that one of the most significant factors in vocational success is the ability to remove the activity, whatever it may be, from involvement in psychic conflict. No matter what the nature of the conflict may have been which caused the individual to become interested in a specific activity in the first place, if it then and thereafter achieves a degree of autonomy it may be developed according to its own requirements with little or no regard for the psychic situation out of which it emerged. The artist is an individual who has special gifts the nature of which we do not understand but which enable him to erect such relatively independent structures according to laws of their own and with such intricacy that the course of their development from the original material may be impossible to trace.

The problem of the artist is complicated further by changing conditions in the medium and the milieu, by new artistic movements and by fluctuations in taste. Those personal qualities which would produce success in one era may be useless in another. We are reminded of the unknown Higgins of Tennessee in Mark Twain's *Captain Stormfield's Visit To Heaven* who marched ahead of Shakespeare in the procession of merit because if he had only had the opportunity he would have written poetry even greater than Shakespeare's. Kris suggests that while specific applications are difficult to make, it is likely that "the artist whose creative capacities are close to potential pathology will find his place more easily in romantic than in classical periods of art," and vice versa.[21] Sometimes it is fertility of imagination and loftiness of inspiration which are most highly valued, sometimes serenity and control of the medium. These changes may not only encourage or discourage certain types of personalities to come forward at certain times but may also actually effect changes in the personalities themselves as they strive to adjust themselves to the demands of the artistic milieu. The artist whose "flexibility of repression" is greatest will probably be most successful at this.

In attempting to understand the nature of the artist it is useful to examine the popular myth about him, the belief in which he himself sometimes shares.[22] In some early literary biographies this bears a close resemblance to the myth of the hero, the chief difference being that the artist's outstanding quality even as a child is not, of course, kingliness but creative power, a mysterious gift of God. Since it is of divine origin, it comprises not merely the ability to rearrange the physical materials of this world but a supernatural quality as well. This appears to be in direct line of descent from myths like that of Daedalus in whom great skill was combined with a daring that led to the defiance of deity. And these two qualities are essential to all artists. Each is either God's rival or His tool.[23] In the creation of his world the artist is supreme. He makes and remakes it according to his heart's desire. There are many legends of sculptors and artisans whose statues come to life, of painters whose pictures deceive birds, animals or men with their realism. The unconscious wish to create like God is apparently part of the artist's equipment. His skill affords him the means symbolically to achieve omnipotence.

The conception of the artist as God's instrument is a more common one, or rather it is more commonly acknowledged. "Its nucleus is inspiration. The underlying psychological mechanism is familiar: an unconscious thought is externalized and when it reaches consciousness is experienced as if it came from the outside." [24] Nowadays it is probably not very often attributed to the Deity but rather to an unspecified force of immeasurable power, like fate. Kris suggests that the chief reason for this is that in the process of creation the artist is made aware of many of the deeper layers of his personality which are not ordinarily accessible to conscious perception. The strength of these id-impulses, which have temporarily been allowed by the ego to emerge, gives them direct sensory expression, and the artist is thus made aware of a sound or a visual image which has not come from outside in the usual fashion but which registers on the sensory apparatus just as though it had. Such an act is almost indistinguishable from hallucination and indeed differs from it only in the use to which it is put. A closely similar phenomenon is the state of ecstasy in which religious revelation takes place. In both there is a feeling of being in full control at the same time that one is doing God's will as His chosen agent.

This relationship between creativity and passivity is the result of a change in the nature of the material which is passing from unconsciousness to consciousness. "Id energies suddenly combine with ego energies, mobile with bound and neutralized cathexes, to produce the unique experience of inspiration which is felt to reach consciousness from the outside." [25] The feeling of power is increased by the large quantity of energy being discharged; the feeling of submission by the reaction to the danger that the ego will be overwhelmed. Flexibility of repression permits such outflowings of the id, but only when the ego is standing watchfully by and has the strength to put a stop to them when it needs to. This always occurs relatively soon, for the id is too powerful to be permitted a free hand; if it were to get out of control the equilibrium of the personality would be destroyed and psychosis would probably ensue. Inspiration is the diametric opposite of such a disaster. The psychic integrity of the artist remains intact.

Both inspiration and the next phase of artistic creation, elaboration, "are characterized by shifts in psychic levels, in the degree of ego control and by shifts in the cathexis of the self and the representation of the audience." [26] Inspiration, by these operations of the ego, performs the essential task of directing the artistic imagination away from the self and toward the work. It establishes the interest of the artist in the theme and its potentialities for expression through the medium. A new focus is set up, a direction suggested, an area delimited which is separate from the artist as man —even as artist—and which contains the embryo of an almost self-sufficient entity. The connection, however, is never broken; something always remains to link it with its source. But in certain kinds of art production this may become a very attenuated filament indeed, while in others the bond may remain close. What matters is that inspiration affords the possibility of a new creation which the artist may then develop with a degree of freedom from his neurosis. Aesthetic requirements are quite different from the laws of the psyche, though they have a fairly large number of traits in common. While he is creating, the artist is still subject to the demands of his psyche, but he is nevertheless able to do his work according to artistic principles.

Having re-directed his artistic attention to the work and away from his emotional problems, the artist then follows aesthetic requirements. His inner life goes on as before, but it is now separated from his artistic activity, except that he is able from time to time to avail himself of the resources of his id and to bring them into the aesthetic pattern. The process of inspiration results in a re-orientation toward a new object, the work of art, which involves conscious as well as unconscious powers in a new relationship. Elaboration of the material, i.e., the art-work, is then possible.[27] Part of this consists of the preconscious mental processes already mentioned, and takes place without awareness. Part is consciously willed. The greater part combines these two, for they are not so much independent actions as phases of a single, complex act, each with its own emphasis.

Since, according to Kris and his co-workers, freely wandering thought processes of the kind which are typical of fantasy tend to discharge more libido and aggression and less neutralized psychic energy, and since purposeful reflection of the kind which is found in creative thinking tends to discharge more neutralized energy, then it follows that reflective—and creative—thinking best serve the "higher, autonomous ego interests." [28] This combination of analysis and synthesis is heavily influenced by the devotion of the artist to his work, by his dedication and concentration. In technical terms, there is a shift in the cathexis, that is, the quantity of emotional energy attached to certain ego functions.

> The inspirational phase is characterized by the facility with which id impulses, or their closer derivatives, are received. One might say that countercathectic energies to some extent are withdrawn, and added to the speed, force, or intensity with which the preconscious thoughts are formed. During the "elaborational" phase, the countercathectic barrier may be reinforced, work proceeds slowly, cathexis is directed to other ego functions such as reality testing, formulation, or general purposes of communication. Alternations between the two phases may be rapid, oscillating, or distributed over long stretches of time.[29]

The ego relaxes its rigor and, for a moment, "entrusts a thought to the id." In this moment the thought is subjected to id forces which elaborate it according to the methods characteristic of that portion of the psyche. The ego thereupon reclaims the elaborated thought for its own—since it retains control of the entire process—

invests it with neutralized ego energy and proceeds to elaborate it further, this time according to the needs of the individual in his relations with the outside world. In this phase it is not the body which rules but the judgment. This process is characteristic of the whole field of reflective thought including the creative. Each kind is, of course, conditioned by the requirements of the medium it uses: mathematics imposes one mode of procedure, politics quite another. Creative thought in art is necessarily different in the various branches of art; a musician characteristically does not think like a poet or a sculptor, although there are individuals who combine two or more of these apparently diverse abilities to a high degree.

*   *   *

In his study of artists' biographies which were written before the sixteenth century, Kris [30] found that the accounts of their early life tended to show remarkable parallels to the pattern established by Rank.[31] Principally they viewed the child's special gifts and accomplishments "not as part of his history, but as premonition of his future character." [32] These gifts were discovered, according to the typical legend, by a famous man, e.g., the discovery of Giotto by Cimabue, who thereupon became the child's sponsor and teacher. Regularly the pupil grew up to outdo the master. Another theme is the relation to the divine. The painter is so skillful that his picture deceives birds into trying to eat the painted fruit; the sculptor falls in love with the statue he carves (Pygmalion). In Genesis God shapes Adam out of clay. God as artist and artist as God are closely related conceptions.

Before modern biography the image of the artist tended to be very like the image of the hero. The child is supernaturally endowed, he outdoes his teacher, he creates the equivalent of life. In later biographies one more feature is added, that of ambivalence. There is an inner struggle going on which causes the artist to alternate between challenges to God and submission to Him. He has moods of despair which, however, do not prevent him from producing triumphant masterpieces. There is a parallel in his social life. He defies the Pope, refuses to complete the Duke's statue, keeps the portrait of the Duchess. For a time he lives at court, but then he leaves and sets up a bourgeois establishment in the city. There he offends the burghers by flouting their moral values while he outrages his fellow artists by conspicuous spending of the munificent commissions he has received from the nobility. He considers himself apart from society and above its demands. He consents to live in it but only within an enclave where he is master. There is at once something of the outcast in him and something of the chosen one.

The public, too, regards him as at the same time blessed and cursed. Along with the disquieting feeling that he is empowered by some mysterious and frightening force to accomplish more than ordinary men there is the notion that all artists are a little crazy. This association with sacredness on the one hand and mental aberration on the other brings with it an uneasy awe, almost uncanniness.

Like other widely held ideas, there is a measure of truth in this one, but it has been magnified and distorted in the popular mind until it seems to the informed to be all falsehood. But the educated, too, suffer from insufficient information since completely adequate means simply do not exist by which the productions of normal artists can be surely distinguished from those of neurotics and even some psychotics. Psychoanalysis has not solved this problem either, but it has advanced to the place where it can say some useful things about it.

One of the difficulties is that there is not even a satisfactory definition of what is normal. A recent attempt to provide one may be provisionally adopted here, although it has not yet been generally accepted.[33] Kubie reports that his clinical observation shows only one feature which always accompanies neurotic behavior. This is the necessity that the act be repeated:

> Whether or not a behavioral event is free to change depends not on the quality of the act itself, but upon the nature of the constellation of forces that has produced it. No moment of behavior can be looked upon as neurotic unless the processes that have set it in motion predetermine its automatic repetition irrespective of the situation, the utility, or the consequences of the act.[34]

According to this hypothesis, when the dominating motive for an act is unconscious (or perhaps partly unconscious and partly preconscious) the goal is most likely to be an unconscious symbol rather than some external reality. Since this goal is never attainable the act is doomed to be repeated endlessly, and fruitlessly, as long as sufficient energy is available for it. Normal behavior is governed by an alliance of the conscious and preconscious systems. Therefore, the action will cease "either when its goal is achieved and satiety is attained, or when the goal is found to be unattainable or ungratifying or both." The normal person (for which we may read "the artist") learns from experience, tests his ideas against external reality, changes his course when he sees it to be necessary, and finally makes an end. His actions are not irrational, erratic and destructive; they have pattern and meaning, and they make sense to himself and to his peers. Between these extreme ends of the scale there are innumerable gradations at any one of which we may find ourselves during a given act. But a few wild swings of the indicator in either direction have little effect on the general level of the performance. In fact, as we have seen, the ability to move rapidly out of one's usual orbit and to bring the psyche back into equilibrium is one of the marks of the creative personality. It is a sign of the ego's strength that it can tolerate brief incursions of the id and turn them to its own purposes.

The psychotic who creates, in contrast to the normal or neurotic artist, does so as a part of his delusional system. His illness involves the fantasy that he has somehow destroyed certain (psychic) objects which are significant to him, and pictorial or linguistic "art" becomes a means by which these may be restored. The intact portions of the psychotic's ego, in other words, take the only channel available to them to re-establish the lost contact with reality. The degree to which they succeed in this depends on how much id strength the disintegrating portions of the ego allow to emerge. This kind of "art" has for its purpose a purely private restitution of reality along with an elaboration of the psychotic fantasy. It embodies the struggle which is taking place within the personality and mirrors both the healthy and the sick tendencies. Thus, the psychotic uses his "art" as a magical means of destroying his enemies as well as rebuilding his universe. But even though the ego is fighting to restore normality, the odds are against it. The id has invaded too-large areas of the psyche and holds sway there; its imposition of the primary process on symbolic expression eventually becomes dominant and cannot be controlled by the weakened ego. Such "art" is the result of compulsion; the patient has no choice. It is a mental battle within the self and not a means of communicating with others. The psychotic "artist" never moves from a direct expression of his conflicts to a concern with the symbolic production for its own sake, as the normal artist does. He never learns new techniques, never becomes aware of social or artistic influences from without. The whole process takes place within and is not intended to reach out to others.

This, however, is stating the case in the most extreme way, which I have done here to make it more easily understandable. It is literally true only of psychotics who are in the last extremity and for whom there is no hope of cure. All manner of combinations become possible at different points on the scale. Some psychotic mechanisms may influence normal creative activity, as is obvious in the work of certain surrealist painters and poets, without thereby enabling us to conclude anything useful whatsoever about the psychic life of the artist. Some may merge with the stronger parts of his personal expression and produce work which is extremely difficult to interpret or appreciate, since it is an admixture of elements which we are familiar with as critics or appreciators, and of elements which are comprehensible only to the clinician. Finally, the degree to which all this is discernible in the work varies according to laws which have not yet been discovered. The point is that art may partake of illness and yet be healthy art. The "art" of the psychotic is of interest to us only in that it shows in extreme form some of the things that go into normal art.

*　　*　　*

In responding to a work of art the audience undergoes a process which is the reverse of that experienced by the artist in creation. From the conscious perception of the work it is led back to the preconscious elaboration which the original elements have undergone, and from these still further back to "the reverberations of the id." [35] There seem to be two phases in this process, the first passive and the second active. The audience at first gives itself to the art work, submitting to the pattern and direction which the artist has set. Psychoanalytically stated, for each member of the audience, the ego relaxes some of its control, as did the ego of the artist in creating, and permits a certain amount of interplay with the id. The amount of this and its intensity of effect varies with the individual. The second phase is the re-establishing of the ego's control, not only for defense against the restrictions of the superego and the dangers arising from the id but also for the assumption by the ego of a creative function analogous to that of the artist. Depending on a host of variables—such as the ego strength of the individual, the relation of art to his own psychic problems, the form and structure of the work, and the aesthetic milieu which expects certain kinds of responses rather than others—the audience then proceeds to re-create an emotional-aesthetic entity which is the resultant of all these forces.

The aesthetic illusion (approximately what Coleridge meant by the "willing suspension of disbelief that constitutes poetic faith") is not a universal phenomenon, or perhaps it would be better to say that not everyone has the ability to a sufficient degree to experience wholly in the imagination and to relinquish the possibility of action. Probably most of the human race unthinkingly seeks motor discharge of tensions most of the time and in general prefers it to the internal kind of reaction induced by an aesthetic experience. The latter, at least in its higher forms, occurs probably as infrequently as the ability to perform any specialized and skilled act, and this restriction refers both to endowment and training. For those who are psychically so constituted that the possibility exists, an aesthetic experience takes place only when psychic energy is discharged as a result of the establishment of a point of identification for the audience with the work of art. This is not by any means the only condition that is necessary, but it is an indispensable one.

A proper psychic distance must be maintained from the work of art for optimum aesthetic effect. When the identification with the emotional situation depicted is too intimate, the response becomes an active one; the work of art is then experienced as reality, and an attenuated aesthetic effect is felt, or none at all. Such a response harks back to primitive participation in religious ceremonials where the physical activities of the dancers or chanters provide sufficient outlet for the accumulated tensions and where the magical character of the ritual makes the audience feel that it is taking part in a real activity which can actually influence the course of nature. A modern counterpart is the small boy at the movies who shoots his toy pistol at the villain on the screen. If, on the other hand, the identification is not great enough the distance from the work of art is too great. No point exists at which the audience may establish an emotional connection with it, and consequently an aesthetic experience is impossible. Our small boy is forced to invent his villains or simply to shoot at any available target that he invests with those attributes which it is desirable for targets to have.

Kris suggests that the reaction of the audience begins with the recognition that some portion of the subject matter resembles a memory of a past experience. A psychic connection is thus made between the complex of associations clustering about the inner world and the imaginary world presented by the artist, an imaginary world which represents both inner and outer reality. A stage follows in which "some experience of the perceived and recognized subject becomes part of the spectator." [36] He reacts with his own body, i.e., kinaesthetically, to what he sees in the work. This reaction may be completely unconscious. Thus bodily experience, the image of one's body,[37] and the sensory perception of the work of art combine to produce an identification with the artist's model, especially when this is a human figure but perhaps for any object. Finally, the unconscious bodily following of the lines produced by the artist, i.e., the apprehending and appreciation of his technique as distinct from the subject matter, may, but does not always, lead to "imitation" of them. In passing into an active role we become co-creators along the path marked by the artist and so identify ourselves with him.

> We soon recognize that what is here described as reaction to representative art is part of the adequate response to all art. The case we chose, i.e., of the reaction to the representation of the human body—by whatever theory this reaction be ex-

plained—proves to be only the case by which our thesis can best be demonstrated. The sequence of reactions described, however, seems to be valid for a wide range of experiences. This sequence will not develop if we miss the aesthetic illusion; it will be impeded by both "overdistance" and "underdistance." It is, we believe, dependent upon and—in circular fashion—frequently responsible for the appropriate distance, and seems a most significant component of the specificity of the aesthetic response.[38]

What the ego contributes to the appreciation of art is, in addition to its knowledge of the world and the self, the relating of the aesthetic object to the unconscious of the spectator. This it accomplishes by its ability to subject the perceptions momentarily to the influence of the primary process, as we have already seen the artist doing. The spectator undergoes a similar experience. He is thus enabled to feel what the artist wishes him to feel and to do so in the way that is of the greatest emotional significance to him. What has just been outlined here is the ideal case; there are great difficulties in fully achieving such a response. If the audience has a high degree of ego control "the result is not re-creation but reconstruction. The experience is . . . 'intellectualized.' " [39] Instead of an aesthetic response, we have a concern with form and interpretation, a dilletantism which lacks the essential ingredient of emotional integrity. A great deal of feeling may be attached to the knowing remarks which are made between the acts or between drinks, but it is not the feeling which the artist put into his work and which properly belongs to it. This is the sort of thing which has been so devastatingly satirized by James Thurber.[40]

When there is too little ego control over the influence of the primary process we are apt to be overwhelmed by inarticulate ecstasy. The proper shift in psychic level cannot take place, and we feel great gusts of emotion relatively uncontaminated by the discipline the artist intended to impose upon us. We do not emerge from the passive stage to the re-creative activity which leads to the highest aesthetic enjoyment.

Psychoanalytic ego psychology is changing the conceptions of artist, art and audience as they existed in the early days of psychoanalysis. Its investigations into the nature of creative mental processes reveal these as evidence of strength, not of weakness, in the personality. The ego of the successful artist handles dangerous psychic material and remains in control of it. The artist is not the victim of his sexual and aggressive drives but their exploiter. This is the central conception which is replacing the former view.

V

Van Wyck Brooks versus
Mark Twain versus Samuel Clemens

The Ordeal of Mark Twain is one of the earliest books in which a prominent American critic makes use of psychoanalytic ideas, although they furnish him neither the central theme of the book nor its chief method. In it Van Wyck Brooks addresses himself to the problem of why Mark Twain's success was accompanied by a bitter feeling of failure and why this developed into a pessimism which grew more marked with age. His conclusion, which he presents as a hypothesis at the outset, is stated in these words:

> It is an established fact, if I am not mistaken, that these morbid feelings of sin, which have no evident cause, are the result of having transgressed some inalienable life-demand peculiar to one's nature. It is as old as Milton that there are talents which are "death to hide," and I suggest that Mark Twain's "talent" was just so hidden. That bitterness of his was the effect of a certain miscarriage in his creative life, a balked personality, an arrested development of which he was himself almost wholly unaware, but which for him destroyed the meaning of life.[1]

According to Brooks this led inevitably to the gloomy mechanistic philosophy of Mark Twain's later years, and he attributes this inevitability solely to psychological causes:

> Mark Twain was a frustrated spirit, a victim of arrested development, and beyond this fact, as we know from innumerable instances the psychologists have placed before us, we need not look for an explanation of the chagrin of his old age.

He had been balked, he had been divided, he had even been turned . . . against himself; the poet, the artist in him, consequently, had withered into the cynic, and the whole man had become a spiritual valetudinarian.[2]

The foundation of the book, however, does not seem to me to be wholly psychological, since it gives at least as much stress to social factors in the America of the Gilded Age and to Mark Twain's relationships with friends and business associates as it does to the primary bases of these in the family constellation. The book, consequently, may be characterized as a combination of criticism and biography using a method which is a combination of sociology and psychology. Its intention is to show the stultifying effect of psychic trauma, maladjustment, and frustration induced by adverse social conditions upon Mark Twain's latent artistic ability. This it does by tracing the ineffectual struggle which he waged against their combined power.

Brooks makes no attempt to account for the genesis of Mark Twain's artistry but confines himself to the almost unending series of rebuffs it received at the hands of both the world and its possessor. He merely states that Mark Twain was a naturally well-endowed individual, that the tie to his mother determined not only his choice of a wife but his submission to her ideas of decorum, that this surrender led him to abandon his artistic aspiration in favor of commercial success, that he was riven by an internal conflict between his impulse and the world's demands, that this caused him to become a popular humorist rather than a serious artist, that he became embittered about humanity and that this bitterness was at bottom an externalized form of his self-reproach. Speaking generally, Brooks succeeds in documenting and proving his thesis. As has been noted elsewhere [3] he is short on aesthetic criticism; he merely tries to relate Mark Twain's desire for public approval to his personal life, and he hardly mentions anything concerned with artistic technique or accomplishment except the tabooed nature of certain themes which were either treated surreptitiously or rejected by our author.

The central concern of my study is with the psychoanalytic ideas which Brooks used and the way in which he used them. His performance must be evaluated in the light of the fact that the book was written in 1920. The bibliographies of Freud and other psychoanalysts show that a large number of their most important works were in print by that time and that psychoanalysis had already attained a high degree of complexity. From internal evidence in *The Ordeal of Mark Twain,* however, there is no reason to suppose that Brooks had read anything more of Freud's than *The Interpretation of Dreams* (1900), *Wit and Its Relation to the Unconscious* (1905), and *The Psychopathology of Everyday Life* (1904), English translations of which appeared in 1913, 1917, and 1914, respectively. He apparently knew something also of the writings of Adler and Jung, but these are both outside the scope of this study. There is no indication that he knew even a single work of any other psychoanalyst, although Ernest Jones, Otto Rank, Hanns Sachs and Karl Abraham, to mention only those who were closest to Freud, had already made significant contributions toward the application of psychoanalysis to literary and artistic subjects. It might be argued in extenuation of Brooks that probably none of these men was known to the lay public— with the possible exception of Jones for his study of *Hamlet*— but to do so would exempt him from the critic's responsibility for getting a sufficient understanding of the materials which he uses in his work. To consider *The Ordeal of Mark Twain* only from the standpoint of the limited number of psychoanalytic books which its author had elected to read would be to condone his omissions, whereas they have no more justification than his misconceptions.

One of the twin foundation stones upon which the structure of *The Ordeal* rests is the relationship of Mark Twain to his mother. (The other is the inhibitory influence of the America of the time upon an artist.) Presumably in preparation for this, we are given the information that the marriage of his father and mother was a loveless one, that the father was a rather ineffectual man, ill and impractical, that the mother was overly concerned with patent medicines and such, and that "Little Sam" was the fifth child and perhaps unwanted. Having placed all this upon the record, Brooks proceeds thereafter to ignore it, making only a few passing references to some (not all) of the items later on. If this be psychology he has made the least of it.

He continues with a confused paragraph listing these facts: The boy was "high strung and neurotic." This is apparently connected (we are not told how) with his "exquisite sensibility." He endears himself to all by his manner and smile. He has very strong emotional reactions. He requires frequent medical care. At the time of his sister's death—he is then four—he walks in his sleep. Later he will have prophetic dreams. Evidently Brooks believed in a vague sort of way that emotional instability is a prerequisite for, if not a concomitant of, art, for he presently asks, "Can we not already see in this child the born, predestined artist?" [4] Now this implies a surprising assumption because up to this point he has said absolutely nothing about any artistic ability in the boy. Were it not for this rather important lapse we would be reminded of the pattern discovered by Kris in his study, "The Image of the Artist." [5] Nearly all the rest is there, the adverse and humble circumstances, the stimulation of imagination by the everyday surroundings (the story-telling of Negro slaves), the stigmata of differentness. The only thing lacking is the essential ingredient, artistic talent. This leap at a conclusion without even a glance to see whether the necessary intermediate steps are there carries no conviction precisely because they are not there. Evidently the writer's enthusiasm has swept him past this obstacle, but the reader has been left no path to follow.

All this is by way of preliminary to the thesis that Mark Twain's mother was a strong-willed woman with an excessive attachment to her son which adversely affected his development as an artist. Here Brooks is on safer ground although his use of psychoanalytic ideas is questionable. It is not a certainty that psychoanalysis is needed in this discussion at all since the evidence he cites from letters, Paine's biography and the recollections of friends seems sufficient to establish the mother's dominance and the father's passivity until his death when the son was about eleven so that Sam Clemens thereafter had to struggle with his feminine identification. The same thing expressed in non-psychoanalytic terms is quite adequate to Brooks's argument. Nor is the subject illuminated when we are told that Sam was "neurotic" without the "neurosis" being either described or identified.

Much is made of the impressive scene beside the father's corpse, when the sobbing boy promises his mother that he will not break her heart, and of his sleep-walking that same night and for several nights thereafter. Had Brooks intended this as a rhetorical device to drive home a point by hyperbole, then this heavy reliance on it might be justifiable. However, he sees more in it than that. In his eyes it is no less than the decisive moment in the boy's life: "We feel with irresistible certitude, that Mark Twain's fate was once for all decided there." [6] From now on the boy stifled the impulse to become an artist and devoted himself to seeking worldly success—with considerable inner resistance, to be sure—succumbing in the end to the national zeal for business and for conventional gentility which were both so admired by his mother. Psychoanalytically, however, there is insufficient evidence for this conclusion. Character is not determined by the effects of a single trauma at the age of eleven. Even in 1920 when the study of child psychology was in its early stages it was recognized that we must begin with constitutional endowment and the child's relation to its environment, particularly to its immediate family, and examine the various phases of development. The most that could be said for this event was that it was probably the most vivid incident in what must have been a long series all tending in the same direction. It was not the last time the struggle between the masculine and feminine sides of Mark Twain's nature took place nor was the victory always with the latter. *Huckleberry Finn* is not a girl's book.

The sleep-walking, too, is given an exaggerated and wholly unscientific interpretation by Brooks. It is offered as proof that "at this moment he became . . . a dual personality." In support it is said that the subject of dual personality was always an "obsession" with him and that he "had shown from the outset a distinct tendency toward what is called dissociation of consciousness." [7] For this we have only the bare assertion; no evidence is offered. Furthermore, it is difficult to know what Brooks understood by the psychological terms or the concepts which they expressed since he uses them either vaguely or inaccurately. The reason the sleep-walking is so important is that Brooks conceives of the Unconscious (which manifests itself in sleep) as another "personality." Consciously Sam Clemens desires to please his mother, the world and himself by becoming the success his father never was. Unconsciously he wishes to become an artist (this Brooks merely states but never proves). Again we must consider the possibility that Brooks is indulging in figurative language, for, considered as psychology, even as the psychoanalysis of 1920, what he says cannot hold water. It is plain that Mark Twain did suffer from an inner conflict which tormented him all his years, but his personality remained intact. He never, as far as we know, became psychotic. It appears certain Brooks could not have known the psychoanalytic meaning of the language he used, for the effect of what he says—and what I am sure he did not intend to say—is that Mark Twain was schizophrenic!

But this blunder may be admitted without detracting from the validity of the book. Brooks announces his intention of showing how the baleful power of the mother over the boy kept him from realizing himself as an artist because he was too weak to follow his natural bent against her wishes. Up to this point Brooks has been sound.[8] He makes another error now, however, which is more serious. Two ideas are confused, and he rests a large part of his argument on the confusion. He has assumed that somehow the unconscious portion of the boy's mind constituted a distinct personality which ardently wished to become an artist. This is psychoanalytically untenable because it is the combination of unconscious and conscious which makes up the personality; neither can stand alone. Further, such a wish never arises in the id (or to use the terminology of 1920, in the Unconscious) which knows nothing of art. It is an ego function and is hardly likely to remain unconscious even if it should originate in the unconscious portion of the ego, which is highly improbable. Such a wish requires a degree of understanding so complex and so involved with outer reality that awareness seems absolutely necessary in order for it to take place. Brooks has evidently assumed that the psychoanalytic meaning of wish is the same as that of its everyday use. He has consequently missed a distinction of considerable importance.[9]

He then proceeds to show in a convincing chapter that the

only opportunity for a morally free and purposive life afforded
by the pioneer culture of the time was that of a Mississippi
pilot. At one point it seems that he is about to escape the
careless attribution of too much to too little. He writes of Mark
Twain's "natural passion . . . lavished . . . upon the only creative—shall I say?—at least the only purposive figure [the pilot]
in all his experience." For a time he seems to recognize that all
purposiveness is not creative, that all problem-solving is not art,
but he soon surrenders to the need of his argument and assumes
the existence of a link where actually there is none. In becoming
a pilot Mark Twain "had naturally gravitated toward the one
available channel that offered him the training his artistic
instinct required." [10] The discipline, energy, self-reliance and
exercise of judgment which piloting demanded were, according
to Brooks's statement, equivalent to artistic training. During his
life on the Mississippi the young man was in process of finding
himself, says Brooks, and he leaves the clear impression that this
mobilization of inner resources was specific preparation for the
profession of writer. The qualities required of a pilot are, of
course, not identical with those needed by a writer; Brooks is
having semantic difficulties here. The independence, initiative
and skill (these are Brooks's words) of the pilot are not, except
in the most general sense, the independence, initiative and skill
of the writer. Psychologically, the channeling of effort into the
mental and motor activities of piloting has only a peripheral
resemblance to the work of the artist. Both attain an autonomy
of their own, but it is doubtful whether they are comparable
to any useful extent for Brooks's purpose.[11]

It is unfortunate that Brooks is so careless in this matter since
it constitutes a crucial portion of his thesis. In another place he
seems to know better, and he speaks of the role the Mississippi
experience ought to have played in Mark Twain's artistic life
as a "nursery for his talent." Had not the Civil War brought
it to an end, it might have served him

> as the streets of London served Dickens, as the prison life of
> Siberia served Dostoievsky, as the Civil War hospitals served
> Whitman. . . . Those great writers used their experience
> simply as grist for the mill of a profound personal vision:

rising above it themselves, they impressed upon it the mold of their own individuality.[12]
In his enthusiastic and fuzzy way, however, he has attributed too much to it, and the result is unconvincing. He intuitively grasps some facets of artistic psychology, but this is not enough to make up for his deficient understanding of the psychoanalytic ideas of his time. That deficiency is further exemplified by his use of certain psychoanalytic concepts and terms. Some of the concepts he uses with a fair degree of accuracy, although he does not name them. Projection, for instance, is a word which does not occur in this book, but Brooks plainly describes some projections of Mark Twain's psychic problems onto the pages of various works, notably the portrayal of his mother as Aunt Polly ("the symbol of all taboos") in *Huckleberry Finn,* and the disillusionment of his old age in *What Is Man?* He does not dwell, as a modern critic equipped with psychoanalytic insights would, upon the detailed fashion in which the private experience becomes the printed account, or the ways in which it is altered for literary purposes, or the extent to which it reproduces what actually took place (as far as this can be determined). He simply assumes that the two are equivalent. This is both general and arbitrary. Even in 1920 a closer correspondence should have been established, with evidence along every step of the way.

The related concepts of repression and sublimation also play a part. The latter, of course, is an important phase of the process by which a portion of life becomes art, and it likewise calls for detailed analysis. But this is not forthcoming. The word itself is not used, nor is the concept even presented.

The case of repression is different. This word appears again and again throughout the book, sometimes used accurately, sometimes not. Brooks falls into two traps. First he often uses repression when he means conscious suppression.[13] This is impossible by psychoanalytic definition. Second, he speaks of repression of "the creative instinct" which is not an instinct at all in the psychoanalytic sense but a highly organized complex of psychic tendencies, some of which are true instincts and some not.

His erroneous notion of the Unconscious as a separate self
we have already seen. He has a romantic view of this self as
something wiser than our conscious selves: "When . . .
one appeals for evidence to Mark Twain's estimate of himself it is
no conscious judgment of his career one has in mind but a far
more trustworthy judgment, the judgment of his unconscious
self." [14] This is exactly opposed to the psychoanalytic view that
unconscious ideas tend to interfere with rational judgment since
they are concerned not with such matters as a critical evaluation
of one's worth but with the maintenance of psychic integrity.
This is not at all the same thing as personal integrity, a concept
involving honor and "higher" social behavior. Our inner life
is conducted on the basis of feelings, not intellect. The latter
may frequently be in conflict with inner wishes (in the psychoanalytic sense) but it is also in better touch with external reality
and better able to bring its awareness of outer necessity to bear
upon the assessment of a situation. A portion of this ability has
been incorporated into the unconscious part of the psyche, but
it is limited mainly to curbs on certain kinds of behavior and
cannot be regarded as a "far more trustworthy judgment" than
that of the total personality.

Brooks devotes several pages (19–25) to illustrating how in
Mark Twain the judgment of this self was always in direct
opposition to that of the conscious self. According to him, it was
Mark Twain's unconscious self that wished to become an artist;
consciously he had no such intention, and this gave rise to
conflict:

> We know that he was always chafing against the scheme of
> values, the whole social regime that was represented by his
> wife and his friends. His conscious self urged him to main-
> tain these values and this regime. His unconscious self strove
> against them, vetoed the force behind his will, pushed him
> in just the opposite direction.[15]

The pleasure he must have felt in writing *Huckleberry Finn*
comes from the liberation he attained in the fantasy of the
raft. "His whole unconscious life, the pent-up river of his own
soul, had burst its bonds and rushed forth, a joyous torrent!" [16]
For Brooks the Unconscious is nothing more or less than the

artist in Mark Twain, the wise judge, the creative and reflective force. This is reminiscent of Rousseau's natural goodness, of which it might be a direct outgrowth, and, in our own time, of the Surrealists. It has nothing to do with Freud, who specifically rejected this doctrine.

Another serious misunderstanding of psychoanalysis occurs in a discussion of the representations of Mark Twain's inner conflicts which are to be found throughout his works "in a sort of cipher, for us of another generation who have eyes to read." [17] With the caution that we have learned from thirty more years of psychoanalysis this seems a risky statement indeed, but it is only an introduction to the rather extensive evidence that the cipher, if it existed, was not Brooks's to command. In order to show the scientific basis for his use of literature as case record he says this about the nature of dreams:

> In the Freudian psychology the dream is an expression of a suppressed wish.[18] In dreams we do what our inner selves desire to do but have been prevented from doing either by the exigencies of our daily routine, or by the obstacles of convention, or by some other form of censorship which has been imposed upon us, or which we ourselves, actuated by some contrary desire, have willingly accepted. Many other dreams, however, are not so simple: they are often incoherent, nonsensical, absurd.[19] In such cases it is because two opposed wishes, neither of which is fully satisfied, have met one another and resulted in a "compromise"—a compromise that is often as apparently chaotic as the collision of two railway trains running at full speed.[20] These mechanisms, the mechanisms of the "wish-fulfillment" and the "wish-conflict," are evident, as Freud has shown, in many of the phenomena of everyday life.[21] Whenever the censorship is relaxed . . . then the unconscious bestirs itself and rises to the surface, gives utterance to . . . slips of the tongue . . . sets our fancies wandering in pursuit of all the ideals and all the satisfactions upon which our customary life has stamped its veto.[22] In Mark Twain's books, or rather in a certain group of them, his "fantasies," we can see this process at work.[23]

This betrays a careless reading of *The Interpretation of Dreams*. Brooks does not understand the nature of the dream, the materials it deals with, nor the "language" it uses. He is satisfied with equating the dream, the fantasy (or daydream), the everyday "thoughtless" action that reveals hidden thoughts, and the story written by an author. He apparently believes that they all say approximately the same thing in approximately the same way. They are indeed connected, but not in the way Brooks imagines.

An example of Brooks's dream interpretation occurs in the final chapter. The passage is worth a close look. He begins with a statement that can heartily be endorsed: "The interpretation of dreams is a very perilous enterprise: contemporary psychology hardly permits us to venture into it with absolute assurance.[24] And yet we feel that without doubt our unconscious selves express through this distorting medium their hidden desires and fears." [25] Evidently, however, he does not estimate properly the degree of distortion which takes place, nor does he seem to comprehend its nature, for he commits two major errors at the outset. Mark Twain had written out three recurring dreams in a memorandum and had told Paine, "I generally enjoy my dreams but not those three, and they are the ones I have oftenest." Brooks omits one of them because it "is long and, to me at least, without obvious significance." [26] The honesty of his confession does not mitigate the arbitrariness of this procedure. We have Mark Twain's own word that they belong together, and in a proper interpretation this is a fact that must be evaluated. So the record we are given is not a complete one. Furthermore, Brooks tells us that the other two have been chosen because "one cannot fail to see in [them] . . . a singular corroboration of the view of Mark Twain's life that has been unfolded in these pages." By his own confession, then, Brooks is seeking only "obvious significance" and support for his own thesis. This is truly Procrustean. Instead of examining the material, as a sound interpreter should, and following where it leads, he announces that he will select those portions of it that he likes, and ignore the rest. The evidence is to be made to fit the argument. This is interesting indeed to those who possess the cipher. Here are the two remaining dreams in Mark Twain's own words:

> There is never a month passes that I do not dream of being in reduced circumstances, and obliged to go back to the river to earn a living. It is never a pleasant dream, either. I love to

think about those days; but there's always something sickening about the thought that I have been obliged to go back to them; and usually in my dream I am just about to start into a black shadow without being able to tell whether it is Selma Bluff, or Hat Island, or only a black wall of night. Another dream that I have of that kind is being compelled to go back to the lecture platform. I hate that dream worse than the other. In it I am always getting up before an audience with nothing to say, trying to be funny; trying to make the audience laugh, realizing that I am only making silly jokes. Then the audience realizes it, and pretty soon they commence to get up and leave. That dream always ends by my standing there in the semi-darkness talking to an empty house.[27]

Brooks begins his interpretation with the remark that "I leave my readers to expound these dreams according to the formulas that please them best." Here he frankly abandons psychology. It even seems like an abdication of his critical function since he says diffidently, "I wish to note only two or three points." This may be disarming to the quick and casual reader, but it seems a weak stand for a serious critic, and it detracts from the effectiveness of the points which follow.

Mark Twain is obsessed with the idea of going back to the river: "I love to think about those days." But there is something sickening in the thought of returning to them, too, and that is because of the "black shadow," the "black wall of night," into which he, the pilot, sees himself inevitably steering. That is a precise image of his life; the second dream is its natural complement. On the lecture platform his prevailing self had "revelled" in its triumphs, and, he says, "I hate that dream worse than the other." Had he ever wished to be a humorist? He is always "trying to make the audience laugh"; the horror of it is that he has lost, in his nightmare, the approval for which he had made his great surrender.[28]

The second major error is Brooks's "interpreting" the manifest dream and almost completely ignoring the latent dream thoughts which can be obtained only from the dreamer himself. There is one honorable exception to this, and it is almost enough to make one believe that he has correctly read *The Interpretation of Dreams* in the face of all the other evidence to the contrary. I refer to the feelings which the dreamer reported as accompanying these dreams and which, for the psychoanalyst, constitute a factor of the greatest importance. However, while the feelings are to be accepted literally, their attachment to the symbols of the manifest dream is not, for the latter are distortions by definition. The original thoughts have emerged from the primary process as well as from the secondary elaboration, and what the dreamer dreams is the transformed result. In order to identify their origin and trace their intricate path to the surface of the mind, both of which are necessary to an adequate interpretation, the dreamer's associations are needed, and it is precisely these which are missing. From the psychoanalytic point of view Brooks has performed with incredible naiveté.

A revealing instance of Brooks's use of psychoanalysis, which contains in a small compass his practice throughout the book, occurs in the chapter on Mark Twain's humor. He is discussing the "innumerable repressions" of pioneer life, and defines his term: "What do we mean when we speak of repressions? We mean that individuality, the whole complex of personal desires, tastes and preferences is inhibited from expressing itself, from registering itself." [29] In psychoanalysis an inhibition is not a repression, nor are "desires, tastes and preferences" concepts of the same order. In fact, the latter three contain so many ambiguities, so many overlapping areas of meaning that they must be carefully defined themselves before they can be useful in a definition. The key to the entire problem of what Brooks has done with those psychoanalytic concepts which he elected to use lies in the beginning of his question and in his answer to it: "What do we mean. . . . We mean. . . ." He has taken a psychoanalytic term and provided it with his own private definition.

He is obviously not concerned with psychoanalysis as a science. His eye is on his critical-biographical thesis, as is fitting and proper for a critic. Psychoanalysis as he understands it is merely a supporting auxiliary. Despite its frequent appearance in his pages, it supplies only a minor part of his argument, so minor that, in my opinion, it could be left out altogether with no loss to either his central idea or its development. One need not have psychoanalytic insight to comprehend that Mark Twain was the child of a time that valued business above art, that this attitude was reflected by those persons who were most influential with him, that he sometimes fought against this pressure but most of the time gave in to it, and that this had adverse effects upon his artistic performance. Psychoanalysis can corroborate, illuminate and deepen this view, but Brooks's cavalier treatment of it does none of these things in more than a rudimentary way.[30] The question, however, is not whether a literary critic may use the findings of a non-literary discipline in his work, but what method he should employ.

Brooks has dealt very carelessly with such psychoanalytic ideas as he had access to. If we are to judge from *The Ordeal of Mark Twain,* he did not grasp the significance of the Freudian works which he read. He seems to have retained only a few superficially understood general notions and unrelated fragments, all of which he has mixed with undigested bits from other psychological sources. The result is an inconsistent mass which cannot possibly furnish a solid base for any critical conceptions.

This seems a hard thing to say about a man whose profession requires careful reading, but the evidence is clear. The question is, why did he do it? I suggest that the reason for his failure is his indifference to psychoanalysis. His chief concern is the establishing of his critical viewpoint on American letters, which is a philosophical and social one, going far beyond the scope of psychoanalysis. With his eye on this goal, he permitted himself to lose sight of some of the intervening obstacles.

What he had read and heard about psychoanalysis by 1920 seemed to him to offer support for ideas which he already held or was in process of developing. This was enough; it led directly to his uncritical use of psychoanalysis and did nothing for his examination of Mark Twain which he had not already done without its help. In later years he came to believe that psychoanalysis was useless, false and, if I read him rightly, pernicious.[31] He became its opponent, not on scientific grounds but because he found that he could draw inferences from it which were injurious to his critical ideas. Naturally, there was no incentive for him to use it in his subsequent books. In *The Ordeal of Mark Twain* he failed to comprehend it and consequently misused it, to the detriment of both psychoanalysis and criticism.

VI
==

Joseph Wood Krutch:
Poe's Art as an Abnormal
Condition of the Nerves

In his attempt to apply psychoanalysis to the career of Edgar
Allan Poe for purposes of literary criticism, Joseph Wood Krutch
exhibited a commendable degree of competence for a layman.[1] He
seems to have had at his command a fairly good, though incomplete, outline of psychoanalysis as it was constituted circa 1926
and a serviceable understanding of the nature of unconscious
conflict as well as certain of its overt manifestations. The psychoanalytic concepts which he uses are interpreted, for the most part,
with a fair degree of accuracy. What is especially noteworthy is
that even technical terminology is correctly employed. By 1926
enough of the basic material of psychoanalysis had reached print
—much of it in English translation—so that it was theoretically
possible to go even further than he did, but although his knowledge of it was not very extensive he seems to have understood
better than most people what he had read. He is nowhere guilty
of the gross falsification of psychoanalytic doctrine which was so
common then, and which even now gives trouble. His competence
served him well—up to a point.

That point is reached when he tries to evaluate Poe's writings
solely as manifestations of psychic conflict without regard for their
aesthetic character. Up to then he is on perfectly solid ground. A
poem is, as he indicates, as much a psychic product as a slip of the
tongue or a hallucination, but it is of course something else be-

sides, and Krutch's application of psychoanalysis does not tell us anything useful about what that something else may be. But perhaps this failure is not altogether his fault. Those portions of psychoanalytic research which bear on this problem were available chiefly in Austrian and German publications; many of them remain untranslated to this day. The researches of men like Kris and Hartmann into the role of the ego in creativity came much later. At the time when Krutch wrote his book there existed only tentative formulations in many parts of this field. No direct psychic connection had been established between the origin of a poem and the final product, but one was popularly assumed by both psychoanalysts and laymen; and the means by which creation takes place, since they were not known, were ignored. Nevertheless, despite the circumstances, this gap in Krutch's chain of reasoning is a major flaw which is not mitigated by the note of caution on which he ends the book:

> The question whether or not the case of Poe represents an exaggerated example of the process by which all creation is performed is at least an open question. The extent to which all imaginative works are the result of the unfulfilled desires which spring from either idiosyncratic or universally human maladjustments to life is only beginning to be investigated, and with it is linked the related question of the extent to which all critical principles are at bottom the systematized and rationalized expression of instinctive tastes which are conditioned by causes often unknown to those whom they affect. . . . [The critic] must . . . endeavor to find the relationship which exists between psychology and aesthetics, but since the present state of knowledge is not such as to enable anyone satisfactorily to determine that relationship, we must proceed only with the greatest caution and content ourselves with saying that the fallacy of origins, that species of false logic by which a thing is identified with its ultimate source, is nowhere more dangerous than in the realm of art.[2]

From a psychoanalytic, as well as a critical, point of view this statement is unexceptionable. The trouble is that Krutch does not faithfully follow his own advice. For over two hundred and thirty pages he develops a thesis which sometimes skirts the danger line and now and then passes over it. The effect of all this cannot be undone by a pious disclaimer at the end. Despite the consistency he shows elsewhere, Krutch here succumbs to the very fallacy that he warns against.

This makes it pertinent to ask how much he actually understood of psychoanalysis. From the internal evidence of this book it would seem that, for one thing (and a very important one) he was aware of the principle of psychic determinism. Exercising the privilege of a biographer to criticize his predecessors, he berates those who had attempted to separate Poe's genius from his moral character. To him, this had resulted in "a silly farce in which the most fantastic and abnormal writings in all literature are assumed to be ingenious toys without meaning, and in which the whole process which created them is dismissed as irrelevant." [3] A large part of his case rests upon his acceptance of the psychic necessity for Poe to write as he did. It is easy to understand Krutch's annoyance with the biographers who ignored or denied this fundamental tenet of psychoanalysis. Those who have learned something new and satisfying are commonly impatient with those who lack this knowledge. In another place on the same subject Krutch is much calmer: "From the effects of such a psychological process no one is wholly free. Given a prejudice rooted deeply enough in the unconsciousness no man has a reasonableness or a sense of justice capable of restraining it. . . ." [4] Although this passage actually refers to Poe's "uncontrollable obsessions," it is applicable here as well. It might lead a searching questioner to inquire how thoroughly Krutch had assimilated the principle he asserts and whether his agreement with it was whole-hearted or merely cerebral. In his favor it must be said that, except for the present lapse, he consistently maintains it throughout the book.

He knew that unconscious feelings could embody themselves in a fantasy or a piece of writing which effectively disguised them until a qualified interpreter discovered their existence. [5] He understood at least the surface aspects of the process of sublimation. He knew that it was possible for such feelings to begin in a childhood relationship and acquire depth and breadth by attaching themselves to later objects. He was aware that "the adjustment of the neurotic is . . . unsatisfactory and incomplete [but that he] prefers his fantasies to the actuality from which they give an escape, since . . . they furnish him satisfactions which his conscious mind may not be able to recognize." [6] He saw the role that the marriage to Virginia played in Poe's defense against the acknowledgement of his impotence and the way in which it lent him a degree of stability.[7]

On the debit side we must record that some of his understanding was shallow by psychoanalytic standards. He insists that Poe was "a true dypsomaniac in the medical sense," but he offers no better explanation than that this was "the result of some obscure psychic cause." [8] Excessive drinking is, of course, a problem on which a sizable quantity of psychoanalytic writing has been done, but Krutch is apparently unaware of it. He speaks of the devastating effect of John Allan's constant reminders of Edgar's origin and dependency, but he does not see that the pride which was thus tortured was intimately related to the boy's feelings about his mother and the father he never knew.[9] He discusses Poe's inability to engage in normal physical love but states only in a general way that this was connected with the fixation on the mother. Some of the obvious clues from the works and from Poe's experiences with women are mentioned, but we are not given a well-knit analysis of this important evidence. In dealing with Dupin's ingenious reading of his companion's thoughts in *The Murders in the Rue Morgue* Krutch points out that "the associations of random thought require so slight and often so unessential connections between succeeding ideas that the possibilities are almost infinite and quite unpredictable." [10] This appears to abandon the principle of psychic determinism which Freud has so convincingly demonstrated [11] and fails to say that the connections referred to here are only seemingly adventitious. For one thing, they depend on the sounds and forms of words. For another—and this is what really matters psychoanalytically—they are established as the result of the emotional values which these symbols have acquired unconsciously. Though the connections may seem "unessential" to our conscious minds, psychoanalysis finds that they are strictly determined by unapprehended psychic forces. Krutch's application of this principle is inconsistent here.

A further example of superficiality is his offhand equating of the stories with dreams: "Dreamlike in their power to make fantastic unrealities seem real, they are dreams in essence. . . . His works [are] characterized at their best by the fantastic illogicality of dreams. . . ." [12] This kind of remark is tossed off as though one needed only to mention it to make it self-evident. Yet, as we shall see, Krutch did not have a thorough grasp of the nature of dreams, and he did not learn from psychoanalysis all that it knew at that time about the difference between dreams and artistic productions. Marie Bonaparte, in her chapter on what psychoanalysis tells us about literature, makes this distinction clearly. [13] She points out that they are analogous kinds of expression but that the dream is private, egoistic and far less coherent than the story, being formed unconsciously. Krutch is aware that the conscious part of the mind is used by Poe, but he restricts its greatest influence to the rationalization shown in the criticism and the philosophy rather than to the construction of the tales and poems, where a psychoanalyst would give it far greater weight than it is accorded here.

These examples illustrate the limitations of Krutch's comprehension of psychoanalysis in his book. He has a gross understanding of some of the basic principles and can apply them adequately to readily ascertainable surface phenomena, but he cannot go very far below these. While he sees the general significance of the psychoanalytic approach to human problems and is clearly convinced of its validity, he does not know specifically and in detail how complex it really is. He has evidently learned a few of its important formulations, but he tends to use them rather mechanically. His sin is that he tries to find instances of preconceived patterns in the material instead of examining it without prejudice to see what pattern, if any, will emerge.

The greater part of his book is not literary criticism at all but may more properly be called psychography. It is an attempt— which is successful as far as it goes—to demonstrate that Poe suffered from a severe neurotic disturbance. Against this Poe erected a series of defenses in a desperate effort to maintain his equilibrium, and for varying periods of time each of these worked until it was destroyed either by external circumstances or by the power of the neurosis exerted from within. This tormented existence continued as long as the marriage to Virginia Clemm, the keystone of the defensive system, lasted. After her death Poe was no longer able to reconstitute it effectively. He deteriorated rapidly, and twenty-one months later, finally overwhelmed by the mysterious forces whose onslaught he had withstood for so long, he was dead.

To this outline Krutch supplies sketchy biographical information and describes the neurosis in a general way as psychic impotence stemming from a fixation on the mother which was complicated by her early death so that a strong element of sadism became a part of the boy's character. This was directed mainly against himself as far as his face-to-face relationships with others were concerned—Krutch emphasizes Poe's gentleness and gentlemanliness—but it appeared in the open now and then in the form of outbursts of temper, notably in the denunciations of Longfellow and Lowell, and of Boston and all its works. Krutch also notes that sadism and horror appeared in many of the writings, but he does not show what connection there was between them. In short, we are given little more than an outline of Poe's life and character together with some circumstantial detail at key points. There are numerous lacunae, some attributable to the sketchy knowledge of psychoanalysis possessed by Krutch and some to the state of psychoanalysis in 1926. It is not necessary to dwell further on this subject here since it is beyond the scope of this study and since it has been competently treated elsewhere.[14]

Where Krutch's book becomes more interesting from a literary standpoint is in his demonstration that an intimate relationship existed between Poe's life and his works. Its connection with psychoanalysis lies in the recognition that the outer events have relatively little psychic significance in themselves. When charged with imitating the Gothic genre, Poe once wrote that the horror he described was not of Germany but of the soul. It was not of Boston or Baltimore either. Krutch is concerned not merely with the fact that Poe's mother died as she did but also with the effect of this experience upon the imagination of the boy. And so with all the other troubles of that unhappy career. They are shadows cast upon a screen, and we must try to comprehend the reality behind them as in Plato's analogy of the cave. It is Krutch's feeling that inner life is reflected in literary works most clearly in Poe of all writers, but while we might question the superlative, certainly we may grant that the contrived fantasies are probably very close to what their originals must have been.

Krutch sees two major forms of expression in Poe and shows that they complement one another. First, of course, is the repeated theme (with variations) of the death of a beautiful woman, and second, the repeated insistence upon the powers of pure intellect. Each has its place in the working of Poe's imagination, and this in turn is stimulated mightily by the unconscious struggle going on within.

Krutch establishes effectively the appearance in the tales and poems of themes which are derived from the inner events of their author's life.[15] His heroes and heroines are frequently of ancient and decaying families. They are identified only as noble, great willed and sensitive, and suffering from a mysterious malady more spiritual than physical. They are "strangely learned in some half specified and forbidden learning," they have sinned in some exquisite and horrible way and they undergo the penalty of death or of enduring the death of a loved one. They are morally lost; they hover on the brink of madness or are precipitated over the edge; they suffer (and enjoy?) the anticipated outcome of their esoteric behavior. They are perverted and evil—and they fascinate Poe. There can be little question that this kind of character represented Poe's fantasies of himself or that the constantly recurring plots and the repetitively gruesome settings were literary versions of the terrible conflict of whose origins and meaning he was never aware and which was at times palliated but never resolved. Krutch is right when he insists upon the compulsive nature of these forces. "Whenever Poe turned to his imagination for material the same vision reappeared to him, unbidden." [16] Else how explain the similarity of Morella and Ligeia, of Berenice and Ulalume, of Prince Prospero and Roderick Usher?

It is not necessary to retrace here the steps by which Krutch spells out in detail the morbidity of the tales and poems and how they reflect (perhaps refract is better) the psychic turmoil.

His conception of the process by which the change from fantasy to literature takes place is more properly our concern. Again we are given a skimpy theory. Krutch believes that Poe's writing was solely a product of the morbidity. The hypothesis upon which the book is constructed boils down to something like this: Poe suffered a great trauma in the death of his mother. This was exacerbated by subsequent experiences as the foster-son of the Allans. As a result he developed into a neurotic young man who quarreled with most men and idealized most women. (We are not told how this came about, only that it happened.) He became impotent from psychic causes (not specified). This caused mental instability so great that there was danger of insanity. In defending himself against the realization of the reason for the impotence on the one hand and the threatened loss of mental powers on the other, Poe translated his fantasies, only slightly disguised, into his morbidly imaginative tales and poems, and devised a philosophy of composition which explained to his satisfaction that what he was doing by inner compulsion in his art was actually demanded of him by aesthetics. In his tales of ratiocination and in his criticism of current books he both exalted the power of intellect—by implication, his own —and denied that of impulse. He married Virginia, with whom consummation of the marriage was impossible for reasons of her ill-health, and thus deluded himself that the outer form of normal sexual relationship was the actual substance. Her death made it impossible for him any longer to sustain this fiction (still unconsciously), and he embarked upon a series of disastrous affairs with other women, in each instance going to pieces as marriage, and therefore actual sexual relations, became imminent. For a long time he had fled to the solace of drink when the conflict became unbearable, and he continued this destructive practice which had caused him to lose jobs and friends. Finally, in the famous and not fully understood episode at Baltimore, it contributed to his death.

It will be noticed that there are many gaps in the story. Krutch has at his command the end results, Poe's works, and a good deal of biographical information from which he selects mainly material that bears upon origins. He reconstructs the broad outlines of Poe's struggle and shows in general where it came from psychically, but how it developed as it did or why it became just this and not something else is passed over. It seems to me that, despite some description of the process and despite the inclusion of material from which even more of it might have been deduced, as Marie Bonaparte has done, Krutch falls victim to that same genetic fallacy against which he warns in the closing pages of his book. Evolution and vicissitudes are every bit as important as origins in the description of a neurosis, but of these he gives us only incidental hints.

An inevitable result of this incomplete analysis of Poe's character is a weakening of the thesis that the works closely represent it. Krutch sees the recurrence of certain themes which are handled in certain ways, and he recognizes that they constitute one form of psychic expression. What is lacking is the close correlating of these with the inner events of Poe's life. We see only the general features, like a portrait observed from a distance; the details may be guessed, but how are we to know that they have been guessed correctly? And are not the details necessary for understanding? In 1926 not enough psychoanalytic information was current in literary and critical circles to do much more than this with Poe, but that the material existed for those who knew how to use it is clear from the publication only seven years later of Marie Bonaparte's book.

Of greater importance than Krutch's deficiencies in psychoanalysis of character—after all, he did better than many of his contemporaries—is his conception of creativity. For this he should be censured because he fell into the trap of oversimplification once more and in a manner that his good sense as a critic should have protected him against. From his quite accurate observation that Poe did not write from a moral or social standpoint and that he was "interested in the soul's relation to itself but in nothing else," Krutch draws the startling conclusion that "nearly all the things which ordinarily give value to a piece of literature are absent from Poe's work." [17] Here he surely mistakes a difference in degree for a difference in kind. It is true that Poe knows only himself, which is the equivalent of saying that "the only springs of action concerning which he reveals knowledge are the morbid ones by which he himself was influenced," [18] and that this is a serious limitation on his art. But is this knowledge so little, after all? How many of us know even this much about ourselves? One of the great lessons of psychoanalysis—and one which Krutch seems to have missed—is that we are all so constituted that we share to a considerable extent the same strengths and weaknesses. No two of us are alike but each has at least a minute quantity of the characteristics of all the rest. The nearly infinite number of possible combinations accounts for the fact that we are individuals at the same time that we are members of one another. The sadism that is so marked in Poe, therefore, is present in each of us to a lesser degree. Neurosis is an imbalance of the factors that in a different combination produce what we call normality. Only the combination is unique; the rest is as common as our basic physical constitution.

An understanding of this principle would have saved Krutch from his final, and fatal, reduction of genius to neurosis: "We have, then, traced Poe's art to an abnormal condition of the nerves and his critical ideas to a rationalized defense of the limitations of his own taste." [19] This estimate could have been avoided by the simple reflection that not all neurotics are geniuses or even unsuccessful artists, or, for that matter, that not all artists are neurotic. To say that "both his genesis and his significance are to be found by reference not to any tradition or environment but instead to the morbid type to which he belongs" is almost to restrict the enjoyment of Poe to sufferers from necrophilia. Krutch comes dangerously close to doing this without realizing it when he discusses the reception of Poe's works by Baudelaire and remarks that the latter's enthusiasm "seems positively insane to those who are, happily perhaps, without even a touch of the morbidity to which he appeals." [20] That the morbidity is there is obvious; that this constitutes the essence of the art is so questionable that Krutch himself seeks another answer.

The best that he can offer is that Poe is somehow talented with words. "His gift . . . is the gift of expression." Furthermore, it is nothing else but that: ". . . his genius was no more than the power to express [his] character in perfect symbols." In some mysterious fashion, which Krutch does not describe, the internal disorder was transmuted into "the more controlled aberrations which gave birth to his art." [21] Krutch's idea that madness is necessary for artistic creation differs in only one major respect from the findings of psychoanalysts like Kris, though it lacks almost completely the subtlety and detail of the latter. As we have seen in the development of psychoanalytic ego psychology, it is precisely such detachment from reality which detracts from the value of art, for it undermines its social nature. [22] Krutch is somewhat inconsistent in his use of the concept of "madness" for in another place he seems to recognize that when Poe "lost his grip upon the fancies which had always haunted him [he] lost, too, the power to give them imaginative form," [23] and was left to cope directly with his psychic disorder. He concludes that, even had Poe lived, he never could have re-established the emotional balance necessary for artistic production, and would have produced only more *Eurekas*. What Krutch saw in art was only its capacity to communicate emotional states. He did not—at least in the case of Poe—distinguish between aesthetic experience and psychic imbalance. Consequently, he insisted that Poe's genius was only the ability somehow to communicate his inner impulses to his readers by means of his elaborated fantasies.

While Krutch understood psychoanalysis better than most of his literary contemporaries, his use of it was shallow when he analyzed Poe's emotional disorder and questionable when he applied it to Poe's writings. In doing the latter he was rushing in where psychoanalysts themselves feared to tread. In the foreword to Marie Bonaparte's book Sigmund Freud remarks, "Investigations such as this do not claim to explain creative genius, but they do reveal factors which awaken it and the sort of subject matter it is destined to choose." [24] With the brashness of the 1920's Krutch conducted an investigation which was not at all "such as this" since it was far too superficial to "explain" Poe's genius. Satisfied at the time with his partial grasp of psychoanalysis, he was not aware of its deficiencies. Some years later he publicly acknowledged that his "explanation" was oversimplified and inadequate.

VII

Ludwig Lewisohn
and the Puritan Inhibition of American Literature

LUDWIG LEWISOHN begins *The Story of American Literature* [1] with a statement of purpose in the light of which the book deserves to be judged. In it his emphasis, as is proper, is upon his critical thesis, but he relies so heavily in its development upon certain psychoanalytic ideas that I must direct the major part of my attention to these at the risk of seeming to slight what is actually more important. He is attempting "a portrait of the American spirit seen and delineated, as the human spirit is itself best seen, in and through its mood of articulateness, of creative expression." [2] The vicissitudes of that spirit are understood by him largely in terms of a moral struggle in which the impulse to the free expression of American experience in literature collided with the powerful inhibiting influence of the Puritan tradition. In Lewisohn's view, Puritanism triumphed throughout nearly all of our national history, to our great loss. "To it, rather than to the harsh but not ignoble struggles of the wilderness and the frontier, is to be attributed all that is unlovely and cruel and grotesque in the life of the American people." [3] Its doctrine of grace for the few and damnation for the many imposed an artificial dichotomy upon everyday living in which the satisfaction of normal appetites was regarded as sinful, and the only acceptable kind of conduct was based upon their suppression, since it was necessary to curb one's worldly desires in order to seek salvation. This denial of natural behavior had its reflections in the writings which Lewisohn chose to study in his book.

As long as the Puritan influence was dominant, runs his claim, it was impossible for our literary men to write about the realities of human experience. They were confined to themes unrelated to the actualities of American life and therefore removed from that passion and urgency which alone can produce great literature. The intellectual revolution of the nineteenth century cracked the shell of the complete and perfect universe postulated by the theocrats and their descendants, and at last permitted a direct view of things as they are. Its literary outcome was the rise of realism and naturalism. A new type of reader also arose, "one to whom literature [is] no longer an elegant diversion or an illustration of the foreknown and fixed, but moral research, a road to salvation, the bread of life." [4] The modern writer addresses himself to this reader, and he writes not of man's relation to God and eternity but of human experience and his kinship through it with his fellows. For an understanding of that experience and its expression in literature Lewisohn calls psychoanalysis to his aid:

> It was . . . inevitable that I use the organon or method of knowledge associated with the venerated name of Sigmund Freud. The portrayer of any aspect of human life or civilization who does not do so today will soon be like some mariner of old who, refusing to acknowledge the invention of mathematical instruments because their precision was not yet perfect, still stubbornly sailed his vessel by the stars. [5]

His recognition that psychoanalysis was not a complete and closed system marks a more mature comprehension of it than was shown by either Brooks or Krutch, and this is further borne out by his specific applications of it to the work of individual writers. Nor does he fall into the error of basing his whole argument upon it. To him it is a tool, a means toward an end. His reliance is first upon his critical judgment; psychoanalysis is a secondary, though valuable, help.

The first important place where it is of assistance to him is in his examination of the Puritan character and the characters of Puritan writers. In the pervasive conviction of sin that discolored everyday life, in the hysteria of many sermons, in the guilt which was so great that it could not be borne and had to be projected onto heretics and witches he sees a pathology not only personal but moral. The ruling delusion of the time, epitomized by Edwards' famous sermon, "Sinners in the Hands of an Angry God," generated the fear that justified the forcible saving of men from the consequences in eternity of their own actions by temporal punishments inflicted with a cruelty which was matched only by the righteousness of the responsible authorities. Psychoanalysis has something to say here about sex and sadism, and Lewisohn says it. Edwards and Mather were sick souls. The violence of their expressed religious feelings was a measure of the dammed-up sexuality which could find an outlet only in the perverted forms of aggression against others and symbolic mortification of their own flesh. For this combination of spiritual self-torture and the physical punishment of nonconformists they found justification in the age-old rationalization of those who scourge the helpless. "To excommunicate an heretic . . . is not to persecute; that is, it is not to punish an innocent, but a culpable and damnable person, and that not for conscience, but for persisting in error against light of conscience." [6] From excommunication to hanging is but a step for such a mind. This was the mentality that regulated daily conduct for the colonists and that, according to Lewisohn's view, stifled any possibility of true literary expression.

Psychoanalysis supports his depiction of the Puritan character, as far as it goes, although a more thoroughgoing examination based on an appreciation of psychoanalytic ego psychology would reveal some things to be said on the positive side. There was a strength, a channeling of energy into work, which was well adapted to the needs of the country, a moral earnestness which might have been carried too far but could not have been wholly destructive—in short, the story has at least two sides. All that we are given, however, is the overwhelming impression that there lay like a blight upon the young nation "the undying Puritan conviction that man and nature and man's instincts are from the beginning evil and without hope." [7] We are presumably meant to conclude that pathology ruled the colonies. Lewisohn's evidence from their own writings demonstrates plainly that certain of the powerful Puritans could not handle their sexual feelings in what we would consider normal ways and that this influenced their actions as public figures. What he does not quite succeed in establishing, at least on psychoanalytic grounds, is any connection between this situation and the inability to write literature.

I believe, nonetheless, that his case is sound, although not for the reasons he gives. If the authorities regard human experience as evil, then it is perfectly natural for them to refuse to tolerate —let alone to encourage—its expression in literature. But for this knowledge one does not need psychoanalytic support. Furthermore, even the psychoanalysis of 1932, the year of Lewisohn's book, gives no ground for such an idea. An inhibition of sexuality and its conversion into symptomatic behavior may be connected with the production of literature, or it may not. And it makes no difference whether we are dealing here with good writing or bad. The choice of writing as a profession and the writer's attainments therein have not been shown to be correlated with a specific type of personality or a specific frustration. The whole field of vocational choice is only beginning to be explored by psychoanalysis; not much is known about it yet from this standpoint. It is questionable whether simple generalizations like those assumed by Lewisohn were valid and whether they affected the quality of the work under discussion. His critical estimate of the Puritan influence is a reasonable one, though somewhat one-sided, but his psychoanalytic "foundation" for it is extremely shaky.

As he carries the story forward from the colonial period, those inheritors of a watered-down Puritan tradition, the Polite Writers, get short shrift at Lewisohn's hands. For him, Irving is the typical example of the kind of mind that, lacking the Puritans' conviction, nevertheless languidly follows in their footsteps. To such men human experiences no longer seem actively evil but merely beneath the notice of the genteel. The passionate wrestling with sin has dwindled to a pretense that what really counts is conformity to the manners of polite society. A stringent code of ethics has given way to rules of etiquette. Consequently, literature can deal only with an unrealistic idealization of human beings which keeps silent about the "major and intenser experiences of life." This affected other writers of the time as well. Lowell, for instance, failed in criticism "through the ancestral Puritan aversion from dealing with ultimate questions in any field except theology and politics." Holmes managed to salvage some honor for a few remarks indicating that his scientific training gave him a hostility to Calvinism, but that is not enough in Lewisohn's eyes to redeem his failure to face reality. On the other hand, P. T. Barnum produced literature in his autobiography, crude and vulgar though it was, because he "wrote out what he thought and saw and dreamed and knew." [8]

We begin here to see the bias of the book emerging. Literature must touch life, not celebrate that which attempts to evade life, as Lewisohn defines it. What cannot be seen so readily is how psychoanalysis supports this thesis or why its support should seem necessary to a literary critic. There seems also to be emerging the implication that technical quality is somehow irrelevant. The worth of writing in this view could depend upon its theme, its fidelity to reality, its concreteness and therefore its power to move the reader, and not on style, skill or polish. I shall not debate this critical position but only point out that psychoanalysis offers very little here to Lewisohn, except peripherally. It does not evaluate literature as literature; that is the function of the critic and the aesthetician. It merely provides certain incomplete bits of information about the place of literature in human life. He who draws conclusions from its store of facts does so on his own responsibility and at his own peril. Lewisohn seems to be overly ambitious for psychoanalysis, and tries to press it into service beyond the point where a cautious psychoanalyst would go.

Things become slightly better in the book as the Transcendentalist Revolt brings the emergence of the individual, although not yet the artist of reality whom Lewisohn admires. Its outstanding figures, Emerson and Thoreau, lack fire, but this is a constitutional deficiency and not the outcome of a struggle to contain fiery natures. They are not prisoners of the bleak

Puritan tradition; they are simply cold. It is not depreciating the power of their intellects to say that their "light was almost polar. It gave no warmth." Such personalities could write only upon "nature and metaphysics and morals" rather than on subjects closer to the human heart, for only upon the first of these could they muster up the equivalent of strong feelings. Lewisohn believes he has psychoanalytic warrant for his contention that the sexual deficiency in both Emerson and Thoreau directly prevented them from treating realistic themes. Emerson's was an attenuated nature, and this thinness could not express what it did not feel. His instincts, says Lewisohn, were trustworthy, even to the extent of understanding his own "lack of intensity, of severity, of absorption in the concrete coil of things." [9] What he wrote under their prompting is worth preserving; the remainder ought to be rejected as old-maidish and therefore of relatively little literary worth. Here again Lewisohn goes beyond psychoanalysis while leaving the impression that he has scientific backing. In point of fact, he is functioning as a critic whose thesis is being satisfactorily developed but who imagines that he needs extra assistance. When closely examined, the outside help proves to be mostly irrelevant, and the original chain of reasoning is not strengthened thereby.

Thoreau is something else again. His bachelorhood is not of the mind alone; he is actively un-sexual. His aversion to marriage is shown by extracts from the Journals and letters.[10] Introducing these Lewisohn remarks: "Yes, excellent reader, I have to 'drag in' sex here as I shall do again and again. God dragged it in from the beginning of things. . . ." This patronizing air is understandable considering the kind of audience he felt himself to be addressing, but it reveals little about the problem. Lewisohn repeatedly states that Thoreau is a great writer and just as often says that he is a defective man. There is an unexplained gap here. If there is a relationship between a man's sexuality and the quality of his writing, as Lewisohn evidently believes, then we are left with a mystery, since the gap has not been bridged by psychoanalysis, and Lewisohn does not bridge it by criticism. He says only: "That they [Thoreau and Emerson] were chilled undersexed valetudinarians, deprived of helpful and sympathetic social and intellectual atmosphere, renders their achievements only the more remarkable." [11] Here again he is too ambitious for psychoanalysis.

He attempts to make it serve his critical ideas in his analysis of *Walden,* a discussion which illuminates Lewisohn more than it does Thoreau. The book is praised as the record of one who practiced what he preached, who followed his own private convictions, who did not conform. It is praised for style, for social analysis, for prophetic insights. There is no doubt that Lewisohn regards it as one of the masterpieces of American literature. And yet:

> Unfortunately *Walden* contains a chapter called, "Higher Laws" which, in the accustomed Puritan way, blunts all the arrows, retracts all the brave and lofty sayings of the earlier and later chapters and makes it necessary for Thoreau to be saved, as by fire, for our uses and the uses of posterity. That chapter is full of the Puritan's cheap unfairness to the senses, his complete unwillingness to bring the whole of human nature under creative and significant control. "There is never an instant's truce between vice and virtue. . . . We are conscious of an animal in us, which awakens in proportion as our higher nature slumbers." Ah, no, good Puritan. *We* are not; you are. We are not conscious of any inner division and have long integrated all aspects of our nature upon the highest or, rather, the most significant and fruitful plane that is attainable by us. Chastity is not "the flowering of man"; it is possible to "eat, or drink, or cohabit, or sleep sensually" and yet nobly. For who told you that the senses are necessarily ignoble? They are ignoble only when, as in yourself, they are abstracted and divided from the faculties of the mind and the soul. But in us they are not; they have never been. We do not have to "overcome nature", for nature is not something outside of or below us, but has long been conquered and cultivated and embodied in the total harmony of life. Our purity is not one of abstention, but of fitting and beautiful use.[12]

Lewisohn here elevates the principle of harmony to a position of the greatest importance in literature, and he makes it dependent upon the writer's honest view of his own nature. The rub lies in his equation of literary value with sensuality which, in spite of his disclaimer, he seems to regard highly for itself and not merely as something integrated into "the total harmony of life." It would appear that in his enthusiasm for the discovery of sensual (including sexual) values, which he has made with the help of psychoanalysis, he has overstated his case. His contention that literature is the less worthy as it stays away from matters which many people do not wish to discuss is at least debatable. Nor have I found any basis in psychoanalytic writings for this position. To state it simply, the value of literature does not depend upon the frankness with which it treats sexual or economic or philosophical problems but rather upon its ability to express and communicate human experience. There is no reason to assume that this does not include Thoreau's un-sexual, un-sensual, transcendental experiences.

Another major group of nineteenth-century American writers is likewise depreciated by him on the ground that their artistic vision did not reveal to them the world as it is, or even a portion of reality which they then took for the whole, but rather a world of shapes and fancies drawn from their imagination. Poe, Hawthorne and Melville are the "troubled romancers" who were so ensnared in their unconscious conflicts that they could not partake of real experience and consequently could not portray it in their writings. What they did, therefore, was to invent private worlds onto which the inner drama could be projected without regard for externals. Art, says Lewisohn, is "first of all [the artist's] personal substitute for lacks and defeats that are otherwise unsupportable." [13] According to this theory the genesis of art lies in emotional unbalance, and it consists of an attempt to make the artist whole. There is a certain amount of justification for this attitude in the psychoanalytic theories of the restitutive function of art, but stated in such blanket terms as he uses, it can have relatively little validity. It is not enough to know that a country is mountainous; we need to know the location of the passes, their accessibility and under what conditions they may be used. By 1932 it was possible to go beyond this general conception,[14] and Lewisohn does take a few tentative steps in the direction of specifics.

He sees Poe almost as Krutch does, and he praises the latter's book as a "brilliant and definitive biography." He asserts that Poe "was confined in his choice of subjects to a few compensatory fantasies," [15] but grants him an artistic quality within this unconsciously imposed limitation that entitles him to be called a genius. The narrowness of range, however, means that he can appeal only to those immature or perverse minds who share the author's psychic problems. Here Lewisohn, like Krutch, comes close to saying that one must be suffering from necrophilia in order fully to appreciate "The Fall of the House of Usher" or "Ligeia." [16] At any rate, he justifies the British and American estimate of Poe as "a writer of narrow and special appeal and therefore of strictly secondary importance" on the ground that his neurosis did not permit him to go beyond his psychic preoccupations to universal truth in his art. What little success he achieved occurs in a few poems "where those qualities of his nature which Poe esteemed the intellectual and consciously artistic were wholly in abeyance," [17] where the elaborately constructed defenses, in other words, were by-passed, and his genuine gift for verbal music expressed itself unhampered. This insight of Lewisohn corresponds roughly to the psychoanalytic concept of the conflict-free sphere of the ego which had not yet been developed in 1932. It must therefore be credited not to his knowledge of psychoanalysis but to his perception as a critic.

In discussing Hawthorne, the second great "troubled romancer," Lewisohn somewhat inconsistently adopts the position of Freud that, although we have "the beginning of an understanding of the inner character of the creative impulse, of subject choice, even of execution," this "leaves wholly untouched the mystery of the splendor of genius." He then proceeds to show how Hawthorne's writings express with "excessive indirection" his neurotic problems, and concludes that he was different from the "more normal artist" who "dwells upon the process of creative justification of himself and . . . hence of mankind." [18] In Lewisohn's opinion, Hawthorne lacked the ability to transcend his own problems in his art so that they could become a creative expression for all men, like Milton's achievement in *Areopagitica* or Dostoevsky's in *The Brothers Karamazov*. He remained entangled in his guilt and, although he had the capacity occasionally to establish a significant connection with reality, as in his marriage, he slipped back into his dark reveries. These were the core of his life and art because they partially satisfied his disturbed soul, and he was therefore compelled to submit to them just as a neurotic clings to his solution which is in reality no solution. It was not his feeling of guilt which made him a lesser writer—for all men feel the same guilt to some extent—but his absorption in it to the exclusion of broader, more varied and fundamental human interests. His writing did the reverse of what a Shakespeare's might have done: "He integrated with his feeling of guilt and its expression all happenings and persons whether of history, legend or life with which he dealt, and substituted for the various experiences of human nature a single one, because it loomed so large in his own soul." [19] Lewisohn believes that Hawthorne was able to reach his audience because he expressed the guilt that is in everyone and so struck a chord which found an echo in others. This is at once a strength and a weakness in that Hawthorne's range did not extend beyond it to other universal experiences.

In all of this Lewisohn emphasizes psychic rather than literary factors. His evaluation of Hawthorne is based upon what he sees of the author's motivation—almost obsessive guilt—and a repeated insistence upon the role played by psychic determinism in the choice of the theme and its treatment. There is nothing wrong with this as far as it goes, but it does not go far enough. What we have here is the beginning of psychoanalytic understanding, but it is a beginning beyond which Lewisohn does not advance. Having shown that Hawthorne clothed his guilt feelings in literary forms [20] and was compelled to use certain symbols [21] he is led to the final conclusion of this position. If a work of art can be "explained" (except for the fact of genius) by the writer's psychic needs, then it follows that *The Scarlet Letter* is successful because it reflects or is the result of some successful psychic integration. And so we read:

> It is but sober truth that we owe Hawthorne's one thoroughly achieved book and unique masterpiece "The Scarlet Letter" to his happy and harmonious union with Sophia Peabody. . . . He is at last able in those earlier years of his marriage really to project, truly to create, to send forth into the world a work separate from himself, living with a life of its own

and therefore easing him of a portion of his inner burden. This book, alone among his books, moreover, deals with central things—with normal guilt, with genuine passion, with the operations of recognizable minds.[22]

Such a one-to-one correlation between life and work is difficult to establish and so general that from a psychoanalytic standpoint it is, even though valid, not very valuable, since it tells us nothing that we did not already know without the help of psychoanalysis. Nor is Lewisohn satisfied with the mere statement that an author puts himself into his work (for that is what it amounts to); a few pages later he tries to extend the insight. But there he becomes once more the critic and passes from the application of psychoanalysis to his own critical judgment:

> Nor will work which thus speaks permanently to men ever be without that beauty of form which is the precipitate of its spirit, which is indeed part of and inseparable from substance, which constitutes in the last analysis, the *act* of artistic communication.[23]

Up to a certain point psychoanalysis serves him. It helps him see the author's gross motivation—plus a few specific insights here and there—and choice of themes; it shows him the universal meaning of some rather common and obvious symbols; it enables him to see the universality of the author's appeal in so far as the work arouses psychic echoes in the reader. But it does not give him clues to what present-day psychoanalysis finds to be of importance: the specificity of not only theme but treatment, not only problem but language, not only symbol but beauty. Lewisohn sees art largely as the struggle of a gifted neurotic. He lacks sufficient knowledge of psychoanalysis to carry the conception further, to explore the ways in which artistic activity is different from daily actions of other kinds, to examine the product as an independent entity as well as a neurotic residue, to understand the role of the ego as well as that of the id.

* * *

Lewisohn's dissatisfaction with American literature stems from his belief that up to the latter half of the nineteenth century it was dominated by a national unwillingness to look facts, especially sexual facts, in the face. He felt that the relegating of this important part of normal life to the limbo of sin by the Puritans caused it to be either ignored or artificially treated in literature, with the result that creative expression was stultified. For this thesis he found support in psychoanalysis, at least to the extent that he understood it. His understanding appears to have been accurate as to generalizations but superficial as to particulars. He apparently has a clearer grasp of psychoanalytic concepts than either Van Wyck Brooks in *The Ordeal of Mark Twain* or Joseph Wood Krutch in *Edgar Allan Poe*. Furthermore, he does not fall into the trap that they blundered into when they tried to make psychoanalysis the basis of their books instead of using it to support and illuminate a critical idea. Lewisohn writes like a critic, not like an amateur psychoanalyst. This appears clearly in his book despite the great number of psychoanalytic references, insights and analyses of authors' private lives, individual literary works, intellectual movements and national "neuroses." The book stands or falls not on the way he has used psychoanalysis but on his critical judgment.

It is well that this is so, for in specific applications of psychoanalytic ideas his practice is, as we have already seen, often questionable. His chief fault is that in his eagerness to prove his thesis he tries to make psychoanalysis do more than even psychoanalysts ask of it. He assumes as an established fact the highly debatable notion that the appearance of (or absence from) literature of certain psychic themes determines the quality of the work. He tends too readily to read from the plot of a book the inner turmoil of the author. There is some validity in this; a connection does exist. But there is as much difference between these two as there sometimes is between the "knowledge" that a man is guilty of a crime and the production of evidence that will stand up in court. Lewisohn is often content with clues that, while they might tell a psychoanalyst a great deal, would still not be sufficient to establish a diagnosis. Straws in the wind are not accurate scientific instruments. A graver matter is his inability to bridge the gap between psychoanalysis and art. He sees certain aspects of personality reflected in the artist's work, but he cannot tell what makes a novel, for example, art whereas the same psychic traits seen in the same writer's diaries and letters are not art. His only acknowledgement of this discrepancy is the feeble statement that we cannot know the nature of genius. Whether this is so or not—and let us remember that Freud himself took the same position—Lewisohn proceeds in his book to act as though such a connection has indeed been established. This is a serious inconsistency of which he does not even appear to be aware.

In the latter half of the book he deals with the rise of realism and naturalism, with the second of which his critical preference lies. Naturalism being defined as the use of symbols of the actual to represent a moral view of the artist's world, it follows, according to Lewisohn, that this honesty regarding both self and society produces good literature. This has been the saving of American literature and has paved the way for the honest acceptance of modern philosophy and science by the artist, from all of which "the emergence of a neo-idealistic literature may be confidently predicted." [24] The "urge toward wholeness" which began with the great figures of the nineteenth century will enable artists to integrate the findings of science, arrived at by a rigidly controlled mechanistic methodology, into a creative moral view of man's place and duty in the universe. Thus the hypocrisy, evasion and falsification of the earlier writers will give way to a proper basis for the creation of literature: a clear vision and a scrupulous honesty. Lewisohn has learned that the golden age did not exist in the past; he has therefore shifted it to the future.

Throughout all this he continues, as he did in the first part of the book, to invoke psychoanalysis. The method is essentially the same, with direct reading of a writer's character from his work,[25] the interpretation of the national spirit in psychoanalytic terms,[26] and the evaluation of the free verse and imagist movements as merely psychological manifestations.[27] Here, however, his tone is different. Literature is now moving in the direction in which psychoanalysis has told him it ought to move, and while he castigates those who still attempt to go against the current, he approves the general tendency which he now sees in process of triumphing. His scorn of the unrealistic, the traditional and the romantic is unabated, but it necessarily diminishes in quantity, for these are merely the rearguard of a retreating army. There are fewer of them than there are of the awakening and the awakened; it is the latter who dominate the remainder of the book. In this argument the role of psychoanalysis is really a subsidiary one. Lewisohn is transparently not deeply concerned with what it has to tell us about human nature or even about literature, that is, he is not concerned with psychoanalysis as a scientific discipline. If he were, he might have availed himself better of its resources and achieved the understanding of it that he seemed on the verge of reaching. Psychoanalysis appears so excellent to him that he does not question it but applies it uncritically wherever it seems to support his ideas. He is primarily interested in his argument that realism and naturalism are good for literature; psychoanalysis has value for him mainly as a sign of the growing tendency toward these. Its significance for him lies not in the clinic but in literary and social criticism. It is merely an aid in his fight for critical standards more to his liking than those of Poe, Lowell and Howells.

Psychoanalysis grows more complex every year, but Lewisohn evidently did not advance beyond its threshold. It is true that he asks some of "the pertinent and crucial questions" and that this is no mean achievement. We need to know, however, not merely that a writer's inner life appears disguised in his writings but how it does and what we may reasonably conclude therefrom. We need to know in what ways the writer is affected by the "national neurosis" and whether his writing attacks or supports it. We need to know if science can tell us what constitutes genius, beauty, and artistic (as distinct from emotional) appeal. And we need to know the ways in which science looks at intellectual, moral and artistic movements. To this last Lewisohn has made a limited contribution, one which has the merit of possessing a degree of accuracy, sense and good will but which nevertheless suffers from vagueness outside its area of competence, from limited scope and from the innocent expectation that it can accomplish more than its resources actually allow. The words of his condemnation of the nineteenth century can be turned against his own too-facile use of psychoanalysis:

The nineteenth century was the century of easy solutions and of eternal truths that lasted ten years. . . . It is now clear, tragically clear, if one likes, that the nineteenth century succeeded solely in asking the pertinent and crucial questions. All its answers were absurdly premature; all its solutions are strewn like withered leaves on an autumnal road. The disillusion, be it remarked, is not with science as an organon; it is with a type of mind that jumped to conclusions suiting its inner climate and then sought to impose its special interpretation, its somber subjective poetry, upon the world as truth and fact.[28]

He has read parts of psychoanalysis and understood parts of what he has read. Then he has behaved as though he has read and understood all of it.

Lewisohn is encouraged by what he knows of psychoanalysis to assert his conviction that art is best considered from the standpoint of its human origins and human uses. "Art is social and moral and religious and metaphysical, not because it has to be made so, but because man is so and because the artist is a man." We need not adopt a philosophical or religious system as the basis for a theory of art. If anything, it would seem rather that these ought to be derived from an adequate comprehension of human nature, and to this, he holds, psychoanalysis is making the most significant contributions. Its importance in Lewisohn's scheme of things is thus very great but only as a means to an end, and this is the role it plays in his criticism. He abhors fixed and closed systems of knowledge and conduct, particularly those which some people feel constrained to impose upon others. His plea is for the development of an ethic and an aesthetic which shall grow out of the true nature of humanity as it is being increasingly revealed by the discoveries of science and the untrammeled operation of free minds. Art must be permitted to emerge by the free choice of the artist among models as well as materials, but his expression must be in accord with his inner nature and not with a received standard external to his own perceptions. The classics, for instance, are not to be regarded "as norms of practice but as examples of the creative spirit in action." [29]

From this man-centered viewpoint, and particularly from the assumption that what is "natural" is good, it is easy to understand Lewisohn's enthusiasm for psychoanalysis. He sees it as a kind of twentieth-century justification for attitudes much like those of Rousseau, a position which is not wholly supported by its clinical findings. He sees it also as an aspect of the movement in modern thought toward realism and naturalism as well as of the literature that these may ultimately lead to. In his view, therefore, it has importance not so much for its scientific usefulness as for the encouragement it offers to those who think as he does. Science is thereby subordinated to ethics, surely a possible and reasonable procedure, but one which, in the wrong hands, can lead to disaster, as we have seen in our time. Whether its service to literature is necessarily thus enhanced may also be questioned. Lewisohn is on safer ground in his insistence upon a moral reference for art. He has not succeeded, despite his good will, in establishing a workable relationship between art and psychoanalysis.

VIII

Edmund Wilson and Psychoanalysis
in Historical Criticism

EDMUND WILSON, a widely read man, has at various times brought to bear upon literature the insights of other disciplines, notably economic and political theory, history and psychology. In preparation—or justification—for the first of these he has written the admirable *To The Finland Station,* tracing the development of Marxist thought. The place of literature in society from this point of view is a fundamental and recurrent theme of Wilson's criticism, but he obviously knows too much about economics, politics, history—and literature—to have followed the orthodox "Marxist" critics down their narrow blind alley. Despite the rather sneering indictment of Wilson's taste by Hyman [1] I feel that it still remains the chief criterion by which he judges literature and that even his Marxist erudition does not stand in its way. I have the same impression of his use of psychoanalysis, although he has produced no work on this subject comparable with *To The Finland Station* from which erudition could be so easily demonstrated.

Nevertheless there is considerable psychoanalytic knowledge underlying many of the evaluations he makes in passing whose focus is other than psychoanalytic, and there is, of course, a Freudian basis of a sort for his famous "wound-and-bow" theory. But how much does Wilson actually know about psychoanalysis? How much does he not know? What use does he make of his information? Is this use valid in the light of (a) psychoanalysis and (b) Wilson's intentions as a critic? He has a reputation for understanding psychoanalysis. This reputation is well-founded, although it must be qualified in certain respects. Some students of criticism tend to regard him with awe-tinged respect for his application of psychoanalytic concepts to literary theory. He is generally thought of as the successful practitioner of a difficult art—which he is—and his judgments are accepted much as the general reader accepted his explanations of *Ulysses* and *Finnegan's Wake* in the days when even fewer people than today understood what Joyce was driving at. Perhaps I can here establish the boundaries of his field of competence in psychoanalysis and evaluate his performance within them.

*   *   *

Wilson's formal approach to literature is set forth in an essay which explains that he is interested in its "social, economic and political aspects." [2] He traces the development of this kind of criticism from Vico to Marx and from Dr. Johnson to Taine, its object, as he sees it, being the study of the origins of works of literature in historical terms. "Another element of a different order has, however, since Marx's time been added. . . . I mean the psychoanalysis of Freud." This is a natural extension of the interest in what Samuel Johnson called "the biographical part of literature" which can now receive the benefit of scientific investigation into the nature of personality. In Wilson's scheme, then, psychoanalysis is a part of the historical method; its value in his criticism, presumably, lies not in what it is itself but in the contribution it can make to an understanding of the larger view.

The chief formulation of this portion of his theory occurs in "Philoctetes: The Wound and the Bow," an exposition of the idea that artistic ability is necessarily related to illness. Wilson states it in these words:

> I should interpret the fable [of Philoctetes] as follows. The victim of a malodorous disease which renders him abhorrent to society and periodically degrades him and makes him helpless is also the master of a superhuman art which everybody has to respect and which the normal man finds he needs.[3]

Furthermore, the outcast is able to transform himself into a hero by an act of self-abnegation. Philoctetes allows himself to be persuaded that he must overcome his natural resentment against those who exiled him on account of the loathesomeness of his wound, and place his unerring bow at their service. He does this; the battle for Troy is won; he himself is cured. The artist, says Wilson, serves humanity by his art and at the same time cures his neurosis.

The fatal defect of this theory is that it does not explain what connection there is, if any, between artistic talent and emotional maladjustment. Wilson merely asserts in several places that such a connection exists. Other than his own word for it we have only the Philoctetes story, but this remains unconvincing for the excellent reason that analogy is not proof. There has been some precedent for this point of view, as Hyman points out, in Mann, Gide, Schopenhauer and Nietzsche.[4] However, the present study is concerned not with literary but with psychoanalytic sources, and for these we must go to the writings of Freud.

What we find there sustains our objections. In a number of places Freud states explicitly that he has been unable to establish any such connection and that he considers the problem to lie outside the proper sphere of psychoanalysis.[5] The most he will say is that some writers—but by no means all—suffer from neuroses of one kind or another, just as other people do. Art may be influenced by neurotic elements in the writer's person-ality, but it may just as readily spring from fantasies of a normal, emotionally healthy kind. Some artists are ill, but it is not at all necessary to be sick in order to be an artist; illness may even diminish the artist's power. Some works of art may be used by their creators as—among other things—curative agents, but this tells us nothing since any idea may be involved in a neurotic system and may either advance the neurosis or help to counter-act it. Nor does psychoanalysis provide any support for the assumption that neurosis always finds expression in art. On the contrary, it specifically describes a great variety of behavior pat-terns, neurotic in origin, which have nothing directly to do with art. It is plain that, although the theory is widely regarded as a psychoanalytic one, it is not fully entitled to this designation.

Wilson has used mythological material which is also susceptible of psychoanalytic interpretation, and he has acknowledged Freud as a force in the thought of our time. This combination has probably led to the notion that the theory has psychoanalytic sanction. It has been strongly reinforced by the widespread familiarity with Freud's famous statement that

> the artist is originally a man who turns away from reality because he cannot come to terms with the demand for the renunciation of instinctual satisfaction as it is first made, and who then in fantasy life allows full play to his erotic and ambitious wishes.[6]

This has made a great impression on the literary and scholarly world, so great that apparently it has interfered with a proper understanding of the sentence which follows it:

> But he finds a way of return from this world of fantasy back to reality; with his special gifts he moulds his fantasies into a new kind of reality, and men concede them a justification as valuable reflections of actual life.

At first glance this seems like a corroboration of the wound-and-bow theory. However, a closer look reveals some differences. The gratification by fantasy described here is not restricted to artists but is shared by the entire human race. The rest of us are equally reluctant to relinquish such pleasures and will often accept in imagination what we may not have in reality. This is not neurosis, however, and it does not become neurosis unless we remain content with the fantasy and give up the attempt to achieve healthy gratification in the ordinary way. Neurosis involves the withdrawal of emotional values from objects in the outer world and their partial transfer to elements within the psyche. This attenuation of the usual meaningful relationship to our surroundings reduces the possibilities of normal functioning and enables us to receive and accept substitute gratifications from internal sources. As a result of such weakening of connections we may then behave as though the impetus for our actions still continued to come from outside even after most of it has ceased to do so. While this may afford us temporary satisfaction, to an external observer it will be clear that we are acting as though the imaginary were the real. If this is to be avoided—and it must be if we are to remain healthy—the psyche and its environment need to be kept in a proper relationship to each other. This is the psychic function of art referred to in the second sentence we have just quoted from Freud. The artist achieves a relationship to the reality he has created which can serve, at least for a time, as a substitute for the kind of relationship all men have to their world. But it seems to me that something more is meant here and that Freud's remark needs to be taken at more than face value. The fact that the work of the artist is accepted by the rest of us surely implies that it is more than merely a "reflection" of "actual life," however valuable that may be. By the act of creation art becomes a new facet of reality and not just an unreal imitation of it. The proof that this is so lies in the reality of the response which it has the power of eliciting. The work of art gives us what amounts to a new view of the world. Moreover, it is a view on the basis of which it is possible to form new, significant and valid relationships with the reality we knew before. In this it differs from the new view of reality which results from a neurotic or psychotic distortion, for the latter is based on avoidance of the environment—and even of certain elements in the self—and leads to dissociation rather than to integration. To equate artistic ability with inadequacy is a denial of its value which was certainly far from Freud's intention.

My use of the word "reality" here does not carry any emotive load. Conversely, when I refer to the artist's involvement with his creation I do not mean it pejoratively, nor is there any evidence that Freud so meant it. However, the view that he did seems to be widely accepted in literary circles where it is resented as an attack on the virility of the artist. To anyone familiar with Freud's respect for artists such an interpretation would be impossible. His clinical evaluations are not to be taken either as pronouncements on literary criticism or as belittlings of the creative character nor is his reference to works of art as "reflections" of reality to be construed as excluding them from reality. The contrary is true, as we can see in the development of Freud's idea later on by Kris and Hartmann.[7] The artist.

even though he sometimes begins by seeking to escape from his human connections, ends by maintaining and strengthening them.

There is an insufficiently appreciated distinction between the everyday preserving of one's mental equilibrium—as the artist does by means of his art and as we all do in our several ways—and curing an emotional illness. It seems to me that what Freud is saying is that the artist is using this means to maintain his psychic health, not simply to restore it after it has already been lost. His original turning away from ordinary reality is not yet neurosis, although it may become neurosis if it is not checked. The point is that the artist checks it. Freud speaks elsewhere of the artist's superior ability to pass psychic boundaries,[8] and this quality, which is the artist's by right of endowment, has been overlooked by those who have penetrated no further into psychoanalytic thought than Wilson evidently had at the time he wrote *The Wound and the Bow*. This "flexibility of repression"[9] permits the artist to achieve certain things psychically that are beyond the powers of others who were less fortunately born. We must try to understand the concept of normality so that its dependence upon constantly shifting variables can be appreciated.[10] In short, an experience which might impel a psychically less gifted person toward neurosis could be well within the capacity of an artist to handle.[11] If there is anything left of the "wound" after such an understanding is reached, it can be hardly more than a barely visible scar. What is important for Freud is the bow.

*   *   *

Wilson's adherence to the "Wound-and-the-Bow" theory is by no means as mechanical or rigid as has sometimes been supposed. In his studies of individual writers he departs from it whenever it suits his purpose to do so, which is often. The most important influence on his criticism is the over-all approach indicated in "The Historical Interpretation of Literature," and psychoanalysis is not by any means the most prominent feature of this view. It has been suggested that his method "has always embraced both sociological and psychological factors, with greater emphasis on the sociological in his early criticism and the proportion gradually shifting in favor of the psychological as he developed." [12] The appearance of *Classics and Commercials* and *The Shores of Light* since this statement was made, although they contain material from as far back as the twenties, enables us to see that there was no such neat progression. It is true that psychological ideas appear with some frequency throughout both collections, but no chronological pattern emerges except that, beginning with the appearance of *The Wound and the Bow* in 1941,[13] psychological considerations of various kinds are present. Wilson's major effort in this direction seems to have gone into the formulation of the theory; his subsequent uses of psychology are, for the most part, incidental.

The theory receives its most concentrated application in the essays on Dickens and Kipling [14] in which an effort—successful, in my opinion—is made to establish connections between the works and the psychic traumas suffered by the authors. "Wound," in these instances, seems to be equated with a single traumatic incident or closely related sequence of incidents. Dickens, for example, suffered as a child the humiliation of being made to work in the shoe-blacking warehouse of a relative instead of being permitted to attend school and acquire an education suited to the station in life which he ardently desired. From this "wound," with its attendant attitude towards his father whose economic ineffectiveness had brought about his shame, he never recovered, according to the theory.[15] Inevitably, results of it appeared in his works. It lay behind his choice of certain themes such as that of the benevolent old gentleman in *Pickwick Papers* and in *Oliver Twist* and the almost direct representation of his childhood difficulties in *David Copperfield*. Wilson remarks that "Dickens' personal difficulties make themselves felt like an ache at the back of Little Dorrit," and he makes a case for the identity of Dickens and Jasper in *Edwin Drood*.[16] Not only is this traceable in the writings, but the projection of Dickens' feelings onto his relations with his public is also evident.[17] A similar analysis of Kipling's "wound," the childhood desertion by his parents, shows it to be the chief cause from which springs all that is typical in his stories, most especially the ones that "nobody reads." In the same fashion the neurosis of the writer and the results of it in his works are described for others. Hemingway, says Wilson, fears impotence and death; therefore he frequently portrays submissive women who live only to do the bidding of their men, and he protests too much that one should not be a coward in the face of a malevolent universe. Samuel Butler wages a lifelong fight with various surrogates for his own domineering father. Henry James's writings become more and more intricate as he seeks to hide, from himself and the world, his inability to partake of human experience, particularly sexual experience, a pattern which appears in increasingly "perverse and mysterious forms." [18]

It is never made explicit whether the "wound" as Wilson conceives it is to be taken at face value as the only begetter of the neurosis or whether it is merely the most eye-catching of a long series of antecedent and subsequent events which influenced, if they did not determine, character. The latter, of course, is the psychoanalytic view. In the early days of psychoanalysis the plausible theory that a single traumatic event was sufficient explanation for many psychic disorders was held by some psychoanalysts; today it seems to be confined to laymen. In *The Wound and the Bow* Wilson adheres most closely to the view that the single traumatic event with its cluster of associated shocks is the "explanation" of much of the writer's choice of subjects and themes and his depiction of character. In other criticisms, however, he has drifted away from this oversimplification,[19] although I have not been able to find any formal statement of such a change. It is as though his original enthusiasm for the idea has gradually worn off and he has quietly abandoned it while still continuing to use psychoanalytic concepts in more limited ways.

In his essay on Proust, for instance, he writes:

> The real elements, of course, of any work of fiction, are the elements of the author's personality: his imagination embodies in the images of characters, situations and scenes the fundamental conflicts of his nature or the cycle or phases through which it habitually passes. His personages are per-

sonifications of the author's various impulses and emotions: and the relations between them in his stories are really the relations between these.[20]

This is very early Freud and is by now so well established as to be almost platitudinous. It is to be noted that Wilson does not say—as Freud did not say, either—that this is all there is to art. It is precisely at this point, as we have seen, that the wound-and-bow theory breaks down. This is also where Freud himself asserted that the limits of psychoanalytic illumination lay. In the retreat from the untenable portions of his theory Wilson has thus come back to his psychoanalytic source. Sometimes, though, he makes statements that contain ambiguity and raise the question of how accurate his understanding of psychoanalysis really is.

> Well, art has its origin in the need to pretend that human life is something other than it is, and, in a sense, by pretending this, it succeeds to some extent in transforming it.[21]

This remark, which is tossed off in passing, sounds plausible and can be true if its terms are suitably defined, but Wilson does not define them or even give us any clues in the context. It makes some difference whether he is expressing, as a critic, the idea that we cannot live without our illusions, as Eugene O'Neill has done dramatically in *The Iceman Cometh,* or whether he is making an assertion for which he claims psychoanalytic support. If it is the latter, then he is dealing with the distinction between normal and neurotic which, we have seen, is quite difficult to define, even given a psychoanalytic orientation.[22] None of this complexity is so much as hinted at. The remark has an authoritative ring, however, and the reader is ready to take for granted what it says about art, until, upon reflection, he discovers that he is not really sure what it says.

Wilson accepts the psychoanalytic idea that at least one purpose of art is the alleviation of psychic tension in the artist, though only temporarily: "Poor Shelley and poor Byron, to have carried in their hearts the consciousness of such guilt as no wine could for long disguise, no songs could forever relieve." Such direct applications of Freudian concepts occur frequently throughout Wilson's work, but they never again attain the status of the wound-and-bow theory. Following its appearance he seems to have restricted himself to occasional references of this kind, usually in an incidental way, while chiefly concerned with some other aspect of the subject under discussion. What he says is for the most part solidly based on the work of Freud through the 1920's, with some exceptions which are not so solid, like the one we have noted. Wilson's understanding of Freud is superior to that of Brooks, Krutch, or Lewisohn, but it shares with them the limitation of the earlier bias toward the role of the id. He does not give any indication in his criticism that he is aware of the implications of the later emphasis on the ego for which the groundwork was laid by Freud as early as 1900 in *The Interpretation of Dreams* and which was brought prominently to the fore in 1922 with the publication of *The Ego and the Id,* to say nothing of other, if lesser, writings on the same subject.

The greater part of the present study is necessarily concerned with psychoanalytic ideas in Wilson's criticism. Except for *The Wound and the Bow,* where they furnish the rationale for an entire book, they occupy a minor place in his evaluations of literature. His greatest critical interest, as we have noted, was— and is—the historical study of literature, and his preference is the social, not the psychological, viewpoint. In his criticism of *For Whom The Bell Tolls,* for instance, he is more concerned with the fact that Hemingway "has largely sloughed off his Stalinism and has reverted to seeing events in terms of individuals pitted against specific odds" [23] than he is in studying and evaluating those individuals from a psychological standpoint. He admires Van Wyck Brooks's "bitter insight of *The Ordeal of Mark Twain*" but the admiration is for Brooks's analysis of society, not for its author, as is made plain when Wilson contrasts this with the later "sugaring" of anything that might contribute to a usable past.[24] This attitude comes out very clearly in his remark that:

> What is wrong with the younger American poets is that they have no real stake in society. One does not want them to succumb to society; but one *would* like to see them, at least, have some sort of relation to it. . . . As it is the conflicts of

feeling and the criticism of society are left largely to the novelists and the dramatists; and the poets content themselves with expressing the chagrin of sterility.[25] Wilson's use of psychoanalysis in passages such as these is incidental. Furthermore, he does not rely on psychoanalysis—nor for that matter on sociology—for his criticism. Both have their place in his work, but Wilson is a critic, and his feet are always on literary ground. When dealing with Poe, his judgment is not primarily a psychological but a literary one.[26] He notes the sexual aberrations but does not dwell on them, and he points out that Poe can be understood quite adequately as a participant in the romantic movement. The emphasis is upon literary analogues, not psychic ones; Wilson here is particularly interested in Poe as a precursor of Symbolism and not as a pre-Freudian instance of pathology. In another essay he puts away the temptation to discuss Byron as a scandalous individual and focuses on the work rather than the man when he asserts that "what should be most interesting at any time is to find out to what actuality of human ideals and adventures a creation like Childe Harold corresponded." [27] In a third, he castigates Upton Sinclair for asking the artist to concern himself with irrelevancies:

> If somebody . . . is constructing from the phenomena of experience a satisfactory artistic system, it should not be demanded of him that he construct either a political or a moral system, and the critic should not take him to task if his pattern fails to match the patterns of other people's political and moral systems. The artist has his own technique for formulating his vision of truth, and he cannot be expected to worry about the constructions of other people who are working in different materials.[28]

This can stand as Wilson's critical creed to which, with the single exception of *The Wound and the Bow,* he has consistently adhered.

*   *   *

I have said that Wilson's understanding of psychoanalysis is superior to that of Brooks, Lewisohn or Krutch. In evaluating

the work of the latter, for instance, he was able to say that the
Poe was "a rather half-baked performance . . . depending too
much on a Freudian oversimplification," [29] that is, he was able
to see the flaw in its "scientific" assumptions rather than to reject
in horror the whole idea that psychoanalysis had anything valuable to say about literature, as so many of his contemporaries
impulsively did. This knowledge stood him in good stead in his
battle with the humanists. He adopted the line that they were
simply evading the truth because they found it unpleasant, and
that they were putting forth what seemed to him inadequate
explanations for phenomena in literature which could be more
satisfactorily accounted for psychoanalytically. "The moral philosophy that the humanists profess to derive from Sophocles
seems to me pure boloney." [30] Antigone's regard for her brother
was an incestuous love; it was this, not simply religious duty,
that was her motive in burying his body.

> Sophocles did not call it that, and he did not consider it from
> our clinical point of view; but his comprehension of human
> motives was profound and realistic, and it seems to me impos-
> sible not to conclude that he emphasized deliberately for his
> dramatic purpose the difference between Antigone's attitude
> toward Haemon and her attitude toward Polyneices.[31]

Moreover, Wilson insisted that Sophocles was presenting this
situation "consciously," which I take to mean that as an
intuitive person he was aware of its sexual nature. The luke-
warmness of Antigone to her betrothed lends some weight to this
view, even taking into account the fact that Haemon was not her
own choice for a husband but had been selected for her, and it
justifies Wilson in adhering to classical Freudian doctrine. In
the same essay he uses as another weapon against the humanists
the significant fact that Freud went to Sophocles for the name of
the psychic complex that his dramas so effectively portrayed.
    Wilson understood that emotional life follows universal laws
and that its manifestations in different people are matters of
"mere gradation" rather than of kind.[32] He understood that the
apparent modifications of this universality in literary characters were due to the operation of both unconscious and
conscious factors. Henry James's women, for instance,

are not always emotionally perverted. Sometimes they are apathetic. . . . Or they are longing . . . for affection but too inhibited or passive to obtain it for themselves. . . . James' men are not precisely neurotic; but . . . they have a way of missing out on emotional experience either through timidity or prudence or through heroic renunciation.[33]

Wilson comprehended the fact that a limited constitutional capacity for feeling might prevent fulfillment as effectively as acquired social attitudes. How much of this he derived from studying psychoanalysis and how much from his own observation is not clear. In the absence of proof the available evidence seems to me to point to the latter.

One of the touchstones of psychoanalytic understanding is insight into the nature of dreams. Although *The Interpretation of Dreams* was Freud's first major published work, it still remains the basis of psychoanalysis, and with one notable exception [34] its chief formulations still stand. Wilson's understanding of this exceedingly complex subject is remarkably good for a layman. He knows, as some other readers of *The Interpretation of Dreams* do not, that what appears on the surface of the dream is never to be taken at face value no matter how closely it resembles everyday reality. He knows that what really matters in dreams is not the apparent "message," the rebus which may, with some difficulty, be deciphered, but the feelings which accompany it, and he knows that the interpretation of a dream cannot properly be said to be satisfactory until the psychic meaning of each significant symbol has been established together with its appropriate affect.

This enables him to see that Poe's short stories are literary equivalents of dreams even when not acknowledged as such by their author. "Many are confessedly dreams; and, as with dreams, though they seem absurd, their effect on our emotions is serious. And even those that pretend to the logic and the exactitude of actual narratives are, nevertheless, also dreams." [35] The *Alice* books and *Sylvie and Bruno* of Lewis Carroll likewise reveal resemblances to the dream. Wilson realizes that one of the chief reasons for their appeal to us is exactly this quality which takes advantage of our fondness for the childhood—and therefore

more primitive—aspects of our minds. In *Sylvie and Bruno*
the opening railway journey portrays the alternations of dream
and reality through the account of the dozing narrator. In
Alice, Wilson suggests that we regard the entire story as a little
girl's dream of her reality.

> The shiftings and the transformations, the mishaps and the
> triumphs of Alice's dream, the mysteries and the riddles, the
> gibberish that conveys unmistakeable meanings, are all based
> upon relationships that contradict the assumptions of our con-
> scious lives but that are lurking not far behind them.[36]

He even goes a bit further, as is proper with dreams, and proposes the theory that the story, "the creatures that she meets,
the whole dream, *are* Alice's personality and her waking life.
They are the world of teachers, family and pets, as it appears to
a little girl, and also the little girl who is looking at this
world." [37] Although he does not develop this idea, a case could
be made for it by using the material in the books, even though
Lewis Carroll is not here to give us his associations. This would
admittedly have some limitations, but in these stories as in
dreams there is, as Wilson well knew, more than meets the eye.

Wilson is much sounder than most of his contemporaries on
the more difficult subject of the language of dreams, which seems
destined to go on being profoundly misunderstood for the fore-
seeable future. Here and there, however, its nature appears to
have been fathomed. Wilson quotes T. S. Eliot approvingly:
"It is characteristic of dream poetry . . . that it never means as
much as it seems to." [38] This is, of course, the expression of the
same principle that governs the interpretation of dream symbols.
The mere language of dream poetry counts for much less than the
feelings it conveys. Consequently, a close examination of its
intellectual content leaves the reader disappointed; the expected
correspondence of form and meaning is defective, if not wholly
absent. Even if the author has succeeded in transcribing his own
dream symbols and producing in the reader the feelings which
they aroused in him, there is no way in which the reader can
reconstruct the associative links which connected them in the
author's mind. The analogy with the dream is close. Not only
the ultimate "meaning" but the psychic road by which it was

reached must be known for full understanding. In dream poetry this is, by definition, very difficult if not actually impossible. One of the greatest difficulties is the fact that language does not always behave in dreams as it does elsewhere. When a writer like Joyce, for instance, tries "to make his hero express directly in words . . . states of mind which do not usually in reality make use of words at all," [39] he is faced with the problem of translation as well as the conveying of sense. Such communication must be imperfect at best.

The symbol system of the dream is composed chiefly of visual images with a relatively small admixture of musical tones, odors, pressures and similar impressions derived from various sensory sources. Words play a small part in dreams directly. Most of the time the dream expresses visually what we would use words for if we were awake, that is, it composes a visual pun. For example, one of Freud's patients dreamed that his uncle gave him a kiss in an automobile. When analyzed, this scene was found to represent auto-eroticism.[40] The dream mechanism is compelled to make use of its memories of perceptions, and it chooses primarily visual ones. Even when words actually appear in dreams, Freud warns us, they are never to be taken literally. If they are real words they always stand for something else. If they are invented words (like Freud's *autodidasker*) they must be separated into their component parts on the basis of sensory associations as well as psychic ones. Interpretation is often accomplished by the discovery of resemblance in mere sound without reference to sense at all. Words in dreams lose most of the qualities which make them words in waking life, and they are manipulated by the dream apparatus in accordance with the laws governing the dreamwork.[41]

Starting from these basic considerations, Wilson is able to identify Joyce's debt to Freud and to look beyond even that advanced work. He is aware of the dangers of separating ideas from experience, and suggests that modern poetry may be driven toward the expression of dream-like states because the "old kind of lyric feeling, which used to embrace the world," is being pushed inward and "the deliberate formulas and attitudes derived from the study of external reality which the younger poets are trying to impose upon their poetry have a way of yielding nothing but rhetoric." [42] Whatever the merits of this critical judgment—Wilson's quarrel with the younger poets is in any case beyond the scope of this book—this statement shows an acceptable application of psychoanalysis to a literary problem. The rhetoric against which he inveighs is, of course, an attempt to impose externally derived patterns upon works of art whose form ought to be determined by their inner natures. It results in a great many artistic failures. "Who knows," asks Wilson, "but we may not, in the long run, have to depend on our dreams for lyrics?" If this should come to pass it would make communication between poet and reader increasingly difficult because such dependence would severely limit the subject matter of art to an area of experience in which our primitive rather than our civilized selves hold sway, and poetry as we know it would simply cease to exist. It would be almost impossible to arrest its retrogression toward primitive tribal chants. If Wilson's judgment is accurate, then his alarm is justified; no good can come of abandoning our hard-won advance posts. His position is strongly supported by psychoanalysis which has a stake in strengthening the influence of the ego everywhere.

*   *   *

Wilson's appreciation of symbolism in the dream and its manifestation in literature equipped him to deal with the difficult problem of the relation of the author to his work and the extent to which personal psychology is reflected in writing. On the whole, he adhered faithfully to standard Freudian conceptions and successfully avoided the ludicrous oversimplification of which Brooks, Krutch and Lewisohn were guilty. He objected, rightly, to "the modern school of social-psychological biography . . . [which] seems inevitably to tend to caricature the personalities of its subjects." On the basis of our information about Poe, "it is possible to follow Mr. Krutch in admitting that the atrocious sadism of many of Poe's later tales must have been due to some emotional repression." [43] The inner life of the author, as psychoanalysis sees it, is always represented in his works, although we do not always possess the ability to discern it. But having identified some deviation from "normal" behavior, even a morally discreditable one (this last is, of course, not a psychoanalytic idea), we are not therefore justified in thinking the less of his writing. Such judgment must be based upon non-psychoanalytic criteria. Wilson himself, for instance, states that Kafka was "as neurotic as" Poe or Gogol, but that he was not as good a writer as either because of his spiritual defeat and emptiness, which resulted from the fact that he was "denationalized, discouraged, disaffected, disabled." [44] This judgment is not softened by the success of a few stories which are "realistic nightmares that embody in concrete imagery the manias of neurotic states." [45] Furthermore, Kafka's symbolism must be understood with reference to himself and not to some solely cosmic significance. He is not writing theologically—as we can see now that nearly all of the relevant source material is available and as Wilson, with his sound approach to symbolism, could see even before this—but "satirizing the absurdities of his own bad conscience." [46] Such attention to scientific details would have saved certain other critics from indulging in free-floating flights of fancy which can no longer be sustained now that the evidence is in.

But its merit is positive as well. For example, it enables Wilson to acquire an interesting insight about George Saintsbury:

> Emotional deprivation sometimes drives people to eating and drinking as a substitute for what has been lost, and this may have been the case with Saintsbury, who certainly loved the pleasures of the table . . . and seems to have taken to letters as both a gourmet and something of a glutton. . . . It was as if he had transferred to literature his whole emotional and moral life, so that presently he appeared as an artist whose contacts were all with books instead of with places and people.[47]

In this instance the new view is neither very startling nor very important, but it illustrates the process. On a subject of more consequence for contemporary literature, Ernest Hemingway, it offers more food for consideration—and debate. Wilson traces the strain of murderous impulses in Hemingway's writing and shows how they developed from the killing of trout to larger and more savage game and from these to "Chinamen and Cubans" and finally to white men who are labeled Fascists.

> Hitherto the act of destruction has given rise for him to complex emotions: he has identified himself not merely with the injurer but also with the injured; there has been a masochistic complement to the sadism. But now this paradox which splits our natures, and which has instigated some of Hemingway's best stories, need no longer present perplexities to his mind. The Fascists are dirty bastards, and to kill them is a righteous act.[48]

From the psychoanalytic point of view this reflects an upsetting of the healthy equilibrium which not only kept the destructive impulses in partial check but also permitted expression to them only insofar as they served moral ends. Wilson raises the question whether Hemingway's later development has not permitted more expression to ideas of killing than is good, and whether the Fascist (or any other) label provides sufficient justification for them. In literature, at least, the triumph of the impulses dissolves the tension which produces the best aesthetic effects and leaves only the reader's conscience, undirected by the writer, as the guide. When the artist suffers in this sense, his art suffers also.

There is one place, however, where Wilson finds himself in direct opposition to psychoanalytic thinking about literature, particularly as exemplified by Freud and Jones. He says, "It does not occur to us today to try, as was at one time a critical fashion, to examine the creations of Shakespeare as if they were actual persons about whom it would be possible to assemble complete and consistent biographies." [49] But this is exactly what Jones argues for in *Hamlet and Oedipus*. While neither he nor Freud ever assembled "complete" biographies for any literary characters, both felt it justifiable on psychoanalytic grounds to assume that they would have behaved in other situations in a manner consistent with the laws of human psychology. Such assumptions, indeed, are implicit in the artist's treatment of characters between the acts or offstage. Wilson quotes J. Dover Wilson to the effect that the personality of Falstaff is created as long as the play progresses, and exists only in terms of the play. In one sense this is true, but it is obviously not the same sense intended by Freud and Jones, the latter of whom admires J. Dover Wilson greatly and uses his Shakespearean critical ideas in his book. It would be interesting to have Edmund Wilson's comments on Jones's reconstruction of Hamlet's "neurosis." This unwillingness to accept a mode of procedure which is considered necessary by psychoanalysts, however, must be taken into account (together with several instances of loose usage of technical terms) when Wilson is referred to as a psychoanalytic critic. Like so many other labels, this one conceals something important.

The key to Wilson's understanding of psychoanalysis, it seems to me, lies in the simple fact that he has not kept up with Freud. Up to a certain point (which I would guess was reached in approximately 1927 with the first appearance in English of *The Ego and the Id*) he apparently understood psychoanalysis as an intelligent layman might but not as well as a close student or a practicing psychoanalyst. He has evidently not advanced beyond this conception. As a result, some of his psychoanalytic ideas are valid, having stood the test of time, while others have been superseded under the pressure of clinical necessity.[50] Wilson knows that psychoanalysis is a branch of biological science, a fundamental fact that seems to have escaped many other people who evidently regard it as armchair theorizing which they are free to contradict from their own armchairs. He understands the conception of "the unconscious" as developed by Freud in *The Interpretation of Dreams,* but apparently is not aware that this has since been replaced as inadequate by the tripartite structure of ego, id and superego. He knows the rudiments of the psychoanalytic theory of dreams and has an elementary understanding of the significance of dream symbolism, but he never gets very far below the surface. He can interpret dreams and their literary equivalents in terms of the simple basic outline of the Oedipus complex and the Electra complex, but except for a few flashes of insight,[51] his analysis does not pass beyond the general pattern to the specific meaning in the case of a particular author. Although he has gone further in comprehension than have most other critics, he has not, from the standpoint of psychoanalysis, gone far enough.

This leads him into inevitable errors, such as praising Van

Wyck Brooks's *Ordeal of Mark Twain* as "one of the best examples I know of the application of Freudian analysis to literature." This is based upon Wilson's feeling that

> Brooks really had hold of something important when he fixed upon that childhood incident of which Mark Twain gave so vivid an account to his biographer—that scene at the deathbed of his father when his mother had made him promise that he would not break her heart. If it was not one of those crucial happenings that are supposed to determine the complexes of Freud, it has certainly a typical significance in relation to Mark Twain's whole psychology.[52]

As a figure of speech, as a part standing for the whole, the incident will serve. But this is rhetoric, not psychoanalysis. A complex is not determined by a simplex. A single trauma will not necessarily ruin a person's life. It is true there was a time when Freud thought so, but even as early as 1900 he had advanced to a better appreciation of the intricacy of psychic life and of the meticulous, painstaking work which was necessary before a pattern such as this one could safely be regarded as typical for an individual. To put it briefly, Brooks has generalized from insufficient evidence, and Wilson has accepted his conclusion. In justification he writes:

> The stories that people tell about their childhood are likely to be profoundly symbolic even when they have been partly or wholly made up in the light of later experience. And the attitudes, the compulsions, the emotional "patterns" that recur in the work of a writer are of great interest to the historical critic.[53]

This is perfectly true psychoanalytically, if the word "likely" is defined in the usual way, but Wilson here seems to equate it with "proven." We cannot, therefore, know from this argument whether Brooks's contention is valid. Wilson's eagerness to make a point has betrayed him into a slight lapse in logic. This is not an isolated instance [54] but it illustrates the danger, which even so perceptive a critic as Wilson cannot avoid, of mishandling ideas of a scientific order in the process of bringing them into a critical context.

One more questionable ideological tendency must be mentioned here, since it attained some currency in the thirties and since Wilson himself evidently saw nothing wrong with it. Indeed, he seemed to regard it as a promising critical technique, although the only passage I could find in which he refers to it is this one:

The recent scientific experimentation in the combining of Freudian with Marxist method, and of psychoanalysis with anthropology, has had its parallel development in criticism. And there is thus another element added to our equipment for analyzing literary works, and the problem grows still more complex.[55]

The fact is that Freud and Marx are oil and water. No combination of the two is possible except by doing violence to either or both. It is true that attempts have been made, but only in unacceptable ways. Freud was at some pains to repudiate those that came to his attention, just as he did with the Surrealists and any others who attempted to amputate any of the essential characteristics of psychoanalysis and to fit the mutilated remains into some Procrustean formula of their own. The Kremlin, too, saw the incompatibility of its faith with scientific investigations of human nature; today there are no psychoanalysts in Russia. It is noteworthy that the only significant pronouncements on this subject from Communist sources since World War II are anti-Freudian polemics. The realities of politics can sometimes be instructive to literary criticism.

It is unfortunate that Wilson places "scientific" Marxist method in the same category as Freudian and anthropological investigations. Whatever the standing of the latter two may be in the minds of traditional scientists, they are attempts to observe natural phenomena objectively and systematically rather than to impose preconceived notions upon them.

* * *

It has been necessary to point out the places where Wilson has missed the point in psychoanalysis and where his application of it to literary problems has been faulty. However, to end on this note would be misleading. Wilson's deficiencies are, so to speak, honorable ones, given his basic outlook as an historical critic and not as a scientific student of human nature. The question whether he is intellectually obligated to acquire as thorough an understanding of psychoanalysis as he has of, say, Marxism, is quite another one. What psychoanalytic knowledge he had, he used in essentially sound ways. In his theory of the "wound" of the artist he has attained such insight as is possible for one who is not acquainted with ego psychology. In the essay on Hemingway, for instance, he shows how the psychic equilibrium between feelings about killing and feelings about being killed produce, as long as they are kept in balance, the possibility for the author to express "the resolution of this dissonance" in his prose. When Hemingway finds what seems to him a moral justification for killing—i.e., that these people are, after all, Fascists—the murderous impulse gets the upper hand—and the prose suffers. The tautness is gone; the balance of ambivalence has been destroyed; there is no longer any conflict to engage the reader. Hemingway's lesser works must therefore be regarded as mere journalism and escape-literature. This is creative use of psychoanalysis in criticism, and in this Wilson does very well indeed.

IX

Kenneth Burke's
Terminological Medium of Exchange

KENNETH BURKE is in process of synthesizing a number of disparate disciplines into what he hopes will be a workable tool for the analysis of poetry. Believing that literary criticism ought to make use of all available knowledge from relevant sources, he has undertaken the difficult task of mastering the several fields, integrating them and using the product to study literary works. In a sense, it is impossible to understand any single portion of the intricate fabric which he has woven, even in its present incomplete form, without knowing the whole, for if he continues in the manner that he has followed thus far its essence will inevitably turn out to be its totality. However, an examination of one important strand can be instructive not only for its own design but also for what it reveals about the pattern of the rest. Accordingly, this chapter will look at the way Burke has used one of the contributing disciplines, psychoanalysis.

In order to do this it is best to begin with his first major treatment of the subject, which occurs in a chapter entitled "Secular Conversions." [1] The title is very instructive. In two words it condenses his entire approach to the problem of human motives circa 1935, summarizing both his ideas and his method. Briefly, he regards motives as religious, or at least as analogous to religious ones, "religious" being used here not in the literal but in a metaphoric sense. In Burke's figure it does not necessarily signify adherence to a theological doctrine but rather to any set of beliefs (which may also include theological ones) that constitute the individual's view of the universe. The word consequently refers to the assumptions upon which men act. These "pieties," as Burke calls them, are for the most part tacitly—i.e., unthinkingly or even unconsciously—held. They provide both the impetus for acts and the means of judging their appropriateness. In Burke's view, all people grow up within a framework of such ideas which gradually harden until they control all actions. It then takes an extraordinary effort to break out of the mold.

Such efforts together with their effects he speaks of as "conversions." A conversion is the adoption of an entirely new set of assumptions, that is, a new set of values. What was permitted the pagan is forbidden the Christian; what the child may do the adult may not; and what causes joy or fear in one setting may evoke the reverse in another. A given act, therefore, may either calm the individual or upset him, depending upon the way he looks at it. An inescapable corollary is that conduct need not be altered provided that the manner of judging it is suitably modified. Upon this line of reasoning Burke approaches psychoanalysis.

He develops this view in a section labeled "The Fundamentals of Psychoanalysis," which is remarkable both for the ingenuity with which he makes an analogy between it and religion and for the almost complete absence of any reference to the fact that it is a scientific discipline. Certainly the resemblance of the psychoanalytic patient's experience to a religious conversion is clear— at least from a special and limited standpoint such as Burke's— but it might with equal justice be compared to a re-education process, and many psychoanalysts do so regard it. Other interpretations are also possible, but Burke ignores them. "From our standpoint," he says, "psychoanalysis can be treated as a simple technique of non-religious conversion." Since it is a great deal more than this, we must inquire further into the standpoint from which he takes his view.

As we know from his later books, Burke is striving for an ideological synthesis. But even in his earlier work he seems to have encountered semantic difficulties, at least in his treatment of psychoanalysis. He does not regard it as an outgrowth and branch of biology but as a purely verbal formula very much like an ethical system derived from speculative philosophy instead of from observation of nature. Or rather he does not regard its scientific orientation as of much importance since the terms which it uses "are wholly incongruous with the unscientific nature of the distress." This ignoring or minimizing of perhaps the most important fact about psychoanalysis—its intention of being as objective as it can be about human nature—skews his subsequent treatment so that thereafter we are presented only with isolated fragments of it, in each instance from a special point of view. Burke's system, then, loses whatever benefit it might gain from the derivation of psychoanalytic theory from observed behavior, a considerable handicap for an attempt to deal with motives.

A question of relative values arises here. If conversion takes place, is the patient better or worse off than he was under his previous system of "pieties"? Burke occupies himself so thoroughly with the technique of conversions that he seems to slight their worth or the worth of the "solutions" to which they lead. As a result we are left with the impression that such shiftings of moral ground may follow one another indefinitely and that it does not particularly matter whether the patient ultimately lands among, say, the rationalists or among the true believers. All that Burke seems interested in is the pressure which drives him to seek a change and the means by which he achieves it. He is concerned exclusively with the therapeutic aspect of psychoanalysis; the vast potential which it holds for a larger understanding of motives necessarily lies beyond his horizon.[2]

Even within his self-imposed limitations, however, it is questionable how sound his grasp of psychoanalysis really is, for he persists in treating it merely as a system of verbal symbols whose chief functions are, first, to give a new, and "incongruous," name to the patient's problem and, second, to supply other, and more favorable, names for the things which he must do anyway. Freudian theory and "the various schools of thought that have descended from it" [3] share these features:

the *conversion downwards* of the patient's distress by means of an unfit, incongruous terminology—and the positive development of a substitute terminology until it has provided the patient with a brand-new rationalization of motives.[4]

Conversion downwards, in Burke's special vocabulary, means "the opposite of magnification . . . reduction of scale." It is clear that he is talking about orientation to words alone, not to deeds, and that he means words, quite literally: "By selecting a vocabulary which specifically violates the dictates of style and taboo, it [psychoanalysis] changes the entire nature of his problem, rephrasing it in a form for which there is a solution." This is itself a conversion downwards of the transvaluation of psychic values which has taken place in the neurosis and which is restored to a proper balance in a successful psychoanalysis. What Burke seems to have missed is the psychoanalytic understanding of the relation that a verbal symbol has to a psychic state. An emotional re-education therefore appears to him as simply an exercise in the juggling of logical terms, abetted (if not corrupted) by some of the tricks of propaganda. This makes it possible for him to say of psychoanalysis that, "insofar as it is curative, its effects seem due to the fact that it exorcises the painful influences of a vestigial religious orientation by appeal to the prestige of the newer scientific orientation." [5] Verbal symbols constitute for him a kind of universal medium of exchange, like money but with added magical properties.

It seems to me that he has reasoned fallaciously from the analogy which a financial system bears to his symbol system. The medium of exchange has no necessary organic relationship to the commodities for which it is traded but an arbitrary and shifting one. At the very least Burke is guilty here of inadequately defining his terms, and few things are more unsettling than attempting to follow an exposition in which the meanings of key words are vague. Burke speaks, for instance, of the patient's "basic psychosis" when the context makes it perfectly clear that he is referring to neurosis (and perhaps to something else as well). Since he has used the word neurosis correctly elsewhere, we are at a loss to know why he uses "basic psychosis" here, and he does not tell us. The suggestion has been

made that he adopted the term from Dewey who used it to mean
something like the outlook a person has on the world when it
is colored by his occupational bias, but nowhere does Burke say
so. And yet there is a crucial difference between psychosis and
neurosis as the terms are used in psychoanalysis. It is a common
practice of Burke's to use a familiar word in a special way which
he indicates by enclosing it in quotation marks or italicizing it.
His pages are freckled with such usages. His long-range plan
was to issue a glossary in which all of them would be explained,
but they multiplied until nobody knows their number, and
when the glossary finally appeared he sadly admitted that it
was hopelessly incomplete. There does not appear to be much
chance that he will catch up with his own verbal innovations in
time to make them clear to his readers. This casts considerable
doubt on the validity of the very means by which he hopes to
achieve his great synthesis as well as on his understanding of
psychoanalytic concepts.

An illustration of the difficulties encountered occurs when
Burke presents what he calls "Freud's doctrine of the six abnormal tendencies in everyone: autoeroticism, homosexuality,
sadism, masochism, incest, and exhibitionism." But unless both
elements of the phrase "abnormal tendencies" are carefully defined it is impossible to be sure how they are being used, and
Burke does not define them at all. Instead he goes on to praise
Freud for having promulgated the doctrine since (a) "it is hard
to imagine a single manifestation of human interests which could
not be reduced to one of these six terms," and therefore (b) "if
the six abnormals applied to everybody, it followed that everybody was abnormal, hence it followed that it was normal to be
abnormal." [6] Burke is employing verbal tricks here and imput-
ing them to psychoanalysis which, to his mind, evidently "said
that *everyman* was in essence a pervert." He is not the only one
to have interpreted the findings of psychoanalysis in this way,
but this does not make the interpretation valid. Neither does it
justify him in charging that psychoanalysis seeks to reduce all
conduct to morally repugnant terms. In his difficulties with the
concept of normality he has confused neurosis with perversion
and psychic tendency with overt behavior. Moreover, he does

not see the psychoanalytic view of their respective roles in society.[7]

In all this Burke neglects to consider whether a "reduction downwards" actually does take place in psychoanalytic cures. He offers no proof beyond his assertion that the new context so provided for moral judgments is less complex than the one that has been discarded. He does not examine the relation of each of them to the kind of reality with which it attempts to deal. And he does not propose any measure of efficacy, that is, of psychological, social or moral value, or even appropriateness. The difference between a scientific orientation and a personal, idiosyncratic one is never mentioned. Burke apparently regards psychoanalysis as merely another cult, subject to the vagaries of popular taste and not susceptible to measurement by any objective criteria:

> The pansexuality of Freud's formulae seems to have been especially effective because sexual emphases were already outstanding in the orientation of the day, hence a sexual symptom could most easily recommend itself as the *core* of the entire situation, with all else as mere incidental by-products.[8]

This disregards the scientific intention and basis of psychoanalysis, and places it in the same category as, say, the latest theory of social causation or decay. And it ignores the fact that Freud was not very much interested in what either the general populace or the intelligentsia—to say nothing of the medical profession!—thought of him or his findings. What counts in psychoanalysis is not what the world thinks of it but the psychoanalyst's understanding of what happens both in the clinic and in the world.

These considerations provide a perspective in which to place Burke's mention of McDougall's theory that important aspects of motivation for the citizens of a given country are patterned after its political structure. Burke admires this conception because he feels that McDougall, "in rebuilding the 'master personality' along the lines of the nation's political pattern . . . is socializing the patient's new mental structure by anchoring it to an obvious feature of the *group psychosis* [sic]." [9] This presumably affords an added source of strength. There are some important implications here for the role of national character (if there really is such a thing) in motivation and for the behavior of large masses of people under totalitarian dictatorships, but it is not clear whether Burke is prepared to trace them. All that he says in this connection which concerns psychoanalysis is that

> Freud wrote for a people who had, for many centuries, accommodated themselves to imperial decay—perhaps he wrote for something which we might call the "psychosis [sic] of the Strauss waltz." Hence his devices for reorientation would be differently formed [from those of McDougall], to correspond with differences in the local orientation of his group.[10]

This is a somewhat more sophisticated version of the earlier objection to psychoanalysis, which asserted that it need not be taken seriously since it merely reflected the notorious sexual looseness of the Viennese and was obviously not applicable to people who lived in other cities. Burke has added to it the weight of a psychological theory. By this maneuver the wind is taken out of Freud's sails, a shift in emphasis is made from the psychic to the social component in motivation, and several obstacles are removed from the path of the forthcoming synthesis.

In Burke's view, then, a traumatic fear—by which he apparently means what psychoanalysts call a neurosis—can be cured by giving it a label which does not carry the original injurious connotations, that is, by misnaming it. The patient can then abandon his "piety" toward the object or situation which aroused the fear and no longer see it in its harmful context. All of the former dangerous associations are broken by the magical act of misnaming, and an entirely new cluster of harmless ones is implied, or at least made possible. In Burke's words, the feared object has thus been exorcised by "the impious devices of incongruity," and its meaning in the patient's system of motives altered, presumably for the better.

Such conversion can take place either upwards or downwards, depending upon which point is selected as the *essence* [the italics are Burke's] of the entire scale. "One's choice usually flows from other aspects of his orientation, or from the particular purpose which his series is designed to fulfill."[11] What this process leaves unsettled is the issue raised before, namely, the relevance of the attempted solution to something beyond itself, to such aspects of reality as we can know, scientifically or otherwise, or to which we can react morally. Burke does not make this clear in *Permanence and Change* but leaves the impression that he adopts a relativistic position. In his view people react to the realities of words whose relationships to their referents are constantly being redefined. What matters to them is not the intrinsic significance of the thing or the situation but the name which is given to it. Connections with reality which have no verbal component apparently do not count. He seems to be trying to extend into a universal principle of human action the tendency of some people to place a high value on their verbal experiences and the inability of others to distinguish clearly between words and things.

*   *   *

Burke's second major treatment of Freudian psychology, "Freud—and the Analysis of Poetry," continues to suffer from his difficulties with psychoanalytic ideas, difficulties which stem partially from his attacks on all science as reductionist.[12] It is interesting that whereas up to this point in his writing he has made no mention of the clinical basis of psychoanalysis, treating it as though it were a purely abstract and almost completely arbitrary construction, he now grants it scientific standing and proceeds to attack it with the same weapons that he directs against science in general. His first criticism is that the strategy utilized by Freud tends toward an "essentializing mode of interpretation. . . . That is, if one found a complex of, let us say, seven ingredients in a man's motivation, the Freudian tendency would be to take one of these as the essence of the motivation and to consider the other six as sublimated variants." He points out justly that this cannot lead to a tenable position for the good reason that "the simple is precisely what the complex is not." This is followed by the assertion that, for Freud, "the sexual wish, or libido, is the basic category." [13] Anything else, no matter to what it may have reference, is merely a sublimation of this.

Both the major and minor premises of Burke's argument are faulty. Science does not claim to "explain" the complex in terms of the simple. It only examines one simple element at a time in order to learn as much as possible about it before it is replaced in its context where the acquired information can then contribute to the understanding of the whole. Science analyzes in order to synthesize, not to disintegrate, and the essentializing strategy therefore governs not the whole of scientific method but only its preliminary phase. Science can attain fruition only by putting back together the elements which it has studied separately and by giving each its proper place in the whole. This is nothing more or less than the "mode that stresses proportion of ingredients," so strongly advocated by Burke. His argument against science, and therefore against psychoanalysis, thus collapses.

The second weakness in Burke's position is his insistence that psychoanalysis sees the sexual wish as man's sole motivation. Although he uses the term libido, the context makes it clear that he is really talking about genitality; he makes no reference here at all to Freud's much broader conception.[14] But aside from this, Burke commits the fundamental error of omitting the other basic, and complementary, part of Freud's theory, the proposition that all living things tend toward death. He attacks Eros as inadequate but ignores the existence of Thanatos, which completes it.[15] Freud's view of motivation is, of course, based upon the interaction of these two, not simply upon one alone. In attempting to reduce this dualism to a monism Burke is himself using an "essentializing strategy."

This is seen again in his attempt to equate Freud's idea with the oversimplified proposals of others who seek to explain all motivation as stemming from a single source. He lumps in the same sentence "the sexual emphasis of Freud, the all-embracing ego compensation of Adler, or Rank's master-emphasis upon the birth trauma, etc."[16] It is only necessary to recall that Freud objected to these theories—including the one here attributed to him—for the same reason that Burke does.

Another gross misconception of psychoanalysis which Burke sets down as preliminary to his consideration of its role in literary criticism calls for quotation. Since he is convinced that "the sexual wish, or libido, is the basic category," he has no difficulty in demonstrating it to be an example of the essentializing strategy and therefore not comprehensive enough for the present task.

A writer deprived of Freud's clinical experience would be a fool to question the value of his category as a way of analyzing the motives of the class of neurotics Freud encountered . . . and the especially elaborate process of diagnosis involved in Freudian analysis even to this day makes it more available to those suffering from the ills of preoccupation and leisure than to those suffering from the ills of occupation and unemployment (with people tending to be only as mentally sick as they can afford to be). This state of affairs makes it all the more likely that the typical psychoanalytic patient would have primarily sexual motivations behind his difficulties.[17]

Burke is here attempting to replace a psychological by a socioeconomic motivation (and is this not in the essentializing mode?). On the one hand he disclaims clinical experience, but on the other he categorically states (a) that Freud analyzed only patients from the moneyed strata of society and (b) that their positions permitted them to indulge in the luxury of a neurosis. The implication is that, had Freud analyzed people from the working (or hard-working professional?) class, another kind of psychic constitution would have been discovered.[18] But neurosis nevertheless occurs in all classes of society and cannot be understood without reference to its biological basis, although the specific forms which it takes are strongly influenced by socio-economic and other factors. It is hard to conceive of any qualities which "typical psychoanalytic patients" could have in common except those which are part of their common humanity. And ability to pay for treatment has never been an absolute requirement, as many a psychoanalyst, beginning with Freud himself, can attest. Burke attempts to strengthen his position by citing the remark of Henry James that sex is something about which we think a great deal when we are not thinking about something else. This loses some of its plausibility after its first impact has passed and we realize that it can be taken in more ways than one. Following the passage we have just examined, Burke executes an abrupt about-face: "Furthermore [why "furthermore"?], I believe that studies of artistic imagery, outside the strict pale of psychoanalytic emphasis, will bear out Freud's brilliant speculations as to the sexual puns, the *double-entendres,* lurking behind the most unlikely façades." [19] The extent to which the analysis of symbols may be regarded as speculations, however brilliant, varies with one's distance from clinical reality. Burke is here admiring Freud for the wrong reason. He does not seem to grasp the fact that psychic life is affective rather than symbolic. That is to say, that it consists of states of feeling for which sensory impressions, words, etc. serve as vehicles. The important thing psychically is not the symbol—like a poker chip, it can have only the meaning that is assigned to it—but the emotional value with which it is more or less temporarily invested. People who are interested in literature and who have a highly developed relationship to words, when they come to learn about psychoanalysis, commonly and naturally tend to attach great significance to the verbal symbols which are utilized for psychic expression and either minimize or ignore their emotional connotations. Much of this significance, and hence symbolic value in the literary sense, is the product of intricate, conscious thought as well as of reference to tradition, convention or a writer's private system. Such symbols, however multi-leveled their interpretation may be, differ from the symbols discovered by psychoanalytic investigation in that the former are fixed while the latter are interchangeable. This holds true even for the "universal" symbols, like that of wood for femininity or money for child, because what matters psychoanalytically is not that the one is equated with the other in every context but that it is the façade, or perhaps better, the vehicle, for an emotional state. The relevance of the feeling which the word represents to the referent of the word (in the semanticist's sense) varies, of course, with the psychic situation.

Burke concludes his preliminary "placing" of psychoanalysis with a mysterious allusion to an event which, despite the assurance with which he states it, never took place. The critic, he suggests, cannot rely wholly upon symbolism for his understanding of literature. Another approach is necessary.

The important matter for our purposes is to suggest that the
examination of a poetic work's internal organization would
bring us nearer to a variant of the typically Freudian free-
association method than to the purely symbolic method toward
which he subsequently gravitated.

Freud, of course, never abandoned the psychoanalysis of neurotic
patients by free-association, and there is no record that he ever
contemplated doing so. On the contrary, he always regarded the
analysis of the dream by this method as the "royal road to the
unconscious." He never adopted a symbolism in which meanings
were fixed and completely predictable—since they necessarily
alter in significance according to variations in the context—nor
did he "gravitate" toward one. If Burke has any authority for
saying so, he does not cite it. He ignores Freud's objections
to those who, like Stekel, did adopt a dream-book technique
in which each symbol had a fixed interpretation. On the other
hand, Burke's suggestion to literary critics that they use a
"variant" of the free-association method in studying structural
aspects of poetry seems to have some possibilities. His statement
is certainly in accord with Freudian ideas:

> One obviously cannot invite an author, especially a dead
> author, to oblige him by telling what the author thinks of
> when the critic isolates some detail or other for improvisation.
> But what he can do is to note the context of imagery and ideas
> in which an image takes its place. He can also note, by such
> analysis, the kinds of evaluations surrounding the image of a
> crossing; for instance, is it an escape from or a return to an
> evil or a good, etc.? Until finally, by noting the ways in which
> this crossing behaves, what subsidiary imagery accompanies it,
> what kind of event grows out of it, what altered rhythmic
> and tonal effects characterize it, etc., one grasps its significance
> as motivation. The motive of the work is equated with the
> structure of interrelationships within the work itself.[20]

This is the kind of literary analysis which, notably in the work
of Rosamond Tuve, William Empson and Caroline Spurgeon,
has become a familiar part of the contemporary critical scene.
It has its uses, particularly if one remembers, as Burke warns,
that "one can never know what a crossing means, in a specific

book, until he has studied its tie-up with other imagery in that particular book." The method, if carefully applied, can reveal aspects of a literary work which can be seen in no other way short of the author's own free-associations. But even such a turning-up of hitherto concealed relationships falls short of telling us everything that we would like to know about motivations. It ignores the reader who is, after all, concerned with his own part in the process of response to these hidden stimuli. If literature is, among other things, communication, then close analysis of the medium in isolation from the sender and the receiver of the message does not help us very much. Psychoanalysis would pursue a study of all three in a particular aesthetic relationship, a conception which is larger than the role Burke envisions for it.

* * *

Burke proposes a critical method based upon the "analysis of an act in poetry" as dream, as prayer and as chart. Dream includes the "unconscious or subconscious [sic] factors in a poem," prayer "the communicative functions of a poem, which leads us into the many considerations of form," and chart "the realistic sizing-up of situations that is sometimes explicit, sometimes implicit, in poetic strategies." [21] He contends that dream has been slighted by the Aristotelians, prayer by the expressionistic critics and chart by the psychoanalysts. His method is designed to correct these inequities and to give each element its due proportion. This would produce a comprehensive analysis of a literary work for which all relevant fields of knowledge had been laid under contribution.

It is in the first of these that Burke finds psychoanalysis most useful. Insight into the poem as dream is obtained from those meanings of our acts which are hidden from us, from their childhood origins, from our growth through various crises, both developmental and adventitious, to maturity. Here, however, he offers a critique of psychoanalysis on terminological grounds. He feels that Freud's formulations, while they are well suited to scientific situations, prevent us from applying to literature our

knowledge about the phenomena which they symbolize. There is
no point, he says, in challenging the clinical reports; what we
need to do is to see them in a special light.

Revise Freud's terms if you will. But nothing is done by simply
trying to refute them. . . . One may complain at this procedure, for instance; Freud characterizes the dream as the fulfillment of a wish; an opponent shows him a dream of frustration, and he answers: "But the dreamer wishes to be frustrated." You may demur at that, pointing out that Freud has
developed a "heads I win, tails you lose" mode of discourse
here. But I maintain that, in doing so, you have contributed
nothing. For there are people whose values are askew, for
whom frustration itself is a kind of grotesque ambition. If
you would, accordingly, propose to chart this field by offering
better terms, by all means do so. But better terms are the only
kind of refutation here that is worth the trouble.[22]

By way of example he cites the "profitable answer to Freud's
treatment of the Oedipus complex" by Malinowski, who studied
its variants in a matriarchal society. Such a recharting of the
field in "more appropriate terms" will, in Burke's view, prevent
the concealment of what goes on in art by Freud's "overemphasis
on the patriarchal pattern." [23] It is necessary, he says, to see only
that portion of a phenomenon, or that cross-section through it,
which has relevance to one's immediate interest.

Nevertheless, it is possible to do a certain amount of direct
translation, or lifting, from one level to another. "I submit that
we should take Freud's key terms, 'condensation' and 'displacement,' as the over-all categories for the analysis of poem as
dream." For the artistic uses of language have something in common with the ordinary uses, and this is made visible to us in
exaggerated form by the neuroses, so much, in fact, that psychoanalytic insights "can be carried over, *mutatis mutandis,* to
the operations of poetry." Precisely in what these necessary
changes consist is the question which Burke ultimately answers
by nothing less than his entire system. He condenses it in this
way: "In so far as art contains a surrealist ingredient (and all
art contains some of this ingredient), psychoanalytic coordinates
are required to explain the logic of its structure." [24] The study

of imagery, essential to the understanding of the poem as dream, is best approached with the help of the concepts of condensation and displacement. The language of art, in so far as it mirrors psychic processes, can be usefully considered by the technical terminology applied to the latter. The poem as prayer is Burke's view of poetic organization as it embodies and manifests the poet's desires and his transmission of them to an audience. Burke makes an easy transition from the religious orientation ("prayer is also an act of communion") to the secular. This brings us back to the familiar problems of expression and communication in art, with emphasis on the latter.

Considering the poem from this point of view, we begin with the incantatory elements in art, the ways of leading in or leading on the hypothetical audience X to which the poem as a medium, is addressed. . . . We move here into the sphere of rhetoric (reader-writer relationships), an aspect of art that Freud explicitly impinges upon only to a degree in his analysis of wit.[25]

But we have already seen that psychoanalysis has much more to say about matters of rhetoric, form, style, meter, rhythm and the like than appears even in the fruitful pages of *Wit and Its Relation to the Unconscious*. In the writings of Freud and other psychoanalysts on clinical and theoretical matters, whether or not art is mentioned directly, there are many ideas which are provocative and suggestive for the study of literature. It is probable that Burke has read some of these, but if so, he gives no evidence that he has seen any of their implications for his critical theories. This raises the question whether the poem as prayer is not more intimately related to psychoanalytic conceptions than Burke thinks it is.

The "incantatory elements" are by no means as exempt from psychoanalytic examination as Burke would wish them to be. However, in evaluating his system we must first of all respect his intentions as a critic. Given his quasi-religious orientation, the poem may indeed be considered a secular "prayer." Its reaching out to the members of the audience and its attempt to generate in them responses analogous to those which motivated the author have their being on an ideological level to which science need not aspire. But Burke himself has provided it with an entering wedge by adopting condensation and displacement, and it is questionable whether, having gone this far, he now has either the power or the right to call a halt. As he himself insists, much depends on vocabulary. How far can he be "religious" and still utilize scientific terminology?

The poem as chart is the product of the poet's "explicitly discussing his situation." When this element is uppermost Burke wishes us to take the poet's statement at face value. Since the message is given to us on the surface, he argues, it would not be proper to look below it for hidden meanings because this would be unfair to the poet, who is here revealing rather than unconsciously concealing or consciously suggesting, and besides it would actually distort the plain sense of his words. A whole poem may be predominantly chart with only slight traces of dream and prayer. Or the three may occur in some other proportions. Burke's point is that psychoanalysis has least to say about chart in any context. He has constructed a graded sequence in which the usefulness of psychoanalysis to him is greatest in dream, less in prayer and negligible in chart.

As "the primary category, for the explicit purposes of literary criticism . . . [he prefers] that of communication rather than that of wish." This relegates psychoanalysis to a minor role in his system, but he goes even further: "Wishes themselves, in fact, become from this point of view analyzable as purposes that get their shape from the poet's perspective in general (while this perspective is in turn shaped by the collective medium of communication)." Thus he is having his cake and eating it too, for he forbids psychoanalysis to examine the wishful aspects of communication on the ground that it would then claim these as the most significant ones, while at the same time he advocates the examination of wish only from the communicative point of view because he regards this as really the most significant one. What is sauce for the goose is evidently not sauce for the gander. To bolster his position he falls back on his socio-economic convictions: "The choice of communication also has the advantage from the sociological [sic] point of view, that it resists the Freudian tendency to overplay the psychological factor." The reason that he finds psychoanalysis of limited usefulness in literary criticism is that, according to his system,

> we should require more emphasis than the Freudian structure gives, (1) to the proportional strategy as against the essentializing one, (2) to matriarchal symbolizations as against the Freudian patriarchal bias, (3) to poem as prayer and chart, as against simply the poem as dream.[26]

We have already examined the misconceptions upon which this summary is based.

*   *   *

In his later books Burke has built upon the foundation of the earlier ones.[27] The method he devised is brought to a higher degree of development, but the basic principles remain the same. Of that method it would be proper in a comprehensive study to ask several questions. Since it partakes of the nature of philosophy, how valid are its assumptions and its applications of logic? Within its entire framework, so far as it has been presented to us, is the place assigned to psychoanalysis consonant with its character? How much does Burke actually know about this character? How much of what he knows does he use? How much does he omit? Why?

It is not my purpose to conduct a full examination of Burke as a critic but merely to describe and evaluate his use of psychoanalytic ideas in his criticism. Consequently, complete answers to these questions cannot be supplied here. One of the basic problems which they pose, however, is relevant to this study. He is setting out to produce a synthesis of disciplines some of which are at such odds with others as to be mutually contradictory. Can Freudian and Marxian ideas, for instance, be integrated into a meaningful whole without destroying what is essential for one, or both? It seems to me that, for these two, peaceful coexistence is impossible; the only integration which could conceivably be managed is the integration of the lamb with the wolf. The same question can be asked about all the other elements in his projected synthesis. How can he combine the several psychologies, sociologies, philosophies and theologies and still retain the essence of each?

If I understand his intention correctly, it is to find among these disparate entities some point, or area, at which they can be seen to intersect. He seems to ignore the fact that some do not intersect at all, but even for those that do, has he the right to assume that the coincidence occurs precisely at the point where the central significance of each happens to be the strongest? And if this meeting place is off the ideological center, is there not the danger that what is most important in the discipline being so manipulated will be distorted or forgotten? What price synthesis?

It is possible to argue for the consistency of Burke's system, but not at the same time to claim that it embodies the essential values of all its components. In the case of psychoanalysis it seems that such consistency as it possesses has been ignored by Burke. He has fragmented it and tenderly picked a few surviving morsels out of the rubble. But he has not kept even these intact. They have been reshaped and forced into a new context where there is serious doubt that they can perform any useful function having a significant relation to their former state. It is as though a golden statue had been melted down and cast into blocks which were then used to build a wall. In this way they might well acquire a new, architectural value—but in the meantime what would have become of the statue?

Throughout his writings Burke seems to have effected a neat "conversion downwards" of phenomena into terms. His system is, it seems to me, essentially a verbal one which treats words at what is often a great distance from the reality of things and people. It would be interesting (though not within the province of this chapter) to study Burke semantically and to examine, among other things, the fluctuations in verbal level which he employs. His theory of poetic performance leads through the ascending order: poetry, act, motive, power, reality. This scale might well be applied to his critical system. Were this to be done, I have the impression that we would find it to be as much a poetic as a critical performance. If this is indeed the case—and I think there is strong evidence for this quality of mind in Burke—then scientific and logical objections are beside the point, and the proper approach to his work is the kind that a literary critic takes toward a poem. But he has published it as serious literary criticism relying in part on psychoanalytic ideas and has thereby left himself open to censure for his lapses in handling those ideas. A clinically based scientific discipline cannot be dealt with as though its essence were verbal, despite the metaphoric quality of some psychoanalytic terminology. Psychoanalysis cannot exist without words, but this does not mean that words are the only things in it that matter. Burke has been guilty of taking the part for the whole, and this has thrown his entire critical view out of focus.

X

Lionel Trilling's Creative Extension of Freudian Concepts

LIONEL TRILLING is one of the few critics of any standing to have actually written at some length on the relationship between psychoanalysis and literature. Aside from the incidental use which he makes of psychoanalytic ideas in the regular course of his criticism, he has several times directed his attention specifically to evaluations of what this relationship has been in the past and may be in the future. In particular, there are three essays which may well serve as milestones in his consideration of the subject.[1] Each constitutes a clear statement of a position—even when the position is somewhat ambivalent—and, taken in chronological order, they show a steady progress toward mastery of the scientific ideas themselves and their integration into criticism.

Trilling begins from strength. Even in the earliest of the essays it is evident that he has more knowledge about psychoanalysis than most other critics have so far demonstrated. His careful formulation of its concepts in non-technical language shows that he understands their boundaries as well as what they contain; his conclusions are conservative and judicially stated; his suggestions for new uses of these ideas in criticism are brilliant. And yet in this same essay his manner leaves the impression of a mind not wholly made up, of matter not wholly assimilated, of positive assertions weakened by reservations which are stated just as positively—in short, of a reluctance to follow to its logical conclusion his announced acceptance of Freud's ideas. This striking series of advances toward and retreats from psychoanalysis diminishes in the later essays—although it does not disappear—and they show a surer grasp of the ideas, less disposition to quarrel with them, and a smoother handling of the whole subject.

In the first essay, "Freud and Literature," the ambivalence is most noticeable. The opening sentence asserts that

> the Freudian psychology is the only systematic account of the human mind which, in point of subtlety and complexity, of interest and tragic power, deserves to stand beside the chaotic mass of psychological insights which literature has accumulated through the centuries.[2]

This seems unequivocal enough, and yet it is followed immediately by an attempt to show that "psychoanalysis is one of the culminations of the Romanticist literature of the nineteenth century" on the ground that "this literature, despite its avowals, was itself scientific in at least the sense of being passionately devoted to a research into the self." [3] It is at this point that he first becomes entangled in the difficulty which affects the remainder of the essay and raises some fundamental questions about the ways in which critics ought to use psychoanalytic ideas. As Trilling himself remarks at the very outset, these belong to a different order of thought from literary ideas. This awareness, however, does not prevent him from using them at times as though they belonged to the same order, a practice which weakens much of his otherwise valuable commentary.

Although he devotes a good deal of space to tracing the "connection between Freud and this Romanticist tradition," it turns out to be a tenuous one indeed. What actually emerges from this part of the discussion is a historical summary—inadequate by Trilling's own admission—of tendencies in certain European writers toward self-examination by introspection, an outstanding feature of the Romantic period but not by any means confined to it. We know that Freud quoted at least two Romantic writers, Diderot and Schiller, and that he was familiar with others. Trilling seems satisfied that this is enough to establish the validity of his proposition, and his discussion thereupon turns to the influence of Freud on literature and criticism, another topic altogether. Perhaps it is significant that the latter occupies more space than the former.

What has actually been demonstrated, of course, is only a temporal association, but it has been treated as though it were a causal relationship. There is nothing to show that it was primarily the literary temper of the time which caused Freud to leave physiology and turn to psychology, even though it is true that he was profoundly influenced by Goethe's famous essay on nature and equally true that he had not only the literary background which the educated person of his day might be expected to have but also a special fondness for literature apart from his scientific interest in it.[4] Also, it should not be forgotten that he was interested in history, archeology, painting and sculpture. All of these felt the influence of the times and might, with the same justice, be regarded as movements, "one of the culminations of which" was psychoanalysis. This may be an instance of a careless use of words. However, it seems unwarranted to go beyond the most conservative conclusions which might be drawn from the facts: that psychoanalysis was one of the culminations of nineteenth-century science, not literature; that this science, like other cultural phenomena of the time, was influenced by various tendencies growing out of the upheaval in Western thought represented in politics by the American and French Revolutions and in literature by the Romantic Movement; and that each developed according to its essential nature with such modifications as prevailing cultural forces imposed upon it. Trilling's habit of thinking in the language of literary criticism and his commitment to the critic's point of view has here apparently caused him to look upon literature as the most significant cultural development of the nineteenth century, if not to place it at the very center of nineteenth-century thought. The claims of science, of religion, of political and social thought cannot be so easily dismissed. But what is in question here is the quality of the relationship between psychoanalysis and literature.

Although some Romantic writers did manage now and then to contribute isolated fragments to the "chaotic mass of insights," it is certainly going too far to call their kind of looking inside the self scientific. And it seems utterly impossible to say, as Trilling does, that psychoanalysis grew out of this literature and was merely a by-product of a literary movement. The fact is that the relation of Freud's thought to the intellectual and cultural currents of his time has been only superficially investigated and that no comprehensive view of it exists as yet. We simply do not know to what extent the genesis of psychoanalysis was facilitated and its development influenced by cultural factors; we do not know how much Freud owed to specific artistic, intellectual and scientific events, how much to general tendencies which were in the air and how much to the unaided achievement of his genius. The best, therefore, that can be said so far for Trilling's suggestion is, "possible but not proven."

The reason for dwelling on this seemingly minor, or even tangential, point is that throughout the essay a similar confusion between scientific and literary ideas prevails. It appears to result from a too-exclusive preoccupation with a literary or critical viewpoint which inevitably causes some distortion of terms and concepts taken bodily from a psychoanalytic context. It is necessary to be aware of this confusion because of the danger which it might hold for Trilling's subsequent argument.

He next takes up Freud's attitude toward art.[5] He recognizes the important fact that it emerges from psychoanalysis comprehended as a whole and not simply from those few writings in which Freud discussed specific artistic problems. Apparently well informed on the development of psychoanalysis, Trilling knows that clinical advances brought about the revision of certain early hypotheses which could not account for later discoveries. Even by 1940 his acquaintance with the technical, "non-literary" portions of Freud's writings was considerable and provided him with a large quantity of indispensable background information. However, his treatment of the material leaves some question as to the extent of his understanding, and consequently casts some doubt upon the validity of the adverse criticisms which he makes about Freud's views on art. Some of the criticisms are sound, particularly that of the presumed philosophical ground upon which psychoanalysis—along with other scientific disciplines—rests. He praises Freud's rationalistic positivism for the clear goal which it sets as the aim of psychotherapy, i.e., suitable adjustment to reality. "But upon the rationalism must also be placed the blame for the often naive scientific principles which characterize his early thought— they are later much modified—and which consist largely of claiming for his theories a perfect correspondence with an external reality." [6]

They are later much modified. It is curious that the argument which follows proceeds to ignore this fact and confines itself to the inadequacies of Freud's earlier writings. There is some justice in Trilling's strictures on any theory of art based solely on the pioneering and tentative formulations of psychoanalysis. It is an interesting and provoking suggestion, for instance, that Freud was impelled by his therapeutic intention to view art at times as an illusion—Trilling insists that this necessarily carries a pejorative connotation—or even a "narcotic." However, it is well known that Freud did not think of art only in those terms even in the early days, nor was the therapeutic direction the only one taken by psychoanalysis.[7] Freud considered the greatest potential benefit of his science to be not merely the curing of individuals suffering from neuroses, important though this is, but the promise that it could lead to a better understanding, and perhaps control, of larger human affairs. The effect of this upon the great social institutions such as war, religion and politics might be their modification so as to bring them into better accord with basic human needs. Not merely the interior life of the individual but the reconstitution of society was Freud's ultimate concern. This is the lesson of the studies in group psychology which occupied Freud increasingly in his later years. It is stated clearly in a number of the "non-literary" writings which Trilling slights here.

His essay therefore leaves the impression that Freud looked down on the artist as a man who could not meet the ordinary demands of the world and who consequently retreated into the easier substitute gratifications of art. In support of this contention, which embodies a portion of the truth, Trilling quotes

Freud's own words.⁸ But this quotation, separated from its context, seems to imply something which the whole passage does not. He is constrained to qualify his remarks soon afterward—he admits, as we have already seen, that the ideas "are later much modified"—when he makes the statement that Freud speaks "of artists, especially of writers . . . with admiration and even a kind of awe"; and particularly when he concedes that "what may be called the essentially Freudian view assumes that the mind, for good as well as bad, helps create its reality by selection and evaluation." Each time, however, he seems to forget what he has just said, and goes on as though the argument contains no inconsistency. He concludes with the remark that "so far I have done little more than try to show that Freud's very conception of art is inadequate." ⁹ I do not think Trilling has been successful in this.

One of the difficulties he has encountered lies in the translation of Freud's ideas into the language of criticism. Sometimes this difficulty is avoided by not translating them at all, an omission which has its own dangers. Take, for example, the fact that, for therapeutic purposes, the psychoanalyst regards reality and illusion as opposites. The patient suffers because he acts as though his illusion were outer reality. He thus is able to put off facing his problems, but this bit of self-deception does nothing to solve them. The goal of therapy then becomes the re-educating of the patient so that he can break through the distortion, distinguish the false from the true, and behave in appropriate ways toward both. It follows, therefore, that when art is used for this kind of evasion, the psychoanalyst must regard it with disfavor *in the therapeutic context,* for it has then been perverted from its proper function and made into a defense against reality. Like all such defenses, it needs to be scrutinized and analyzed solely for its role in the psychic equilibrium; this is psychoanalytic common sense. But to assert that this therapeutically necessary objection to the neurotic misuse of art means that Freud personally considers art only an illusion, and therefore less creditable than other kinds of activity, is unwarranted.

We have Freud's own words on this subject in a scientific context. Trilling has transferred them intact into another con-

text altogether and attempted to prove that the adverse therapeutic evaluation meant the same as a pejorative aesthetic
judgment. Trilling writes, "Freud speaks of art with what we
must indeed call contempt." [10] But must we? No evidence is
cited here, nor have I found any in Freud's psychological writings, that the psychoanalytic attitude toward substitute gratification or any other aspect of neurotic behavior is anything
but clinical. He had opinions about art, but he did not let
these interfere with his work, nor—to return to the point—
did his work cause him to de-value art and artists. As psychoanalysis advanced and as his knowledge of human nature increased, his opinions on a variety of subjects were affected by
his discoveries, but in the early days with which Trilling largely
deals the connections were less well established.

The attempt "to show that Freud's very conception of art is
inadequate," therefore fails because Trilling attributes to psychoanalysis and to its founder a view of reality which they do not
hold. Freud did not imagine that the neurotic aspects of art
accounted for all of it, nor did he regard the writer as simply
a neurotic. On the contrary, as has already been shown by
Ernest Jones, he was very much awake to artistic values. Furthermore, in spite of his use of the word, he did not reduce art to
the status of a "narcotic," although he recognized that certain
individuals may at times use it as one. Trilling seems to over-
look the fact that when such a distortion occurs it is the patient's
idea, not Freud's.

An important part of Trilling's argument in this essay rests
upon his repudiation of the psychoanalytic interpretation of
Hamlet as suggested by Freud and carried out by Jones. He
praises Jones's scholarship and "really masterly ingenuity," and
states the purposes of the study to be the "clearing up of the
mystery of Hamlet's character [and] also the discovery of 'the
clue to much of the deeper workings of Shakespeare's mind.' "
He cites in this connection also Freud's partial analysis of
King Lear. The Oedipal pattern in *Hamlet* and the refusal of
Lear to "make friends with the necessity of dying" contribute
to the tragic effect of both plays. "There is something both
beautiful and suggestive in this, but it is not *the* meaning of

King Lear any more than the Oedipus motive is *the* meaning of
Hamlet." [11] Now this is a curious objection considering that
neither Freud nor Jones ever said that all other interpretations
of literature ought to be replaced by psychoanalytic ones. Nor
did they even imply that the psychoanalytic interpretation of a
given work was somehow more valid than any other. A careful
re-reading of both Freud's original remarks on *Hamlet* and
Jones's book did not enable me to find a single instance of this
alleged oversimplification. In *Hamlet and Oedipus* the aim of Jones, following Freud,
is not what Trilling imagines it to be at all. This is Jones's
own statement:

> In the present excursus . . . the problem to be discussed,
> namely, the meaning of Hamlet's conflicts and suffering, has
> been widely recognized by literary critics to be a pathological
> one; the play is mainly concerned with a hero's unavailing
> fight against what can only be called a disordered mind.
> Hence it is surely appropriate for a medical psychologist to
> offer a contribution based on his special knowlege of the
> deeper layers of the mind where such disorders arise.[12]

There is no mention of any wish to deal with other problems
customarily regarded as being within the province of literary
criticism. To interpret this omission as the equivalent of an
assertion that these other problems are not relevant to the play
is clearly going too far. But Jones evidently suspects that he will
be misunderstood, for he is at pains to state a second time the
framework within which he operates:

> The particular problem of Hamlet, with which this essay is
> concerned, is intimately related to some of the most frequently
> recurring problems that are presented in the course of psycho-
> analytic work, and it has thus seemed possible to secure a fresh
> point of view from which an answer might be proffered to
> questions that have baffled attempts made along less technical
> lines.[13]

This kind of apparently groundless interpretation occurs again
in Trilling's contention that Freud and Jones "do not have an
adequate conception of what an artistic meaning is." Whether
or not this is so—and the point is by no means proven—it is not

relevant to the thesis of Trilling's essay. For he goes on to discuss the effect of *Hamlet* on its audiences, insisting that Freud claims this to be the same at all times and in all places. He says that Freud speaks "as if, historically, *Hamlet's* effect had been single and brought about solely by the 'magical' power of the Oedipus motive to which, unconsciously, we so violently respond." Trilling easily refutes this view by pointing out that "there was, we know, a period when *Hamlet* was relatively in eclipse, and it has always been scandalously true of the French, a people not without filial feeling, that they have been somewhat indifferent to the 'magical appeal' of *Hamlet*." [14] This would seem to settle the matter, but unfortunately for Trilling's argument, it is neither what Freud says nor, in my opinion, what he means. What he says is:

> Another of the great poetic tragedies, Shakespeare's *Hamlet,* is rooted in the same soil as *Oedipus Rex*. But the whole difference in the psychic life of the two widely separated periods of civilization, and the progress, during the course of time, of repression in the emotional life of humanity, is manifested in the differing treatment of the same material. In *Oedipus Rex* the basic wish-phantasy of the child is brought to light and realized as it is in dreams; in *Hamlet* it remains repressed, and we learn of its existence—as we discover the relevant facts in a neurosis—only through the inhibitory effects which proceed from it. [15]

It is perfectly clear that Freud has here allowed for differences between cultures flourishing at different times. It also seems reasonable to me to interpret his remark about the progress of repression as applying to contemporary cultures in which that progress occurs at different rates of speed. I cannot believe that Freud was so naive as to imagine that all European nations had developed exactly the same methods in their artistic handling of the great psychic themes.

As for the notion that psychoanalysts see only the Oedipal situation in *Hamlet,* Trilling seems to have forgotten the remark of Freud that

> just as all neurotic symptoms, like dreams themselves, are capable of hyper-interpretation, and even require such hyper-interpretation before they become perfectly intelligible, so

every genuine poetical creation must have proceeded from more than one motive, more than one impulse in the mind of the poet, and must admit of more than one interpretation.[16] Furthermore, this is not merely a passing thought; it is a fundamental tenet of psychoanalysis and rooted in its very conception of the mind. It means that psychoanalysis is not satisfied simply to trace a psychic act to its origin. This would be to fall into the genetic fallacy in which source is equated with significance. What has happened to the impulse or wish in its meeting with the forces of the environment is equally important, and this brings us into the field of ego psychology, including conscious acts of the mind. The necessity for taking this development into account was obvious from the very beginning of Freud's work with neurotic patients, as is shown in his earliest writings. Its extension to artistic problems is an inevitable step, and this is accomplished in his first major book, *The Interpretation of Dreams*, as these quotations attest. Trilling, unfortunately, pays little attention to this important developmental sequence in the history of psychoanalysis.

Despite these weaknesses, the essay shows a superior understanding of larger psychoanalytic issues in at least three areas. Freud's apparently unquestioning reliance upon a rationalistic positivism may indeed be a vulnerable philosophical position, as Trilling suggests. Whether this invalidates it as a frame of reference within which psychoanalysis can operate effectively and legitimately is another matter and one that he touches upon only briefly in a single sentence.[17] It need not be pursued here. Of more immediate interest is his understanding that Freud studied irrational behavior without endorsing it, a fact that would hardly be worth mentioning except that some, like the surrealists, apparently are under the impression that the study by itself constitutes a recommendation for unrestricted use of the dark side of the mind in the production of art. Trilling knows that there is more to writing literature than transcribing verbatim one's preconscious ideas. He also knows the role of illusion in neurotic collisions with reality, although, as we have seen, he has some trouble in applying this technical information to the consideration of artistic problems.

In dealing with Jones he is guilty of what appears to be a lapse in logic. He objects, with some amusement and justice, to Freud's acceptance of the theory that the Earl of Oxford wrote Shakespeare's plays. Then he uses his refutation in an attempt to undermine the position of Jones, who believes that Shakespeare wrote them. Trilling appears unaware throughout that Jones is not guilty of this particular charge.

He is sounder when he objects to some of Dr. Jones's literary judgments, particularly the overvaluation of *Hamlet* as the epitome of Shakespeare's thought. However, this is not, as Trilling himself admits, solely Jones's idea; it is supported by the opinions of others in a well-documented chapter.[18] Trilling is soundest of all when he reminds us that *"Hamlet* is not merely the product of Shakespeare's thought, it is the very instrument of his thought, and if meaning is intention, Shakespeare did not intend the Oedipus motive or anything less than *Hamlet."* [19] I am not aware that Jones disagrees with this conception or that he insists upon a purely unconscious motivation for the play. Contrary to Trilling's expressed opinion, this would be most un-psychoanalytic.

The great strength of Trilling's essay is its recognition of the contributions which psychoanalysis has made and can make to the study of literature and even to its production. Most important of all, I think, is the demonstration that the regular processes of mental functioning are poetic in nature. As Trilling puts it:

> Of all mental systems, the Freudian psychology is the one which makes poetry indigenous to the very constitution of the mind. Indeed, the mind, as Freud sees it, is in the greater part of its tendency exactly a poetry-making organ. This puts the case too strongly, no doubt, for it seems to make the working of the unconscious mind equivalent to poetry itself, forgetting that between the unconscious mind and the finished poem there supervene the social intention and the formal control of the conscious mind. Yet the statement has at least the virtue of counterbalancing the belief . . . that the very opposite is true, and that poetry is a kind of beneficent aberration of the mind's right course.[20]

It is obvious that Trilling has a grasp of what psychoanalysis tells us about the mind and its functioning that is rarely met with outside professional psychoanalytic círcles. One of the striking aspects of mental life is its tendency, almost its compulsion, to compare all things that it knows, consciously or unconsciously. Sometimes these comparisons are based on shallow or trivial similarities, even irrelevant ones, such as puns on words that only sound alike but have no common areas of meaning. This power of association, nevertheless, when it is exercised on a more meaningful level, is what makes metaphor and multiple meanings of a symbol possible in dreams, symptoms and works of art. It is to Trilling's credit that he sees this.

He also recognizes the potential value for literature of Freud's concepts of the repetition-compulsion and the death-instinct. The former, Trilling remarks, "stands beside Aristotle's notion of the catharsis, in part to supplement, in part to modify it." The repetition-compulsion is the discovery, reported in *Beyond The Pleasure-Principle,* that the pleasure motive was not sufficient to explain all dreams, as Freud had at first thought it was. Certain dreams which caused anxiety were found to occur repeatedly in some neurotics. It was also observed that certain children's games tended to repeat situations which were in themselves emotionally painful. Freud concluded that these and similar activities had the purpose of reconstituting the painful situation so that the individual might have another, and yet another, chance to master it. The repetition was necessary because of the strength of the original motivation, only a little of which could be overcome at a time. This produced a "higher" form of pleasure than simple wish-fulfillment in the form of feelings associated with control over one's anxieties, one's self and one's environment.

Freud's conception of tragedy was, as Trilling points out, more or less analogous to the Aristotelian idea "which emphasizes a qualified hedonism through suffering." This, however, is not altogether adequate since sometimes the catharsis may be "the result of glossing over terror with beautiful language rather than an evacuation of it. And sometimes the terror even bursts through the language to stand stark and isolated from the play, as does Oedipus' sightless and bleeding face." Freud did not carry his idea beyond this, but Trilling suggests that the effort of mastering difficult situations by repetition has further meaning for our experiencing of tragedy. He calls it the mithridatic function and describes it as the use of tragedy "as the homeopathic administration of pain to inure ourselves to the greater pain which life will force upon us." [21] This is a fine example of the creative use of psychoanalytic concepts in criticism which extends our understanding in appropriate directions through both psychological and literary experience. If mastery through repetition is a commonplace in psychic life, then it is certainly possible that it constitutes one of the values of tragedy. Aristotle's theory has thereby been broadened and deepened, and Freud's idea has at the same time been given a logical extension and application. Trilling's contribution here may be small, but it is significant.

Trilling also sees in Freud's idea of the death-instinct— whether or not it can be accepted on psychoanalytic grounds alone—"its grandeur, its ultimate tragic courage in acquiescence to fate." The conception that all living things tend toward death is, of course, repugnant; witness the passionate clinging to ideas of immortality in all ages and places. In Freud's ability to conceive it Trilling finds both an intellectual honesty and a freedom from many of the limitations which hamper others who attempt an examination of the human condition. These qualities are characteristic of Freud's thought in general, and they contribute to his greatness as a critic of human nature. The whole weight of the Freudian conception is against a simple optimism on the one hand and an overwhelming pessimism on the other. It takes the position that man is worthy of dignity, although, to be sure, not wholly on his present grounds for thinking himself so worthy. To cite one common instance, man's feeling of shame about his sexuality is an unnecessary inversion of its potential value to him. Properly understood and accepted, it can become the basis for a suitable emphasis upon the power of love as a creative force in human affairs far transcending the relation between two individuals. Freud's strength is not merely that he knows the power of love but that he also recognizes the potency of hate. He is aware that what makes us human is neither one by itself but rather the conflict between them within ourselves. Trilling understands that man is seen by Freud as "an inextricable tangle of culture and biology," and not simply as a creature at the mercy of his unconscious drives, a view widely held among the ill-educated. He also understands the more subtle point that, although the works of love are ultimately overcome by death, Freud insists that man's dignity and worth stem from his magnificent battle against the inevitable: "His best qualities are the result of a struggle whose outcome is tragic." Finally, Trilling knows that Freud regards man as "a creature of love," that what is most characteristic of him is the affirmation of life and creativity in the face of insurmountable odds.

This grasp of a view which is not sufficiently understood by others is a great asset to Trilling. With such a comprehension of the larger meanings of Freud's thought he is able to see that its promise for literature is vast, perhaps vaster than we know.

> [Freud's] desire for man is only that he should be human, and to this end his science is devoted. No view of life to which the artist responds can insure the quality of his work, but the poetic qualities of Freud's own principles, which are so clearly in the line of the classic tragic realism, suggest that this is a view which does not narrow and simplify the human world for the artist but on the contrary opens and complicates it.[22]

Trilling's acceptance of Freud is not, as we have seen, without reservations. Along with greater understanding than most, and with the ability to make creative applications of psychoanalytic conceptions to literature that is unique among critics in its high quality and originality, there is a hesitation, a gingerly handling and a series of hedgings or denials. Sometimes these have strong external reinforcements, like the philosophical questioning of Freud's rational positivism, but most of them appear to have little visible means of support. What this signifies I cannot guess, but it must be recorded because it is so obvious. I recall my first reading of "Freud and Literature" and the impression it left that Trilling had somehow said more against Freud than for him. But this was later balanced by Trilling's stimulating suggestions concerning the critical uses of the concepts of the death-instinct and the repetition-compulsion. Their potential value and the possibilities which they open for further extensions of psychoanalysis into literary study more than make up for the ambivalence.

*   *   *

In "Art and Neurosis" [23] there is a surer grasp of specific psychoanalytic concepts as well as of the whole tendency of psychoanalysis, and there is far less inconsistency. This is due partly to the theme, which demands close organization and does not lend itself to the rambling treatment that characterized "Freud and Literature." Most of it, however, stems from Trilling's better handling of scientific ideas, which are here brought under control and placed in the service of his critical thought with happy results. The theory that the artist is a poor weakling who is unable to deal with everyday reality as well as solid citizens can and who therefore beats a cowardly retreat into art where he finds an easy substitute for life is demolished here on both scientific and critical grounds. What is more to the point, this is accomplished by criticism using psychoanalysis merely as an auxiliary.

Trilling makes the important observation that the primitive idea of sacrifice for the sake of gain has its derivatives in our culture in the popular beliefs that power may be obtained through suffering and that frustration in one sphere leads to over-fulfillment in another; for example, a blind person will compensate for his loss of sight by developing a keen hearing. This is shown to lie behind the wound-and-bow theory. Edmund Wilson and its other adherents apparently believe the artist to be suffering from an illness of the soul for which he is compensated by the artistic gift, each of these, according to the extreme form of the theory, being a necessary concomitant of the other. As is typical in his criticism, Trilling recognizes the importance of social factors. Here he points out the interesting fact that the theory is socially advantageous both to artists and

to philistines. Many of the former accept it as at least compelling acknowledgement that they have talent and are therefore
entitled to a privileged position, while it enables the latter
simultaneously to listen to the artist and to reject whatever
is repugnant to them in his art.[24]

Having established the social, mythic and pseudo-aesthetic
basis of the theory, Trilling then attacks it from the standpoint
of psychoanalysis. He contends that there is no such thing as
"the psychology of the writer," insisting that writers live the
same psychic lives as the rest of mankind.[25] This view, while not
going as far as Ernst Kris goes into ego psychology, nevertheless
is based on Trilling's sound understanding of the nature of
neurosis and its relation to normality.[26] In the largest sense,
psychoanalysis sees all men as partially involved in neurosis.
This does not mean, as is popularly supposed, that all men are
ill but only that, as a natural consequence of our need to accept
less than full and immediate gratification of our impulses, we
must live by psychic compromises. As we have already seen, the
dividing line between those compromises which are "normal"
and those which are "neurotic" is difficult even for psychoanalysts to define, but Trilling understands this meaning of
"neurotic" and is able to relate it to his estimate of the artist.[27]
With this orientation he shows that

> the current literary conception of neurosis as a *wound* is quite
> misleading. It inevitably suggests passivity, whereas, if we fol-
> low Freud, we must understand neurosis to be an *activity*, an
> activity with a purpose, and a particular kind of activity, a
> *conflict*.[28]

This conflict is the struggle of the social, the human side of our
selves against our animal natures, or as psychoanalysis puts it,
the conflict of the ego with the id. In this sense, to say that we
are all ill is true, but "we are ill in the service of health, or ill
in the service of life, or, at the very least, ill in the service of
life-in-culture." Since this is the normal state of man, it follows
that art is not a product of neurosis according to the popular or
gross usage of the term and that the artist is not necessarily
more maladjusted than the scientist or the salesman. A man may
be neurotic no matter what he does for a living, but it is not his

neurosis which makes him skilled at his job, nor must his private woes necessarily interfere with the quality of his vocational performance. With these considerations Trilling has scientifically refuted the wound-and-bow theory and demonstrated that, given its origins and functions, it provides a comforting, though inaccurate, explanation of a disturbing phenomenon. It is, in short, a rationalization.

In place of it Trilling offers his own solution, and it is one which is in accord with psychoanalytic thinking about the psychic situation of the artist. This sees him as the possessor of a special ability to command his material—his reality—and not as a craven evader of human responsibility. As psychoanalysis turns its attention toward the study of everyday success in life and away from its preoccupation with everyday failure, it is beginning to view the artist as the possessor of extraordinary psychic powers. Insofar as he is an artist he is, psychically speaking, anything but a failure. As Trilling puts it:

> the artist is . . . unique in one respect, in the respect of his relation to his neurosis. He is what he is by virtue of his successful objectification of his neurosis, by his shaping it and making it available to others in a way which has its effect upon their own egos in struggle. His genius, that is, may be defined in terms of his faculties of perception, representation, and realization, and in these terms alone. It can no more be defined in terms of neurosis than can his power of walking and talking, or his sexuality.[29]

Trilling's understanding of psychoanalysis enables him to see the fallacy in the oversimple equating of art with illness. From here he continues the search for the meaning of genius not in the direction of science but in that of society, mythology and literature. The contributions of psychoanalysis may be added to any insights thus gained.

In "The Meaning of a Literary Idea" he sets forth his critical doctrine that the writer should have a creative relationship to the meaningful ideas of his culture. In order properly to be utilized, however, these ideas must not be regarded as mere "pellets of intellection or crystallizations of thought, precise and completed, and defined by their coherence and their procedural recommendations." [30] Literature derives a part of its power from ideas as such because, no matter how abstract or autonomous they may seem, they are always connected with the sources of emotion. The aesthetic experiencing of this power is therefore not dependent upon belief in the validity of the ideas themselves.

> Intellectual assent in literature is not quite the same thing as agreement. We can take our pleasure in literature where we do not agree, responding to the power or grace of a mind without admitting the rightness of its intention or conclusion —we can take our pleasure from an intellect's *cogency*, without making a final judgment on the correctness or acceptability of what it says.[31]

Here Trilling approaches the psychoanalytic view that our response to a writer is based both on our pleasure in his verbal skill and on the re-awakening of fundamental psychic themes by his work. We need not accept Milton's theology in *Paradise Lost* in order to enjoy his poetry. And yet these ideas of man's fate are but a particular way of regarding problems which each of us sees from his own point of view. Consequently, the one awakens echoes of the other and of the accompanying psychic values.

> For in the great issues with which the mind has traditionally been concerned there is, I would submit, something *primitive* which is of the highest value to the literary artist. . . . The ultimate questions of conscious and rational thought about the nature of man and his destiny match easily in the literary mind with the most primitive human relationships. Love, parenthood, incest, patricide: these are what the great ideas suggest to literature.[32]

This facet of Trilling's criticism is grounded firmly upon the same base as the psychoanalytic ideas of Sachs and Kris, i.e., "the elemental *given* of biology." [33] He recognizes that human desires arising from physical sources, surely the most prosaic of origins, infuse even the most spiritual ideas with what is probably the largest component of their literary value. This is not simply the echoing of bodily sensitivities—Trilling's knowledge of psychology is too good for that—it consists in part also of pleasure deriving from conscious intellectual processes themselves. What at first appeared to be the extremes of the scale are now seen to be merely two different ways of responding to human necessity, each intimately involved with the other.

Trilling's collection, *The Opposing Self,* in general demonstrates a surer touch in relating psychoanalytic ideas to criticism than his earlier books. There is more use of ego psychology, although this is not uniform throughout the volume, the high point being the essay on Keats.[34] In it the poet's life, his mind and his art are all illuminated, in part, from a psychoanalytic viewpoint which is kept within the framework of the critic's insight. Trilling is interested not merely in establishing specific connections between biographical events and tendencies in the poetry (i.e., the "genesis of Keats's preoccupation with a felicity of 'dainties', kisses, and coziness") but the larger ways in which family and philosophical influences worked together in the mind of the poet and were expressed in his poetry.

> What I have called Keats's geniality toward himself, his bold acceptance of his primitive appetite and his having kept open a line of communication with it, had its decisive effect upon the nature of his creative intelligence.[35]

Trilling holds that this effect was to strengthen it. He clearly approves Keats's active acquiescence in the direct and open manifestations of life, a view which is wholly compatible with psychoanalysis when properly qualified. As a critic Trilling also points out how this affected the development of the poet's thought:

> He did not . . . suppose that mind was an entity different in kind from and hostile to the sensations and emotions. Rather, mind came into being when the sensations and emotions were checked by external resistance or by conflict with each other, when, to use the language of Freud, the pleasure principle is confronted by the reality principle. Now in Keats the reality principle was strong. . . . And it was strong in proportion to the strength of the pleasure principle.[36]

This is in direct opposition to the popular conception of the artist as a weakling, the condition of whose art is illness. Keats's poetic ideal was health, spiritual and poetic, based solidly upon the *given* not only of biology but also of the human condition.

For we must understand about Keats that he sought strenu-
ously to discover the reason why we should live, and that he
called those things good, or beautiful, or true, which induced
us to live or which conduced to our health. (He had not
walked the hospital wards for nothing.) [37]

Like so many others, Keats sought an awareness of the self
through literature which grew out of reflection. In an admirable
passage Trilling traces Keats's achievement in self-realization
and shows how it leads to the heart of his thought, the confrontation of the problem of evil. His conviction that "there is
something real in the world" to challenge the reality of death
and evil grows from this.[38]

Trilling's interpretation of Keats's thought as presented here
is closely parallel to or in harmony with certain psychoanalytic
ideas. There is, for example, the concept that self-identity is
achieved by cathexis, that is, by the attachment of emotional
values to external objects or events or ideas. If the cathexis is
sufficiently meaningful—if the self has achieved sufficient identity
—then there is correspondingly less need to incorporate more
external values since there are fewer gaps in the personality
(perhaps "image of the self" would be a better phrase) that
clamor to be filled. The sense of one's own reality is then great
enough to be satisfying; one has a pleasing set of connections
with the world that enable one to function normally; internal
fantasies can be measured against external reality. There is no
need to submerge one's self in another's personality, as Hitler's
more rabid followers did, or in a contrived and closed system
of ideas within the limits of which one can remain happily
imprisoned while imagining that one has been released from
bondage, like the adherents of certain perennially popular
ideologies. Keats was never in danger of falling into either of
these traps because he possessed the rare quality of "negative
capability," the strength to refrain from total commitment to
such personalities or such systems, to live without insisting
upon, while still seeking, final answers to the great questions
of life and death.

Lesser men, with their powerful urge for certainty, lack this
restraint. Their inner resources are so meager that they actively

hunger for a relation, however humiliating, to something external which will at least provide the sense that they exist. As a consequence they are frequently satisfied with a referent whose objectivity is extremely limited; it may be an illusion or even a projection of an inner wish upon an empty screen. Trilling praises Keats for his successful attempt to base his self-image on a combination of psychic experience and external reality. This accomplishment, which is also the ideal of psychoanalysis, is so difficult that Trilling rightly regards it as heroic.

In his lecture, *Freud and the Crisis of our Culture,* before the New York Psychoanalytic Society Trilling continues his concern with the relation of literature and psychoanalysis. For this new audience he reiterates his previous assertion that the mind as Freud described it is "in the greater part of its tendency, exactly a poetry-making faculty." The necessary background having been provided, he then proceeds to his theme: the relationship between the conception of the self, which is always more intensely perceived in literature than in the general culture, and the limitations which the latter places upon it. "The first thing that occurs to me to say about literature, as I consider it in the relation in which Freud stands to it, is that literature is dedicated to the conception of the self." [39] This being so, then the ultimate test of the self's sense of reality and identity, a record of which appears in literature, must be the effect upon it of the idea of death.

Trilling here calls upon Freud's hypothesis of the death instinct, Thanatos, and, without commenting on its scientific standing, points out that it is very useful in this connection, provided that it is understood as not pathological but positive. "For literature has always recorded an impulse of the self to find affirmation even in its own extinction, even by its own extinction." [40] Although this may be thought of as referring to a kind of apotheosis or the attainment of Nirvana, Trilling does not wish to accept such a notion. It would not be in accord with the vision of artists who are not so easily satisfied. He reminds us that

> the poets call it death; it has much of the aspect of death; and
> when we take into account the age-old impulse of highly

developed spirits to incorporate the idea of death into the experience of life, even to make death the criterion of life, we are hard put to it to say that the assertion of the death instinct is nothing but a pathology, that it is not the effort of finely tempered minds to affirm the self in an ultimate confrontation of reality.[41]

Death, then, must be a part of life, and the realization of this truth contributes to self-discovery and self-definition. In literature it is manifested in tragedy, in the paradox that the annihilation of the self, as represented in art, teaches us to live.

On this and on the question of the opposition between love and power, another theme shared by Freud and literature, Trilling finds support for his basic argument. Our culture, he says, while wanting to provide the self with the greatest opportunities for growth—it is a "generous" culture—nevertheless is handicapped in this because it does not properly understand the real nature of the self and its proper relation to culture and consequently cannot arrange and maintain the optimal conditions for the attainment of this ideal. "This progressive deterioration of accurate knowledge of the self and of the right relation between the self and the culture constitutes what I am calling a crisis in our culture." It is, of course, a crisis which has been troubling the West for at least two hundred years. The significance of Freud's work is that its biological orientation affords a position from which the culture itself can be judged. As culture succeeds or does not succeed in adequately meeting the biological needs of the organisms which comprise it, it allows or does not allow full realization of the self. The various demands of culture—such as the current one for conformity—frequently cause a discrepancy between the need of the individual to be himself and his need to live in society. Trilling suggests that we are ignoring biology at our peril, that Freud recognized this, and that it is at the heart of psychoanalytic thought:

> In its essence literature is concerned with the self; and the particular concern of the literature of the last two centuries has been with the self in its standing quarrel with culture. We cannot mention the name of any great writer of the modern period whose work has not in some way, and usually in a

passionate and explicit way, insisted on this quarrel, who has not expressed the bitterness of his discontent with civilization, who has not said that the self made greater legitimate demands than any culture could hope to satisfy. This intense conviction of the existence of the self apart from culture is, as culture well knows, its noblest and most generous achievement. At the present moment it must be thought of as a liberating force without which our developing ideal of communtiy is bound to defeat itself.[42]

With the publication of this lecture Trilling has brought psychoanalytic thought further into harmony with his criticism. His concern with the role of culture, of social influences, on literature impels him to make use of psychoanalytic insights as to the nature of culture. His keen awareness of the interaction between a writer's artistic impulse and its environment helps him to avail himself of the findings of ego psychology. No other critic has shown a comparable grasp of the significance of psychoanalysis; no other critic has so well incorporated it into his criticism. It is true that his criticism has gone in a direction that lends itself particularly well to supplementation by psychoanalytic ideas and that this eases his task. But nothing in this should detract from his accomplishment in learning, in understanding and in applying these difficult concepts to a criticism which is altogether his own.

XI

Summary

THE ADVENTURES of psychoanalytic ideas in literary criticism are similar to those of other new and disturbing thoughts in our culture. They arouse enthusiastic acceptance in some quarters and violent opposition in others, but they eventually filter into the general mind, although at the cost of some watering-down of their most unsettling elements. They are enabled to maintain their existence in various states along a spectrum ranging from mere grudging acknowledgement of their presence to an over-eager willingness to substitute them for older modes of thought. It is desirable to trace the manner in which they have made their way in the world, but they must also be understood in the context in which they originally appeared and in relation to the direction in which they set out. Historical study shows us what they have become; technical understanding enables us to see what they might be. Both the actual and the potential uses must be grasped for a full understanding of either.

In the foregoing chapters I have traced the development of psychoanalytic ideas in the works of four men whose contributions have particular relevance for art. While this is not the whole story—a satisfactory history of psychoanalysis has not yet been written—it provides enough information about the subject so that the performance of literary critics who tried to use these ideas can be measured by it. A detailed examination of six representative examples shows that, with some exceptions, our critics did not inform themselves sufficiently about the facts of psychoanalysis. The internal evidence seems to show that most of them, perhaps all, had read at one time or another in the writings of Freud, presumably in English translation. This was unfortunate because the first translation of *The Interpretation of Dreams,* by A. A. Brill, was a poor one, suffering from faulty idiom and outright inaccuracies, a performance which considerably dims his luster as a pioneer in making Freud available to English and American readers. This was the only translation until the definitive one by Strachey appeared in 1953. Besides this, it appears that our critics knew something—whether at first or second hand—about *Wit and Its Relation to the Unconscious* and *The Psychopathology of Everyday Life,* but hardly any of them seemed even to be aware of the existence of the voluminous and growing psychoanalytic literature produced by Freud and his students. Since they did not know how much they did not know, they tended as a natural consequence to overemphasize the significance of those few ideas which they felt sure of, acting at times as though they believed that these contained the whole of psychoanalytic fact and theory or, at any rate, all that had any relevance for their criticism. This was the first source of the distortion which, as we have seen, psychoanalysis underwent at their hands.

The second was intimately related to it. Since the critics regarded psychoanalysis as a closed system which claimed to explain all human motivation, they interpreted those books with which they were acquainted as definitive works rather than as progress reports. Consequently, they did not even look for new clinical discoveries and for the amendments, refinements, revisions and extensions of the theory which these made necessary. Some of them expected too much of psychoanalysis and turned against it when it failed to deliver. The failure, however, lay at their own doorstep, for in their unreasonable demands upon it they had ignored the indispensable "if" that must be used in applying a scientific discipline to any other field. By not distinguishing between the established doctrines of psychoanalysis and its tentative hypotheses, they treated the latter like the former and thereby provided an insecure foundation for the conclusions which they drew from both.

The third major source of distortion was, surprisingly, their inability to grasp the meaning of the psychoanalytic material which they read. Instance after instance occurs of a critic's writing that Freud had said a certain thing when a glance at the text shows that he had taken particular pains to assert precisely the contrary. Certain critics repeatedly combined and confused Freudian concepts and frames of reference with those of other psychologists, like Adler and Jung, who had repudiated the very basis of psychoanalysis and whose ideas were therefore incompatible with it. This is not a matter of doctrinal preference but of straight scientific thinking. From Jung's point of view, for instance, it would be just as bad if his system were to be invaded by Freudian ideas. Matters were not helped very much by attempts at synthesis, either, for the results of these were not very convincing. Occasionally during one of these attempts at reconciliation, or even in the ordinary course of the day's work, ideas were attributed to Freud which were actually outside the scope of psychoanalysis or which were simply unwarranted conclusions from psychoanalytic findings. The difficulties of psychoanalytic theory, though they are real enough, are not sufficient to account for such misreading.

When the psychologists themselves were unable to come to an agreement it was not surprising that the critics could not force one. It may be suggested that the reasons for their failure lie in the nature of the material which is the subject matter of psychoanalysis. Much of its attention is turned on that which is ordinarily thought to be too trivial for serious study or too unpleasant to face. It rakes up and exposes to systematic scrutiny many truths about ourselves which we would rather ignore, explain away harmlessly or keep hidden altogether. So strong is our aversion to such matter that the first impulse of most people is to deny its existence. Freud succeeded in overcoming his own repugnance, and he was well-enough endowed psychically and intellectually to carry out a self-analysis. Others, too, have special ability to deal with their hidden fantasies. The capacity of artists is particularly high in this respect, but, as Trilling points out, the insights which they achieve are "a chaotic mass" of fragments depending upon isolated flashes of internal illumination rather than upon systematic investigation. Rarely, even by artists, is this capacity developed to the point reached by Freud. For nearly all of the rest of us the unconscious mental life is largely *terra incognita*.

It is no wonder then that literary critics reacted to Freud's discoveries as they did. A similar history would no doubt characterize the impact of psychoanalytic ideas on other fields. Intellectual power and professional competence are not always enough in themselves to withstand the strength of the instincts or to enable us to acknowledge something which our entire upbringing has trained us to deny. Then, too, we must remember that most critics do not knowingly use psychoanalysis at all; the ones I have selected represent a minority, although a growing one. They have used it in the face of extraordinary difficulties of a kind which do not attend the utilization of other modes of thought in criticism. These difficulties are largely responsible for the fact that its application to literary problems is so often faulty.

Nevertheless, despite the limitations under which our six critics labored, their misunderstanding of psychoanalysis was by no means total. They comprehended certain portions of it and, at least part of the time, used them properly. In general these tended to be the ideas which were most popular, that is, those which had attained the greatest circulation among educated and interested people. The fact that they seldom ventured beyond the areas of widest appeal does not speak well for their initiative as critics, but this is compensated for somewhat by the reflection that these areas included many major psychoanalytic concepts. Among them were such fundamental matters as the existence of the unconscious part of mental life and the recognition that dreams are a continuation of daytime thinking by other means. Dream symbolism and the hidden meanings of everyday actions proved especially intriguing. So did the ramifications—as far as they were understood—of the Oedipus Complex. In short, certain psychoanalytic ideas which offered the possibility of easy surface acceptance were taken up by some critics and applied to criticism in various ways. Those ideas which aroused greater inner resistances tended to fit poorly into critical contexts. The degree to which they proved useful depended in part on the ability of the critic to accept them emotionally as well as intellectually and thereby to avoid the distortions so frequently imposed from within.

An overview of the practice of Brooks, Krutch and Lewisohn in this respect shows an apparently uncritical acceptance of certain psychoanalytic ideas—not, of course, the same ones by all three men—and a wholesale application of them. The general impression left by a reading of their early use of psychoanalytic ideas is that they feel they have found a method which answers the few critical questions that have not yet been answered and that nothing remains to be done in criticism but to apply Freud's ideas to those obscure corners where they have not yet reached. This is somewhat exaggerated, but not much. Each of these men acted for a time as though he had discovered a magical formula which would solve most of his critical problems for him. This had the effect of placing too heavy a burden on psychoanalysis and leaving Brooks and Krutch, for instance, in the position of being able to repudiate it afterwards because it failed to meet their excessive demands upon it. It is a fair question to ask whether this outcome was not engineered by forces unknown to the critics themselves. By this devious but not at all unusual method the concealed reluctance and the overt assent often achieve simultaneous expression.

*   *   *

Within this general pattern there were numerous differences in detail, all serving, however, to illustrate basic similarities in handling psychoanalytic ideas. Brooks knew a good deal about literature and human nature before he encountered psychoanalysis; it apparently did not teach him much that was new. His acceptance of psychoanalysis, while it lasted, seems to have been based upon its corroboration of ideas which he already held. While he had obviously read some Freud, he was just as obviously not interested in questioning the validity of the new ideas but was satisfied to swallow them whole. He had not kept up with new developments and did not know the psychoanalysis of 1920, the year his book on Mark Twain appeared. His lack of concern with science causes some glaring faults, the worst of which is his ignoring of the need for evidence to support his psychological assertions. Although he often claims psychoanalysis as authority for his statements, he seldom cites its specific application to the point which he wishes to make. His proposed chains of causation in the life of Mark Twain leave too many loopholes. He misuses both the psychoanalytic term and the concept of repression; this is almost a touchstone by which the understanding of psychoanalysis can be judged. He completely misses the essential distinction between the latent and the manifest dream, a gross error which makes it impossible to claim the assistance of psychoanalysis in his "interpretations" of Mark Twain's dreams. When he attacks psychoanalysis in his later years he does so because he feels that it somehow destroys the grandeur and nobility of human values. This complete swing of the pendulum from one untenable position to its untenable opposite leaves psychoanalysis no opportunity to be of service to criticism.

Krutch achieved a much better understanding than this, although his application of psychoanalysis to criticism was still less than adequate. He too was somewhat behind the times scientifically, showing no sign in his book on Poe that he knew about Freud's work on the ego and the new breadth which this gave to depth psychology, but he had evidently read much of the earlier psychoanalytic writing. His account of it was, with certain exceptions, accurate; his application of it was, within certain limits, sound. It was in exceeding these limits that he went astray. Recognizing the presence of psychic forces in artistic production, he attempted to equate art with emotional expression, ignoring the important differences between them and the specific forms which must be given to fantasies before they can acquire aesthetic value. Almost as a corollary to this mistake, he confused dreams with works of art. His failure thoroughly to grasp psychoanalytic dream-theory was one of his few important deficiencies in this respect. In his book he tended to be satisfied, when he had traced a phenomenon to its psychic origins, that he had found an adequate explanation for it. He did not seem to be fully aware of the importance of all the things that happened to it on the long and complicated road from psychic wish to artistic expression. On the technical side this is attributable to his unfamiliarity with psychoanalytic ego psychology which studies the alterations undergone by ideas in their progress through the psyche. Krutch's mistake was to treat his partial information about psychoanalysis as though it were complete and to assume that it explained more than it was actually capable of doing.

Lewisohn's larger view and his enthusiastic praise of Freudian psychology do not help him either, for although he tries, he never succeeds in making psychoanalysis a necessary part of his critical thesis. Like Krutch he is a victim of cultural lag. Despite the relatively late appearance of *Expression In America* (1932), it contains little ego psychology; most of its psychoanalytic ideas come from Freud's earlier writings. Lewisohn must be given credit for his insight into something very like the later concept of the conflict-free ego sphere as it applies to literature, but except for this bit of anticipation his use of psychoanalysis is not only elementary but also largely irrelevant and inaccurate.

He pursues his thesis with a devotion that leads him to seek support for it which psychoanalysis cannot supply, but he is evidently unable to see that it cannot. Insisting on the necessity for art to express the essence, the core reality of life, he concludes that the Puritan inhibition of sensual, particularly of sexual, expression has made literature in America false and therefore worthless. Psychoanalysis would regard Thoreau's un-sexual, un-sensual, transcendental experiences as worth studying because they are his way of meeting or attempting to evade reality; Lewisohn denounces and de-values them because they are not direct confrontations of life. Psychoanalysis is not concerned that a work of art omits any reference to certain human experiences; Lewisohn insists that it is rendered valueless by this absence, and he asserts, without ground, that he has psychoanalytic support for this. He attributes the greatness of *The Scarlet Letter* to its having been written during the happiest period of Hawthorne's marriage; psychoanalysis finds no such easy correlation between biography and aesthetics. In short, Lewisohn assumes too much. He does not distinguish sufficiently between a scientific and a critical idea. His lack of information about ego psychology and his basically unscientific treatment of Freudian ideas doom his well-meant attempt to bridge the gap between psychoanalysis and art.

Edmund Wilson comes closer to doing this but not quite close enough. His theory of the wound and the bow misses the mark when it assumes that artistic ability is necessarily a concomitant of illness and when it therefore ignores the psychic function of art in the normal personality and the fact that some artists are not psychically ill. Although the social value of art is an integral part of his theory—Philoctetes is cured when he puts his unique power at the service of his people—this aspect of it is slighted in Wilson's critical writings. The theory as practiced by its formulator is thus even less complete than in its original state. Wilson has psychoanalytic support for part of his hypothesis, but he goes beyond this and, without saying so explicitly, leaves the impression that psychoanalysis sustains him all the way. But the chief deficiency of the theory from my point of view is that it does not provide any criterion for judging literature as an art. In *The Wound and the Bow* Wilson points out many personal events and influences which manifested themselves in some form in the works of various writers, and he makes a case for a better understanding of their personalities by means of their works. We are enabled to know more about them, perhaps, than we did before, but we are not given many clues as to the meaning of all this for literary value. It is rather surprising that Wilson's orientation toward historical criticism did not lead him to establish a better connection between his knowledge of individual psychology and the sociological, economic and political insights which he utilizes so abundantly. In the context of his critical approach psychoanalysis plays a lesser role than the others, perhaps because he regards it as a collection of fragments.

For example, he sees the distinction between dreams and works of art, and he avoids the error of equating them, while he is at the same time able to recognize that some writings (e.g., *Alice In Wonderland*) are close equivalents of dreams. He is not seduced, as so many others are, into handling dream symbols like simple rebuses, since he recognizes that they are more important for their emotional concomitants than for their dictionary meanings. He understands these specific matters, and a number of others, but nowhere does he place them in a larger framework or indicate that he sees the direction of psychoanalysis or accepts its orientation. Yet he makes creative use of some psychoanalytic ideas in his criticism, such as the warning to poets that if their words do not convey their feelings to the reader this will result in the deterioration of poetry as we know it, or his discussion of the balancing of tensions in Hemingway's better works and the loss in power of those stories in which this balance is upset. It is probable that, had he been interested in learning more about psychoanalysis, he might have done even more with it.

In the work of Kenneth Burke there is a philosophical attempt to integrate psychoanalysis into a system where it has only limited relevance. He is not concerned with it as science but rather as a set of verbal symbols, some of which he seeks to fit into his critical synthesis. This limitation, further complicated by his active polemics against science in general, makes it impossible for him to understand psychoanalysis or its intentions, and causes him to regard its contribution to the elucidation of motives merely from a terminological point of view. The result is that he accuses it of dealing only with the verbal aspects of behavior, and then proceeds to do exactly this in his own synthesis. The kinds of values which he sees in words are not psychoanalytic at all but ethical and spiritual. In his view, the analyst, by receiving the analysand's "confession," becomes a figure of authority and is thereby enabled to bring about therapeutic changes. This conception is closer to the impersonal cathartic aspects of the religious confessional than to the emotional re-education which takes place within the transference situation of a Freudian analysis.

Burke's habit of dealing with motives on a quasi-philosophical basis—it is revealing that he has found it necessary to invent a special vocabulary for this—deprives him of the means of using psychoanalysis fully, and even of properly understanding it. Perhaps this arises from his opposition to science as reductionist; he refuses to see that psychoanalysis is concerned with the complexity of motives. In his earlier writings he preferred a socio-economic-political interpretation of behavior. Later he drifted toward a vocabulary with a strong religious flavor, but his religion is language as much as it is anything. His preoccupation with the verbal world insulates him from many of those aspects of life which are the subject of psychoanalytic study.

Without granting psychoanalysis much value as a systematic account of human behavior, he nevertheless agrees that certain of its ideas are useful to literary criticism. The study of imagery, for instance, can tell us something which does not appear on the surface, and it can do this even if the author is dead or otherwise unavailable to supply personal associations. In his own proposed critical method Burke finds a restricted use for psychoanalysis. It can help him only in the elucidation of unconscious factors in a poem, an aspect of poetry which he designates "dream." In this he finds useful the psychoanalytic concepts of condensation and displacement to assist in the reinterpretation of poetic language into motivational terms. He has selected these two and ignored the vast complexities which are both introduced and studied by means of the other preconscious mental mechanisms of the ego. Limiting himself thus, he says that psychoanalysis can aid in explaining the poet's wishes—especially those which might be unknown to him—that led him to write the poem. "Prayer" and "chart," the other aspects of poetry in his system, are not, according to Burke, accessible to psychoanalytic study. Over two thirds of his analysis, therefore, has no place for Freud's ideas. The reason he gives for this is that his particular interest is in the communicative functions of literature, a position he is able to take simply because he is ignorant of the direct concern of ego psychology with this very subject. As justification for his position he insists that psychoanalysis belongs only to the study of the unconscious life of individuals, and he goes far out of his way (into the field of anthropology) to attempt to show that its ideas on society are faulty and therefore may be safely disregarded. He also echoes the popular notion that psychoanalysis wishes to reduce all behavior to mechanistic categories, a notion that his synthesis is designed to correct.

The critic who has made the most of psychoanalytic ideas is Lionel Trilling. Despite some minor difficulties which he encountered in his earliest studies of Freud's writings about art, he knows more about psychoanalysis than most of his contemporaries and has a more profound grasp of it. He was the first critic to recognize from the similarity between Freud's description of our mental processes and the poet's way of thinking that the mind is a "poetry making organ." Best of all, he is able to work within a psychoanalytic orientation and still retain his critical perspective. With greater skill than the other five critics, he finds and explores the area which psychoanalysis and literature have in common.

His thorough grounding in both fields enables him to achieve more than a simple application of psychoanalysis to critical problems; his use of it is inventive, integrative and creative. One of his outstanding achievements is his extension of Aristotle's cathartic theory of tragedy with the aid of the psychoanalytic concept of the repetition-compulsion, indicating not only the immediate value of the catharsis but also the continuing uses in everyday life of experiences in the theater which can supplement our efforts to master certain emotional problems. His suggestion opens new possibilities for exploring the meaning of the drama as an art form. His comprehension of another psychoanalytic concept, the theory of the death-tendency, made it possible for him to see its implications for the enhancement of human dignity as an outcome of the magnificent struggle waged by man against inevitable dissolution. This larger understanding of the meaning of psychoanalysis and the ability to project his vision onto literary problems of the broader sort make Trilling the most important user of Freud's ideas in criticism.

*   *   *

Each of the six critics approached psychoanalytic ideas from his own critical direction, and each enlisted them in a different effort. Their practice was independent; their intentions divergent. And yet each fell victim, at least part of the time, to similar misconceptions and encountered similar difficulties, difficulties which grew not out of the idiosyncrasies of their critical positions but out of their simple human reactions to psychoanalysis. Of course, further difficulties occurred during the application of psychoanalytic ideas to their critical theses, but the basic trouble was not different from that encountered by these ideas in fields other than literature and criticism.

A notable difference between the first three critics in this study and the last three is that the second group asked less of psychoanalysis. Wilson, Trilling and Burke are past the naive stage in which men like Brooks, Krutch and Lewisohn swallowed large chunks of it whole and digested it badly. The former, either tacitly or explicitly, try to set the limits within which it will be useful to them in their criticism; for them it does not occupy the central place. As critics they view literature not only from their personal standpoints but also from a complex position, characteristic of much present-day criticism, which brings to bear upon their work a variety of non-literary disciplines. Psychoanalysis is only one of these, even though it may at moments occupy the most prominent place.

But even in the work of relatively sophisticated critics like Wilson and Burke there are gross misunderstandings of Freud's words as well as conclusions which are not justified by the psychoanalytic evidence. Furthermore, while they have a comparatively good grasp of certain specific concepts, they also exhibit a tendency to regard each of these as an independent idea, as an isolated fragment having no integral relationship with the rest of psychoanalysis. Sometimes in the course of their arguments they omit essential connecting links, evidently under the impression that their assumptions will be granted without the necessity of demonstration. This practice is curious since it is clear from the context that they wish to treat psychoanalysis as a closed system, complete for all time and therefore automatically equipped to supply such links. What is lacking—and the work of Trilling is an honorable exception to this—is a grasp of the feeling, the central direction of psychoanalysis, an understanding of its spirit and its intentions which provide the necessary setting for its facts and theories.

There seems to be a rough correlation between the progress of psychoanalytic ideas in our culture and the understanding of these ideas by literary critics. In general, those who came later knew more and used it better than their predecessors. There is a constantly growing number of critics who accept psychoanalysis as a part of the cultural milieu and use it freely, with varying degrees of competence. It is no longer the novelty that it was before, say, 1930. But the extent to which these men are influenced by psychoanalytic ego psychology is unknown, and we have yet to feel the impact of potentially important developments like the publication of Ernest Jones's biography of Freud, which has recently been completed, and the Standard Edition of Freud's complete works, an authoritative translation which is still in progress. At any rate, if we may judge from the latter three of our six critics, some improvement in the understanding and use of psychoanalysis has already taken place.

*   *   *

Psychoanalysis is not, of course, essential for literary criticism. Most critics pay little attention to it except as an incidental part of the thought of our time. But more and more are using it either in specific applications or as a tacitly assumed part of their equipment. It may be presumed that most people who read criticism will be able to understand at least simple allusions to it. Some critics, like Robert Warshow and Leslie Fiedler, handle it rather familiarly as one of the "non-literary techniques and bodies of knowledge [used] to obtain insights into literature." [1] The decision to use or not to use psychoanalysis is the critic's own affair; his work deserves to be judged on its own assumptions and its own merits just as literature does. However, if one of those assumptions is that psychoanalysis has a contribution to make to his views, then a new factor enters the equation. In that case, it seems to me, the critic has an intellectual obligation to master it

—just as he does any other non-literary technique or body of knowledge which he wishes to use—for it, like his criticism, deserves to be judged on its own merits. If he elects to use more than one non-literary discipline, then I do not see how he can escape the obligation to become competent in each of them.

Having qualified himself in all, the critic would presumably be prepared to consider the problem of their relationship to each other and to his criticism. The extent of his competence would evidently have to be governed by the extent to which he intends to integrate them into his critical thought, and since there is no way of knowing this beforehand, he is obliged to attain the highest possible level of understanding as early as he can. Such preparation would help him choose the most useful ideas for his purpose and, what is just as important, to decide which are not germane. Having made the selection he would then be in position to judge the ways in which the ideas and principles of one discipline may, and the ways in which they may not, be applied to another. As this process goes on, each would enhance the value of the other by revealing new relationships, and the critical insights, which are after all the critic's goal, would be extended and deepened.

To emphasize what is not always recognized as obvious, I repeat that the effective use of psychoanalytic ideas in literary criticism depends first of all upon a working knowledge of psychoanalysis. This does not mean that the critic must become a psychoanalyst or that he must himself be psychoanalyzed but that he ought to know what psychoanalysis tries to do, how it functions, what its successes and failures have been, what it has firmly established as fact and what it can account for only hypothetically, the limits beyond which it cannot go, the conditions under which it may have validity for fields of knowledge outside its own and finally, the degree of its applicability to a given literary situation. These goals ought, ideally, to be reached by a combination of study and experience. Among the things which should be studied are the fundamental scientific assumptions of psychoanalysis, its clinical methods, its historical and scientific development under the influence of Freud, his followers and those who differed with them, its findings, its interpretations of these in the light of psychoanalytic principles, and its possible direction in the future. The critic who did all this would recognize first of all that psychoanalysis proceeds upon scientific grounds. There is some difference of opinion as to its place among the sciences, a controversy into which I shall not enter here.[2] However, psychoanalysis applies scientific criteria to its work as far as the nature of the subject allows, being comparable in this respect to medicine, which nobody calls unscientific. Whatever one's views may be on this question, it must be remembered that the orientation and aspirations of psychoanalysis are scientific, and that it attempts constantly to uphold and maintain scientific standards in its everyday practice.

With this fundamental matter firmly in mind we may next construct a brief definition of psychoanalysis which will at the same time differentiate it from other psychologies, including those which began with Freudian principles and afterward diverged from them. Freud himself has enunciated these principles several times. One of the most concise statements of them is as follows:

> The assumption that there are unconscious mental processes, the recognition of the theory of resistance and repression, the appreciation of the importance of sexuality and of the Oedipus complex—these constitute the principal subject-matter of psychoanalysis and the foundation of its theory.[3]

Once he had established the frame of reference of psychoanalysis, the critic could study Freud's whole conception of the psyche:

> The description of mental processes involves a threefold approach to the subject. Although the psychologist is not concerned with the locality of the mind, he finds himself compelled to postulate for purposes of presentation a certain degree of mental organization which can be conveniently referred to as mental *structure*. Having done so he is then compelled to describe the *energies* which activate this organization or apparatus. Once embarked on this process he cannot stop short of describing the *mechanisms* by which the mental apparatus regulates these energies. This threefold approach constitutes what Freud termed the *metapsychological* approach to the descriptive data, either reported or introspective, that constitute the raw material of psychology.[4]

He would then be in a position to see that psychoanalysis is not confined merely to pathology or even to individual psychology, but that it has the means for studying all aspects of human behavior. And so he would emerge from a concern solely with the abnormal states of individuals and enter, as Freud did, into the study of social relationships, family attitudes, religion and art with the new insights which psychoanalysis affords into all of these.

An understanding of the help which psychoanalysis is capable of giving for the evaluation of literature and the development of critical theory can probably best be acquired by studying its concept of the ego. Its functions are many and complex, but the ones that have most concerned us here are its regulation of the psychic equilibrium and its role in bringing the individual and his environment into a satisfactory relationship.[5] Since each writer is a unique human being, a knowledge of his personality from this standpoint is bound to illuminate his artistic achievement. His works, in turn, as demonstrations of his way of contemplating and meeting certain aspects of his world, afford insights into his personality. The increasing scope of ego psychology permits greater penetration than ever before into the mysteries of art. In this respect, psychoanalysis accepts the critical dictum that the style is the man.

The extent to which psychoanalysis can illuminate literature is limited in the same way as its explorations into personality. It is only with its capacities as a scientific discipline, likewise, that it has meaning for critical theory. It provides a body of facts along with a number of hypotheses which are subject to clinical testing. The critic who wishes to make effective use of psychoanalysis needs to know how these may both circumscribe and expand his judgments. Its area of competence does not extend indefinitely; there is question how much it can ultimately reveal about the shaping, controlling and creating functions of the mind and about their influence upon finished works of art. A creative criticism will take from psychoanalysis what it has to offer and use it within the larger critical context. The values of the critic can hardly be compromised if they take into account the little that science can tell us about the truth.

NOTES

I

1. Sigmund Freud, "The *Moses* of Michelangelo," tr. Alix Strachey, *Collected Papers* (5 vols.; London: Hogarth Press, 1946), IV, 257.

2. Freud had used literary examples in his letters to Wilhelm Fliess, but these were not published until 1950 in *Aus den Anfängen der Psychoanalyse*, London, edited by Marie Bonaparte, Anna Freud and Ernst Kris. An English translation, *The Origins of Psychoanalysis*, by Eric Mosbacher and James Strachey, was published by Basic Books, Inc., New York, 1954.

3. Joseph Breuer and Sigmund Freud, *Studies in Hysteria*, tr. A. A. Brill (New York: Nervous and Mental Disease Publishing Company, 1947), p. 151.

4. Sigmund Freud, *The Interpretation of Dreams*, tr. A. A. Brill (New York: The Modern Library, 1950), p. 81. The passage refers to the shifting of quantities of psychic energy.

5. *Ibid.*, p. 346.

6. *Ibid.*, p. 354. Brill regularly translates *Dichter* as *poets*, whereas Freud uses it in the German sense meaning all literary artists.

7. Sigmund Freud, *Moses and Monotheism*, tr. Katherine Jones (New York: Alfred A. Knopf, 1939), p. 199.

8. See his assertion that Breuer was the man "who brought psychoanalysis into existence." "The History of the Psychoanalytic Movement," *The Basic Writings of Sigmund Freud*, ed. and tr. A. A. Brill (New York: The Modern Library, 1938), p. 933. See also his allocation of credit to Rank, Sachs, Abraham, Ferenczi, Jones and Brill for their discoveries and contributions, as well as numerous references *passim* to non-psychoanalysts whose work anticipated or corroborated his.

9. Freud, *The Interpretation of Dreams*, pp. 14–15.

10. Freud, *Moses and Monotheism*, p. 198.

11. Freud, "Psychopathology of Everyday Life," *Basic Writings*, pp. 84–85.

12. Sigmund Freud, *A General Introduction to Psychoanalysis*, tr. Joan Riviere (Garden City, N. Y.: Garden City Publishing Co., Inc., 1943), p. 35.

13. Sigmund Freud, "Delusion and Dream in Wilhelm Jensen's *Gradiva*," tr. Helen M. Downey, *Delusion and Dream* (New York: Moffat, Yard and Company, 1917), pp. 121–243. The first part of the book contains a translation of *Gradiva*.

14. Freud, *The Interpretation of Dreams*, p. 9n.
15. Freud, *Delusion and Dream*, p. 123.
16. *Ibid.*, pp. 198–199.
17. *Ibid.*, p. 235.
18. *Ibid.*, p. 239. A portion of Jensen's correspondence with Freud was published as "Drei unveröffentlichte Briefe von Wilhelm Jensen," *Die Psychoanalytische Bewegung*, I (September–October, 1929), 207–211.
19. Sigmund Freud, "Dostoevsky and Parricide," tr. D. F. Tait, *Collected Papers* (London: Hogarth Press, 1950), V, 239.
20. Freud, *Delusion and Dream*, p. 240.
21. *Ibid.*, p. 172.
22. Sigmund Freud, *An Autobiographical Study*, tr. James Strachey (London: Hogarth Press, 1948), pp. 116–117.
23. Sigmund Freud, *Aus den Anfängen der Psychoanalyse* (London: Imago Publishing Co., 1950), pp. 238–239. My translation.
24. He was unable, however, to establish any connection between the dreams or other psychic elements in the fantasy and corresponding events in Jensen's life.
25. Sigmund Freud, "Some Character-Types Met With In Psycho-Analytic Work," tr. E. Colburn Mayne, *Collected Papers*, IV. Part II of this paper, entitled "Those Wrecked by Success," pp. 323–341, contains the analysis of this theme in *Macbeth*.
26. Freud, *The Interpretation of Dreams*, p. 164.
27. Sigmund Freud, "A Childhood Recollection from 'Dichtung und Wahrheit,'" tr. C. M. J. Hubback, *Collected Papers*, IV, 357–367.
28. Sigmund Freud, *Leonardo da Vinci*, tr. A. A. Brill (New York: Random House, 1947), p. 120.
29. *Ibid.*
30. Freud, "Dostoevsky and Parricide," *Collected Papers*, V, 222.
31. *Ibid.*, p. 237.
32. Freud, "The *Moses* of Michelangelo," *Collected Papers*, IV, 279.
33. *Ibid.*, pp. 279–280.
34. *Ibid.*, p. 283.
35. Freud, *The Interpretation of Dreams*, p. 162.
36. *Ibid.*, pp. 162–163.
37. Sigmund Freud, *An Outline of Psychoanalysis*, tr. James Strachey (New York: W. W. Norton and Company, 1949), pp. 95–96.
38. Freud, *The Interpretation of Dreams*, p. 161.
39. Freud, "Dostoevsky and Parricide," *Collected Papers*, V, 235.
40. *Ibid.*
41. Freud, *Aus den Anfängen der Psychoanalyse*, pp. 273–274.
42. Freud, "Some Character-Types Met With in Psycho-Analytic Work," *Collected Papers*, IV, 32.
43. *Ibid.*
44. *Ibid.*, p. 331.

45. *Imago*, V (1918). Reprinted in English in Ludwig Jekels, *Selected Papers* (New York: International Universities Press, 1952). See especially pp. 126–127.

46. Freud, "Some Character-Types Met With in Psycho-Analytic Work," *Collected Papers*, IV, 332, 341.

47. Sigmund Freud, "The Theme of the Three Caskets," tr. C. M. J. Hubback, *Collected Papers*, IV, 244–256.

48. *Ibid.*, p. 253.

49. *Ibid.*, p. 255.

50. *Ibid.*

51. Freud, *Leonardo da Vinci*, p. 120.

52. Freud, *An Autobiographical Study*, pp. 119–120.

53. Breuer and Freud, *Studies in Hysteria*, p. 12.

54. Sigmund Freud, "Formulations Regarding the Two Principles of Mental Functioning," tr. M. N. Searl, *Collected Papers*, IV, 17.

55. Sigmund Freud, "The Relation of the Poet to Daydreaming," tr. I. F. Grant Duff, *Collected Papers*, IV, 181.

56. Freud, *Delusion and Dream*, p. 179.

57. Fantasy is used here in the psychoanalytic sense. It includes all aspects of the author's state of mind, conscious and unconscious, intellectual and emotional, perceived and imagined.

58. Freud, *Delusion and Dream*, p. 240.

59. Freud, "The Relation of the Poet to Daydreaming," *Collected Papers*, IV, 173.

60. *Ibid.*, p. 174.

61. Sigmund Freud, "Civilization and Its Discontents," tr. Joan Riviere, *Civilization, War and Death* (London: Hogarth Press, 1939), p. 31.

62. Freud, *A General Introduction to Psychoanalysis*, p. 327.

63. Freud, "Formulations Regarding the Two Principles of Mental Functioning," *Collected Papers*, IV, 19.

64. Sigmund Freud, "Group Psychology and the Analysis of the Ego," *Standard Edition of the Complete Psychological Works of Sigmund Freud* (London: Hogarth Press, 1955), XVIII, 136–137.

65. Sigmund Freud, "Totem and Taboo," *Basic Writings*, p. 927.

66. Freud, "The Relation of the Poet to Daydreaming," *Collected Papers*, IV, 182.

67. Freud, *Moses and Monotheism*, p. 112.

68. Freud, *An Outline of Psychoanalysis*, pp. 95–96.

69. Freud, *A General Introduction to Psychoanalysis*, p. 89.

70. Freud, "The Relation of the Poet to Daydreaming," *Collected Papers*, IV, 180.

71. Freud, "The *Moses* of Michelangelo," *Collected Papers*, IV, 258.

72. Freud, "The Relation of the Poet to Daydreaming," *Collected Papers*, IV, 183.

73. *Ibid.*

74. Sigmund Freud, "Contributions to the Psychology of Love. A Special

Type of Object-Choice Made by Men," tr. Joan Riviere, *Collected Papers,* IV, 192.

75. Freud, *Delusion and Dream,* p. 171.

76. Sigmund Freud, "The Uncanny," *Collected Papers,* IV, 403–404.

77. Freud, "Psychopathology of Everyday Life," *Basic Writings,* p. 86.

78. Freud, *The Interpretation of Dreams,* p. 164.

79. *Ibid.,* p. 229.

80. *Ibid.,* pp. 229–230.

81. Sigmund Freud, "Wit and Its Relation to the Unconscious," *Basic Writings,* pp. 638, 750.

82. *Ibid.,* p. 803.

83. Freud, "Some Character-Types Met With in Psycho-Analytic Work," *Collected Papers,* IV, 323.

84. Sigmund Freud, *Beyond the Pleasure Principle,* tr. C. M. J. Hubback (London: Hogarth Press, 1942), p. 43.

85. Sigmund Freud, "Das Interesse in der Psychoanalyse," *Gesammelte Werke* (London: Imago Publishing Company, Ltd., 1948), VIII, 416. My translation.

86. Freud, *Civilization, War and Death,* p. 32.

87. *Ibid.,* p. 34.

88. Sigmund Freud, " 'Civilized' Sexual Morality and Modern Nervousness," tr. Joan Riviere, *Collected Papers* (London: Hogarth Press, 1946), II, 92.

89. Freud, *A General Introduction to Psychoanalysis,* p. 327.

90. Freud, *Aus den Anfängen der Psychoanalyse,* p. 222. My translation.

91. Freud, *A General Introduction to Psychoanalysis,* pp. 327–328.

92. Freud, "Das Interesse in der Psychoanalyse," *Gesammelte Werke,* p. 416. My translation

II

1. Sigmund Freud, *Die Traumdeutung* (Leipzig und Wien: Verlag Franz Deuticke, 1900), p. 183. In Brill's translation, *The Interpretation of Dreams* (New York: Modern Library, 1950), pp. 163–164.

2. Ernest Jones, *Hamlet and Oedipus* (New York: W. W. Norton and Company, 1949).

3. *Ibid.,* p. 21.

4. *Ibid.,* p. 20.

5. Jones, "The Problem of Hamlet and the Explanations Proffered," *Hamlet and Oedipus,* pp. 20–44.

6. *Ibid.,* p. 43.

7. Jones, *Hamlet and Oedipus,* pp. 52–53.

8. Cf. the soliloquy "O that this too too solid flesh would melt . . ." which expresses his depression.

9. Jones, *Hamlet and Oedipus,* pp. 64–65.

10. *Ibid.*, p. 70.

11. It is important to reject the notion that Hamlet was insane, for if this were the case there could be no play. The psychotic, having lost touch with reality, cannot furnish any drama except by contrast with his former state, as Lear and Ophelia demonstrate. No development or new revelation of character is possible, and nothing is left but death.

For those who are interested in clinical data Dr. Jones remarks that Hamlet's disorder is not a psychosis but a psychoneurosis: "If I had to describe such a condition as Hamlet's in clinical terms—which I am not particularly inclined to—it would have to be as a severe case of hysteria on a cyclothymic basis.

"All this, however, is of academic interest only. What we are essentially concerned with is the psychological understanding of the dramatic effect produced by Hamlet's personality and behaviour."—*Ibid.*, p. 68.

12. *Ibid.*, p. 18.

13. *Ibid.*, p. 11.

14. *Ibid.*, p. 12.

15. *Ibid.*, p. 114.

16. *Ibid.*, pp. 114–120.

17. Ernest Jones, "The Death of Hamlet's Father," *Essays in Applied Psychoanalysis* (London: Hogarth Press, 1951), I, 326–327.

18. *Ibid.*, p. 327.

19. William Silverberg, review of "*Hamlet*. By William Shakespeare. With a Psychoanalytic Study by Ernest Jones, M. D.," *The Psychoanalytic Quarterly*, XVIII, No. 1 (1949), 85.

20. Jones, *Hamlet and Oedipus*, pp. 81–82.

21. *Ibid.*, pp. 61–62.

22. *Ibid.*, p. 88.

23. Silverberg, *op. cit.*, p. 85.

24. Jones, *Hamlet and Oedipus*, p. 26.

25. This approach has been adopted by Maude Bodkin as the basis for her book, *Archetypal Patterns in Poetry*, but her orientation is Jungian rather than Freudian.

26. Jones, *Hamlet and Oedipus, passim.*

27. Jones, "The Death of Hamlet's Father," *Essays in Applied Psychoanalysis*, p. 325.

28. *Ibid., passim.* Also Jones, *Hamlet and Oedipus, passim.*

29. Jones, "The Death of Hamlet's Father," *Essays in Applied Psychoanalysis*, p. 326.

30. Jones, *Hamlet and Oedipus*, pp. 155–156.

31. *Ibid.*, p. 14.

32. Ernest Jones, "The Madonna's Conception Through the Ear," *Essays in Applied Psychoanalysis*, II, 267.

33. Ernest Jones, "The Problem of Paul Morphy: A Contribution to the Psychology of Chess," *Essays in Applied Psychoanalysis*, I, 194.

34. Jones, *Hamlet and Oedipus*, p. 75.

35. (London: Cambridge University Press, 1935.) In his preface to the third edition (1956) Dr. Wilson remarks that he is unconvinced by Dr. Jones's exposition of the supposed character of Hamlet off the stage. "And when he [Dr. Jones] gathered from these pages that I believed 'personality' in *Hamlet* to be 'consistent' I realized that my chapter VI had been written in vain, as far as he was concerned, and that we must go our several ways each convinced he is being misunderstood by the other."—p. vii.

III

1. Hanns Sachs, *The Creative Unconscious* (Boston: Sci-Art Publishers, 1942), p. 11.

2. Sachs uses Unconscious to include Preconscious as well.

3. He states: "The word 'poet' will be used here indiscriminately, whether the production be lyrical, dramatic or narrative. The words 'fictionist' or 'word-illusionist' would be more expressive, but 'poet' will do."—*Ibid.*, p. 12.

4. *Ibid.*, p. 15.

5. *Ibid.*, pp. 16–23.

6. *Ibid.*, p. 23.

7. *Ibid.*, pp. 24–33.

8. *Ibid.*, p. 37.

9. *Ibid.*, p. 38.

10. *Ibid.*, pp. 44–45.

11. *Ibid.*, pp. 46–47.

12. *Ibid.*, p. 48.

13. He presented a copy to Freud at their first meeting. See Hanns Sachs, *Freud, Master and Friend* (Cambridge: Harvard University Press, 1944), p. 50.

14. After being forced to suspend publication because of the rise of Hitler, it was reconstituted in Boston as the *American Imago* by Sachs, who continued as its editor from 1939 until his death in 1947. Since then publication has been maintained under the editorship of Dr. George Wilbur at South Dennis, Massachusetts.

15. This group consisted of Otto Rank, Karl Abraham, Max Eitingon, Ernest Jones, Sandor Ferenczi, Hanns Sachs and Freud. To each of the others he gave a ring set with a carved stone "as a mark of his special friendship and regard." See *Freud, Master and Friend*, Chapter VIII.

16. *Ibid.*, p. 136.

17. Dr. Richard F. Sterba of Vienna and Detroit.

18. *The Creative Unconscious*, p. 153.

19. *Ibid.*, pp. 153–154.

20. *Ibid.*, pp. 157–158.

21. *Ibid.*, p. 162.

22. *Ibid.*, p. 164.

23. *Ibid.*, pp. 165–171.

24. *Ibid.*, pp. 176–192.

25. *Ibid.*, pp. 195–210.

26. *Ibid.*, pp. 211–219.

27. *Ibid.*, pp. 233–239.

IV

1. Ernst Kris, *Psychoanalytic Explorations in Art* (New York: International Universities Press, 1952), p. 14. The chapter from which this quotation is taken has been rewritten and enlarged from a series of three lectures given at the London Institute of Psychoanalysis. A shorter version, in German, of these lectures was published under the title "Probleme der Aesthetik" in *Internationale Zeitschrift für Psychoanalyse und Imago*, XXVI, 1941. The title and certain parts of the chapter were taken from a paper written for *Psychoanalysis Today*, edited by Sandor Lorand (New York: International Universities Press, 1946).

2. *Ibid.*, p. 17.

3. *Ibid.*, p. 265. The chapter from which this quotation is taken (Chapter 11 of *Psychoanalytic Explorations in Art*) was originally published in *The Psychoanalytic Quarterly*, XV, 1946.

4. *Ibid.*, p. 18.

5. See Ernest Jones's paper on Andrea del Sarto for one approach to this problem.

6. Hanns Sachs, *The Creative Unconscious* (Boston: Sci-Art Publishers, 1942). See also Chapter III of the present book.

7. Kris, *op. cit.*, p. 22.

8. Chapter VI of Freud's *The Interpretation of Dreams*.

9. Kris, *op. cit.*, p. 24.

10. This means, according to Freud, that the artist is able to admit forbidden or painful material to preconscious elaboration to a greater extent than less well-endowed persons can.

11. Kris, *op. cit.*, p. 21.

12. *Ibid.*, pp. 31–32.

13. *Ibid.*, pp. 303–318. See also p. 343n. Chapter 14 of *Psychoanalytic Explorations in Art*, from which this quotation was taken, is based on a paper presented at the annual meeting of the American Psychoanalytic Association in 1949 and was published in *The Psychoanalytic Quarterly*, XIX, 1950. It has been reprinted in *The Yearbook of Psychoanalysis*, VII, edited by Sandor Lorand (New York: International Universities Press, 1951). A slightly different version has been reprinted in part with extensive annotations by David Rapaport in his *Organization and Pathology of Thought, Selected Sources* (New York: Columbia University Press, 1951).

14. Sigmund Freud, "The Anatomy of the Mental Personality," *New In-*

troductory Lectures on Psychoanalysis (New York: W. W. Norton, 1933), pp. 82–112.

15. *Ibid.*, p. 96. Chapter 3 of *Psychoanalytic Explorations in Art* (pp. 87–127), from which this quotation was taken, is based on a paper read to the Academic Association for Medical Psychology in Vienna in May 1936, and published in *Imago*, XXII, 1936.

16. Heinz Hartmann, Ernst Kris and Rudolph M. Loewenstein, "Notes on the Theory of Aggression," *The Psychoanalytic Study of the Child*, III/IV (New York: International Universities Press, 1949), 9–36.

17. Kris, *Psychoanalytic Explorations in Art*, pp. 26–27.

18. *Ibid.*, pp. 27–28.

19. Hartmann, Kris, and Loewenstein, *op. cit.*, p. 21.

20. Kris, *op. cit.*, pp. 28–29.

21. *Ibid.*, p. 30.

22. *Ibid.*, pp. 64–84.

23. Kris offers this as a summary of "what we have learned from myth, folklore, and literary traditions."—*Ibid.*, pp. 165–166.

24. *Ibid.*, p. 166.

25. *Ibid.*, p. 317.

26. *Ibid.*, p. 61.

27. By analogy with the dream work. See Chapter VI of *The Interpretation of Dreams* and *Wit and its Relation to the Unconscious*.

28. Ernst Kris, "On Preconscious Mental Processes," in David Rapaport, *Organization and Pathology of Thought*, p. 485.

29. Kris, *Psychoanalytic Explorations in Art*, p. 313.

30. *Ibid.*, pp. 64–84. Chapter 2 of *Psychoanalytic Explorations in Art*, entitled "The Image of the Artist," is based on a paper read to the Vienna Psychoanalytic Society in 1934. It was published in *Imago*, XXI, 1935, under the title "Zur Psychologie älterer Biographik (dargestellt an der des bildenden Künstlers)" and reprinted in the *Almanach der Psychoanalyse*, 1937.

31. Otto Rank, *The Myth of the Birth of the Hero* (New York: Robert Brunner, 1952).

32. Kris, *Psychoanalytic Explorations in Art*, p. 67.

33. Lawrence Kubie, "The Fundamental Nature of the Distinction Between Normality and Neurosis," *Psychoanalytic Quarterly*, XXIII (April, 1954), pp. 167–204. See especially pp. 189–200 for the author's defense of his definition against various objections.

34. *Ibid.*, p. 182.

35. Kris, *Psychoanalytic Explorations in Art*, p. 62.

36. *Ibid.*, p. 54.

37. Kris adopts this concept from Paul Schilder, *The Image and Appearance of the Human Body* (New York: International Universities Press, 1950).

38. Kris, *Psychoanalytic Explorations in Art*, p. 56.

39. *Ibid.*, p. 256. Chapter 10 of *Psychoanalytic Explorations in Art* (pp.

243–264) from which this quotation was taken was originally published in *Philosophy and Phenomenological Research*, VIII, 1948.

40. James Thurber, "What Cocktail Party?" *Thurber Country* (New York: Simon and Schuster, 1953), pp. 219–229.

V

1. Van Wyck Brooks, *The Ordeal of Mark Twain* (New York: E. P. Dutton, 1920), p. 14.

2. *Ibid.*, p. 25.

3. See Stanley Edgar Hyman, *The Armed Vision* (New York: Alfred A. Knopf, 1948), pp. 106–126.

4. Brooks, *op. cit.*, p. 31

5. See Chapter IV of this book. See also Kris, *Psychoanalytic Explorations in Art,* Chapter II.

6. Brooks, *op. cit.*, p. 40.

7. *Ibid.*, p. 42. It is possible that Brooks had in mind here the work of Morton Prince on dissociated states of personality, but these do not meet the requirements of his thesis, either.

8. Except that he has not yet established the presence of any artistic talent in the young Sam Clemens. The realization can therefore be only as a man, not as an artist.

9. See Freud, *The Interpretation of Dreams, The Ego and the Id*, and Chapter IV of this book, *passim.*

10. Brooks, *op. cit.*, pp. 47, 48.

11. As we have seen in Kris, psychoanalysis holds that the activity of the artist, while it shares certain features with the activity of all other people, is a specific and unique combination.

12. Brooks, *op. cit.*, pp. 51–52.

13. *Ibid.* See pages 33, 34, 175 and 183 for examples.

14. *Ibid.*, p. 17.

15. *Ibid.*, pp. 179–180.

16. *Ibid.*, p. 196.

17. *Ibid.*, p. 186.

18. It is not only or always this. The wishes appearing in a dream may be openly acknowledged and quite acceptable ones. Material other than wishes nearly always comprises part of a dream. The dream is always the fantasied fulfillment of a wish, "suppressed" or otherwise.

19. This is evidently an assumption that a dream contains nothing except the central idea or, perhaps better, the representation of the dominant impulse. It may be stated that there is no simplicity in dreams if one looks below the surface. Even if a dream consists of only one impression which refers to only one psychic fact, clinical experience shows that the dreamer's

associations lead to all sorts of complicated connections with other facets of psychic life and that these must be included in the "meaning" of the dream. Freud made this abundantly clear in *The Interpretation of Dreams*.

20. This is a little better, but it does not show (as Freud does) that the incoherence, nonsense and absurdity appear as such only to our conscious mind with its reliance upon reason and logic. When we learn the laws of the dream, its seeming incongruities begin to make very good sense. Incidentally, the "compromise" is seldom as simple as a train wreck.

21. They are related, but it makes a great deal of difference whether a given wish is dreamed or acted out. A private pictorial representation is not at all the same thing as a public action which reveals what one would rather keep hidden. The revelations to be gained about a literary artist from his work are something else again.

22. It is not ideals which are repressed; these require consciousness for their very existence. Aggressive and erotic wishes may be kept unconscious for psychic reasons. And it is a far cry from overt sexuality to ideals. If by satisfactions he means here not the gratification of bodily appetites to which I have just referred but something more spiritual, moral or aesthetic, then he misconceives the nature of that which is unconscious by reason of its emotional unacceptability (as distinct from that which is unconscious simply because it is not needed at the moment and to which there would be no objection if it should become conscious).

23. According to psychoanalysis this process should be visible (in varying degrees) in everything Mark Twain ever did, not merely in his "fantasies." We reveal ourselves not only through what slips out when we attempt to hide it, but also through what we choose to tell and how we go about doing it. For psychoanalytic purposes all of Mark Twain's works are potentially informative, and so are his letters, speeches and casual conversations. If anything, the non-literary expressions are likely to be easier to interpret as revelations of character since they need not be modified for aesthetic reasons.

24. This is as true today as it was in 1920. See for example Robert Fliess, *The Revival of Interest in the Dream* (New York: International Universities Press, 1953).

25. Brooks, *op. cit.*, p. 264.

26. *Ibid.*, p. 265.

27. *Ibid.*

28. *Ibid.*, pp. 265–266.

29. *Ibid.*, p. 202.

30. I venture to say that his social analysis of the Gilded Age sustains his thesis far better, but this is outside the scope of my study. It would be interesting to have the opinions of historians, social psychologists and anthropologists on the matter.

31. Van Wyck Brooks, *The Writer in America* (New York: E. P. Dutton, 1953). See pp. 127, 153, and 164.

VI

1. Joseph Wood Krutch, *Edgar Allan Poe* (New York: Alfred A. Knopf, 1926).

2. *Ibid.*, pp. 234–235.

3. *Ibid.*, p. 17.

4. *Ibid.*, p. 139. This is rather ambiguous. How deeply is "deeply enough"? Ultimately a psychic level is reached which is so far removed from any thoughts that a prejudgment is impossible. That is, if I am interpreting his use of "prejudice" correctly and if I understand what he means by "rooted."

5. See note 17, below.

6. Krutch, *op. cit.*, pp. 57–86.

7. *Ibid.*, pp. 169–170. See also p. 187.

8. *Ibid.*, p. 7.

9. *Ibid.*, p. 38. David Poe deserted his family when Edgar was 18 months old.

10. *Ibid.*, p. 112.

11. In *The Interpretation of Dreams* and *Wit and Its Relation to the Unconscious.*

12. Krutch, *op. cit.*, pp. 77–78, 113–114.

13. Marie Bonaparte, *The Life and Works of Edgar Allan Poe* (London: Imago Publishing Co., Ltd., 1949), Chapter XLV, pp. 639–668.

14. *Ibid.* See especially pp. 1–206.

15. See, for instance, Krutch, *op. cit.*, pp. 85–87 and pp. 57–62.

16. *Ibid.*, pp. 75, 77.

17. *Ibid.*, p. 200.

18. *Ibid.*, p. 198.

19. *Ibid.*, p. 234.

20. *Ibid.*, pp. 194, 195.

21. *Ibid.*, pp. 64, 182, 201.

22. See Chapter IV of this book.

23. Krutch, *op. cit.*, p. 176.

24. Bonaparte, *op. cit.*, p. xi.

VII

1. Ludwig Lewisohn, *The Story of American Literature* (New York: The Modern Library, 1939). First published in 1932 under the title of *Expression in America* (New York: Harper and Brothers, 1932).

2. *Ibid.*, p. vii.

3. *Ibid.*, pp. 1–2.

4. *Ibid.*, p. ix.

5. *Ibid.*, p. vii.

6. *Ibid.*, p. 8. It was John Cotton who wrote this.

7. *Ibid.*, p. 3. The presence of counter-influences such as those of Roger Williams and the Quakers is acknowledged but minimized since they did not constitute part of the main stream of American development during this period.

8. *Ibid.*, pp. 71–104.

9. *Ibid.*, pp. 108, 112, 116.

10. *Ibid.*, pp. 137–139.

11. *Ibid.*, p. 112.

12. *Ibid.*, pp. 151–152.

13. *Ibid.*, p. 155.

14. A glance at the bibliography of Sigmund Freud alone will show the relatively advanced stage which psychoanalysis had reached by this time.

15. *Ibid.*, pp. 158–164.

16. In so far as art serves a purely psychic function it does so by partial and intermittent gratification of tendencies within us which are latent but which cannot remain forever bottled up. A person suffering from necrophilia who reads certain of Poe's stories would require something stronger than the slight easing of tension which they afford normal readers. The reinforcement which they would give to his already powerful fantasies would probably render impossible the controlled expression necessary for a true aesthetic response and would result only in a pathological one.

17. *Ibid.*, pp. 158–167.

18. *Ibid.*, pp. 170–173.

19. *Ibid.*, p. 174.

20. "Since his soul held few or none of the ordinary interests of mankind his historical touches even in the 'Legends of the Province House' are but the echoes of his inner malady: embodied guilt in the form of pestilence stalks in and the inevitable *Doppelgänger* fantasy appears in 'Howe's Masquerade.' "—*Ibid.*, p. 178.

21. "He jots down the notion, extremely revelatory in its form: 'A man to swallow a small snake—and it to be a symbol of a cherished sin.' "—*Ibid.*, p. 177.

22. *Ibid.*, pp. 180–181.

23. *Ibid.*, pp. 185–186.

24. *Ibid.*, p. 527.

25. See, for instance, the psychography of Jack London.—*Ibid.*, pp. 324–326.

26. As in the discussion of Henry Adams.—*Ibid.*, pp. 342 ff.

27. *Ibid.*, p. 375.

28. *Ibid.*, p. 310.

29. *Ibid.*, pp. 459–460.

VIII

1. Stanley Edgar Hyman, "Edmund Wilson and Translation in Criticism," *The Armed Vision* (New York: Alfred A. Knopf, 1948), pp. 19–48. See especially pp. 24–25.

2. Edmund Wilson, "The Historical Interpretation of Literature," *The Triple Thinkers* (New York: Oxford University Press, 1948), pp. 257–270. See especially p. 257.

3. Edmund Wilson, "Philoctetes: The Wound and the Bow," *The Wound and the Bow* (New York: Oxford University Press, 1947), pp. 272–295. See especially p. 294.

4. Hyman, *op. cit.*, p. 35.

5. See Chapter I of this book, p. 21, *et passim*. See also Freud's *Collected Works, passim*, for other such remarks.

6. See Chapter I of this book, pp. 32, 33 and note 57.

7. See Chapter IV of this book, particularly the references to the advanced work in psychoanalytic ego psychology by Hartmann, Kris and Loewenstein.

8. See Chapter I of this book.

9. See Chapter I and IV of this book.

10. See Chapter IV of this book.

11. This is not to argue that the artist must be normal. The process referred to here may break down at any point and leave only a neurotic "solution" open to him. In this discussion "the artist" means "the successful artist," at least psychically.

12. Hyman, *op. cit.*, pp. 33–34.

13. It should be remembered that the book contains essays written (or copyrighted) in 1929, 1932, 1938, 1940 and 1941, respectively, and, in accordance with Wilson's usual practice, presumably revised for publication in the book.

14. Wilson, "Dickens: The Two Scrooges," and "The Kipling That Nobody Read," *The Wound and the Bow*, pp. 1–104; 105–181.

15. Wilson, "Dickens: The Two Scrooges," *The Wound and the Bow*, p. 6.

16. *Ibid.*, pp. 57, 101–103.

17. *Ibid.*, pp. 69 ff. and 94 ff. This is also the hidden meaning which Lewisohn found in "The Figure in the Carpet." See his *The Story of American Literature*, p. 260.

18. Wilson, "The Ambiguity of Henry James," *The Triple Thinkers*, pp. 88–132.

19. Edmund Wilson, "A Dissenting Opinion on Kafka," *Classics and Commercials* (New York: Farrar, Straus and Company, 1951), pp. 387–388, for example.

20. Edmund Wilson, "Marcel Proust," *Axel's Castle* (New York: Charles Scribner's Sons, 1950), pp. 176 ff.

21. Edmund Wilson, "Byron in the Twenties," *The Shores of Light* (New York: Farrar, Straus and Young, Inc., 1952), p. 62.

22. See Chapter IV of this book, particularly the reference to Kubie, p. 113.

23. Edmund Wilson, "Hemingway: Gauge of Morale," *The Wound and the Bow*, pp. 241–242. This assertion, by the way, is opposed as a question of fact by Carlos Baker in *Hemingway, The Writer as Artist* (Princeton: Princeton University Press, 1952) on the ground that Hemingway never actually became a Stalinist. See Chapter X, pp. 223–263.

24. Wilson, "Van Wyck Brooks's Second Phase," *Classics and Commercials*, p. 11.

25. Wilson, "The Muses Out of Work," *The Shores of Light*, pp. 203–204.

26. He criticizes Krutch's *Poe* as "a rather half-baked performance: incomplete, depending too much on a Freudian oversimplification, insufficiently sympathetic with its subject and somewhat distracted in its judgments by what one might call the despair hysteria of the period."—Wilson, "Reëxamining Dr. Johnson," *Classics and Commercials*, p. 245.

27. Wilson, "Byron in the Twenties," *The Shores of Light*, p. 66.

28. Wilson, "Upton Sinclair's Mammonart," *The Shores of Light*, p. 215.

29. Wilson, "Reëxamining Dr. Johnson," *Classics and Commercials*, p. 245.

30. Wilson, "Sophocles, Babbitt and Freud," *The Shores of Light*, p. 474.

31. *Ibid.*, pp. 472–473.

32. Wilson, "The Historical Interpretation of Literature," *The Triple Thinkers*, p. 270.

33. Wilson, "The Ambiguity of Henry James," *The Triple Thinkers*, p. 96.

34. The topographical revision of the conception of the psyche from that of an unconscious, a preconscious and conscious to that of an id, an ego and a superego. See Freud, "The Anatomy of the Mental Personality," in the *New Introductory Lectures* (New York: W. W. Norton, 1933). It is a curious example of cultural lag that even some psychoanalysts still speak of The Unconscious as though they were not aware that, psychoanalytically, "unconscious" is no longer a noun but an adjective. As a substantive the word is widespread among the laity but in ignorance and not as Sachs, for example, uses it to mean "that portion of the psyche which is unconscious."

35. Wilson, "Poe at Home and Abroad," *The Shores of Light*, pp. 189–190.

36. Wilson, "C. L. Dodgson: The Poet Logician," *The Shores of Light*, p. 545.

37. *Ibid.*, p. 543.

38. Wilson, "Dream Poetry," *The Shores of Light*, p. 691.

39. Wilson, "James Joyce," *Axel's Castle*, p. 227.

40. Freud, *The Interpretation of Dreams*, p. 279.

41. *Ibid.*, pp. 285 ff.

42. Wilson, "Dream Poetry," *The Shores of Light*, p. 693.

43. Wilson, "Poe at Home and Abroad," *The Shores of Light*, pp. 181, 185.

44. Wilson, "A Dissenting Opinion on Kafka," *Classics and Commercials*, p. 391.

45. *Ibid.,* p. 385. This also illustrates one of Wilson's weaknesses in the use of psychoanalysis, namely a lack of precision in terminology. Manias occur only in psychoses, not in "neurotic states." In another place ("James Joyce," p. 228) he speaks of the subconscious. Neither the word, nor the concept which it presumably represents, exists in psychoanalysis. This, however, is a common mistake made by people interested in the arts; it is not unique with Wilson. It is a fair assumption when this word appears in a literary context that the person who wrote it does not understand (a) its meaning, (b) the distinction between it and unconscious or the unconscious and (c) the reasons why Freud objected to its use. Among the latter are: that it would lead to confusion with the revised conception of psychic topography, and that it does not mean unconscious in the psychoanalytic sense.

46. *Ibid.,* p. 390.

47. Wilson, "George Saintsbury: Gourmet and Glutton," *Classics and Commercials,* p. 368.

48. Wilson, "Hemingway: Gauge of Morale," *The Wound and the Bow,* p. 234.

49. Wilson, "J. Dover Wilson on Falstaff," *Classics and Commercials,* pp. 162–163.

50. See, for instance, some of the changes described by Freud in the *New Introductory Lectures on Psychoanalysis.*

51. See Wilson's essays on Kipling, Hemingway and James.

52. Wilson, "The Historical Interpretation of Literature," *The Triple Thinkers,* p. 266.

53. *Ibid.*

54. See *The Wound and the Bow, passim.*

55. Wilson, "The Historical Interpretation of Literature," *The Triple Thinkers,* pp. 266–267.

IX

1. Kenneth Burke, *Permanence and Change* (New York: New Republic, Inc., 1936), pp. 164–193.

2. This was Freud's chief concern in his later years. See Chapter I of this book.

3. Burke does not specify these, a serious omission in the light of the controversy about what is psychoanalysis and what is not.

4. *Permanence and Change,* p. 168.

5. *Ibid.,* p. 165.

6. *Ibid.,* pp. 166–167.

7. Later in this chapter we shall see his ready acceptance of McDougall's suggestion that political life supplies the patterns for motivation. In this way the alleged deficiency in psychoanalytic theory is repaired and the importance of sexuality, so difficult for many people to consent to, is diminished.

8. *Permanence and Change,* p. 168.

9. *Ibid.,* pp. 173–174.

10. *Ibid.,* pp. 174–175.

11. *Ibid.,* p. 191.

12. Kenneth Burke, *The Philosophy of Literary Form* (Baton Rouge: Louisiana State University Press, 1941), pp. 258–292. This essay originally appeared in the Freud number of the *American Journal of Sociology* (1940).

13. *Ibid.,* pp. 261–263.

14. There is one later. See his reference to the concept of the libido.—*Ibid.,* p. 266.

15. See Chapter III of this book for the way Hanns Sachs uses it in his theory of the experience of beauty.

16. *The Philosophy of Literary Form,* p. 266.

17. *Ibid.,* pp. 263–264.

18. It is plain that Burke has no intimate knowledge of American factory workers, a distinct economic and social group who nevertheless exhibit the same psychic disturbances as people from other segments of the economy.

19. *The Philosophy of Literary Form,* p. 264.

20. *Ibid.,* p. 267.

21. *Ibid.,* pp. 5–6.

22. *Ibid.,* p. 272.

23. For his argument in full see pp. 272–277.

24. *Ibid.,* pp. 277, 278.

25. *Ibid.,* p. 281.

26. *Ibid.,* pp. 244, 283n, 283.

27. *A Grammar of Motives, A Rhetoric of Motives* and the projected *A Symbolic of Motives.*

X

1. Lionel Trilling, "Freud and Literature," and "Art and Neurosis," *The Liberal Imagination* (New York: Viking Press, 1950), pp. 34–57; 160–180. See also Lionel Trilling, "The Poet as Hero: Keats in his Letters," *The Opposing Self* (New York: Viking Press, 1956), pp. 3–49.

2. "Freud and Literature," *The Liberal Imagination,* p. 34.

3. *Ibid.,* p. 35.

4. See Ernest Jones, *The Life and Work of Sigmund Freud* (New York: Viking Press, 1955), I, *passim.*

5. "Freud and Literature," *The Liberal Imagination,* pp. 40–46.

6. *Ibid.,* pp. 41–42.

7. Ernest Jones, *op. cit.*

8. "Freud and Literature," *The Liberal Imagination,* p. 42.

9. *Ibid.,* pp. 42, 44, 46.

10. *Ibid.,* p. 42.

11. *Ibid.,* pp. 47–48.

12. Ernest Jones, *Hamlet and Oedipus* (New York: W. W. Norton and Company, 1949), p. 16.

13. *Ibid.*, p. 20.

14. "Freud and Literature," *The Liberal Imagination*, p. 49.

15. Sigmund Freud, *The Interpretation of Dreams* (New York: The Modern Library, 1950), p. 163.

16. *Ibid.*, p. 164.

17. "Freud and Literature," *The Liberal Imagination*, pp. 41–42.

18. Ernest Jones, *Hamlet and Oedipus*, Chapter II.

19. "Freud and Literature," *The Liberal Imagination*, p. 52.

20. *Ibid.*, pp. 52–53.

21. *Ibid.*, pp. 54–56.

22. *Ibid.*, p. 57.

23. This originally appeared in 1945, five years after "Freud and Literature."

24. "Art and Neurosis," *The Liberal Imagination*, pp. 162–164.

25. This brings him into conflict with the theory of Dr. Edmund Bergler, but he shows that Bergler himself later abandons this idea when he postulates his "basic neurosis."

26. *Ibid.*, pp. 169–175.

27. See Chapter IV of this book.

28. "Art and Neurosis," *The Liberal Imagination*, p. 177.

29. *Ibid.*, pp. 178, 179.

30. *The Liberal Imagination*, pp. 281–303. See especially p. 302.

31. Lionel Trilling, "Contemporary American Literature in its Relation to Ideas," *American Quarterly*, I, No. 3 (Fall, 1949), 201.

32. "The Meaning of a Literary Idea," *The Liberal Imagination*, p. 293.

33. "Wordsworth and the Rabbis," *The Opposing Self*, p. 148.

34. See note 1.

35. *The Opposing Self*, p. 19.

36. *Ibid.*, p. 31.

37. *Ibid.*, pp. 36–37.

38. *Ibid.*, pp. 32–45.

39. Lionel Trilling, *Freud and the Crisis of Our Culture* (Boston: The Beacon Press, 1955), p. 17.

40. "The Poet as Hero: Keats in his Letters," *The Liberal Imagination*, p. 40.

41. *Freud and the Crisis of Our Culture*, p. 26.

42. *Ibid.*, pp. 34–59.

Notes to Summary

1. Stanley Edgar Hyman, *The Armed Vision* (New York: Alfred A. Knopf, 1948), p. 3.

2. See, for example, Ernest R. Hilgard, Lawrence S. Kubie and E. Pumpian-Mindlin, *Psychoanalysis As Science* (Stanford, California: Stanford University Press, 1952).

3. Sigmund Freud, "Psycho-Analysis," *Collected Papers* (London: Hogarth Press, 1950), V, 122.

4. Edward Glover, *Freud or Jung* (New York: W. W. Norton and Company, 1950), p. 21.

5. No adequate historical account of the psychology of art has yet been written, but the first four chapters of this book provide a workable outline. For this, plus clinical and theoretical considerations, the following are among the most important sources:

The Standard Edition of the Complete Psychological Works of Sigmund Freud (24 vols.; London: The Hogarth Press and the Institute of Psychoanalysis, 1953–1955). This is a new definitive translation of which 11 volumes have already appeared.

Anna Freud, *The Ego and the Mechanisms of Defence* (New York: International Universities Press, 1946).

Ernst Kris, *Psychoanalytic Explorations in Art* (New York: International Universities Press, 1952).

Sigmund Freud, *The Origins of Psycho-Analysis* (New York: Basic Books, Inc., 1954). This is a translation of his letters to Wilhelm Fliess, drafts and notes from 1887 to 1902.

David Rapaport, *Organization and Pathology of Thought* (New York: Columbia University Press, 1951).

INDEX

Adler: mentioned, 227
Adolescence: fantasy and, 30
Aesthetic distance, 99
Aesthetic experience: as result of
tacit agreement with the artist, 45
Aesthetic illusion, 98-99, 116
Aesthetics: and psychoanalysis, 73-76;
relation between biography and,
232
Antigone: mentioned, 172
Aristotle: on tragedy, 213-14
Art: and psychoanalysis, 1-2; as normal psychic activity, 42; psychic
function, 42-43; and sexuality, 43;
and neurosis, 44; social function of,
stressed by psychoanalysis, 44; as
communication, 45-46; daydreams
and, 66; and vocational choice, 107-
09; as psychic restitution, 114-15;
of psychotics, 114-15
Artist: psychological insights of, 4, 7,
8, 31, 38; and alteration of reality,
24, 38-39; daydreams and, 64; his
work and psychic life, 93; as God's
instrument, 109; as God's rival, 109;
and God, 112; image of, 112-15
Artistic activity: psychic equilibrium
maintained by, 32; fantasty in, 33
Artistic creativity: problem of, 61-63
Artistic experience, 82
Artistic form: as expression of ideas,
45; attracting function of, 69
Art-work: definition of, 94; process of
elaboration, 111
Audience: effect of play upon, 47; its
response to art, 115-19
Author: daydreams of, 36

Barnum, P. T.: Lewisohn on, 149
Beauty: the idea of, 74-75; universal
experience of, 74-75; as experience,
77; and psychic quantities, 77-79;
and sexuality, 77-79; and the id,
79-83; stasis and, 80-83; death-instinct in, 89
Biography: relation between aesthetics and, 232
Bonaparte, Marie, 138, 142, 144
Bound energy, 102-03
Breuer, Josef: mentioned, 3
Brooks, Van Wyck: conception of the
unconscious, 125-26, 128-29; view of
art as a cipher, 129; ideas on dream
interpretation, 130-32; opposition
to science, 132; use of "repression,"
132
Brothers Karamazov, The: as Oedipal
drama of parricide, 20-21
Burke, Kenneth: and motives, 183-85;
and psychosis, 186-87, 189; and
genitality, 191-92; and libido, 191-
92; and psychoanalysis in his critical scheme, 195-201; quasi-religious
orientation, 197-98
Byron: mentioned, 169

Cathexis: shift of, 70-71; and self-
identity, 221
Character: as expression of author's
personality, 47-48
Childhood: and Oedipus Complex, 17
Clemens, Samuel: feminine identifica-
tion of, 123-24
Coleridge: mentioned, 116
Communication: art as, 45-46

259

Concealment in art, 68-69
Condensation, 197, 234
Conflict-free ego sphere, 231
Creative thinking, 99
Creativity: and passivity, 109-10
Critic: and psychoanalysis, 237-40
Criticism, literary: psychoanalysis in, 225

Daydreams: of author, 36; and artist, 64; and language, 65; and literature, 15; formlessness of, 65; and art, 66; mutual, 67-69
Death-instinct: in beauty, 89; mentioned, 213
Death: the approach to, 25
Delusions: in fiction, 7
Desdemona: mentioned, 3
Displacement, 197, 234
Dostoevsky: mentioned, 11, 21; motivations of, 12-13
Dramatic impact: Oedipus Complex as component of, 27
Dream poetry: T. S. Eliot on, 174
Dreams: in fiction, 7; Oedipus Complex and, 17, 228; latent vs. manifest, 230; and works of art, 230-33
Dream symbolism, 228

Ego, 100
Ego, artist's: strength of, 118-19
Ego, conflict-free sphere of: and Lewisohn, 153
Ego functions: autonomy of, 94; secondary autonomy in, 106
Ego psychology, 95, 144, 147, 211, 217, 220, 234, 237
Elaboration (art-work), 110-12
Eliot, T. S.: on dream poetry, 174
Emerson: Lewisohn, 145-50
Energy: bound, 102-03
Equilibrium, psychic: maintained by artistic activity, 32
Eros vs. Thanatos: in Sachs's Theory, 74
Expression: and inhibition, 38-40

Fallacy: genetic, 211
Fantasies: aggressive and erotic, 64-65
Fantasies, hysterical: poetry and, 44
Fantasy: play and, 29, 97-98; and

adolescence, 30; in artistic activity, 33; as used by the artist, 45; mentioned, 48; social role of, 66-68; as a means of gratification, 84-87; psychoanalytic sense of, 243, n.57
Fantasy, psychotic: elaboration of, 114
Fiction: dreams in, 7
Fiedler, Leslie, 237
Form: in art and the psyche, 71-73; inseparable from content, 81-83
Freud, Sigmund: on art, 2-3; analysis of Hamlet's motives, 10; on Michelangelo's *Moses*, 15-17; analysis of *Oedipus Rex*, 18-19; analysis of the theme of the three caskets, 25-26; and Marx, 199; conception of tragedy, 213-14

Genetic fallacy, 211
Genitality: Burke and, 191-92
Genius, 62, 144
Glover, Edward, 92
Goethe: childhood episode, 12; mentioned, 3, 5, 11, 12
Gradiva: corroborates theory of dreams and delusions, 6; mentioned, 8
Guilt: Oedipus Complex and, 24

Hamlet: Freud's analysis of motives, 10; sexual aversion of, 11; as played by Laurence Olivier, 19; irresolution, 47-48; loathing for his mother, 49; applicability of science to his character, 49; aboulia of, 49-50; Oedipal motives in, 50-51; feeling of unworthiness, 51-52; as fictional character studies by psychoanalysis, 52; neurosis of, 245, n.11
Hamlet: mentioned, 19, 20, 21; unworthiness of, 20; incest theme in, 58; parricide theme in, 58; development of, from its sources, 59-61; Trilling on, 208-12
Hamnet: mentioned, 55
Hawthorne: Lewisohn on, 152-55, 232
Holmes: Lewisohn on, 149

Id: and beauty, 79-83
Ideas: artistic form as expression of, 45

Identification, feminine: of Sam
Clemens, 123-24
Id psychology, 95
Image of the artist, 112-15
Incest motive for women: and Re-
becca Gamvik, 21-22; and *Rosmer-
sholm*, 21
Incest theme in *Hamlet*, 58
Inhibition: expression and, 39-40; lan-
guage and, 39-40
Inseparability of form and content,
93
Inspiration, 110-12

James, Henry: women characters, 172;
and sex, 192
Jensen, Wilhelm, 6, 8, 242, n.18
Joyce: debt to Freud, 175
Jung: and *Gradiva*, 6, 227

Kafka, 177
Keats: Trilling on, 220-23
King Lear, impact of, 26-27
Krutch, Joseph Wood: and psychic
determinism, 136; equating of stories with dreams, 137-38; and the
genetic fallacy, 142; conception of
creativity, 142

Language: and inhibition, 39-40; daydreams and, 65
Leonardo da Vinci: vulture fantasy,
12, 14-15; symbolic representation
of his mother, 14-15, 93-94
Lewisohn, Ludwig: and psychoanalysis, 146-48, 157-60; on Holmes, 149;
on Lowell, 149; on P. T. Barnum,
149; on Emerson, 149-50; on Thoreau, 149-52; on Melville, 152; on
Poe, 152-53, 156; on Hawthorne,
152-55; on Mark Twain, 156
Libido: Burke and, 191-92
Literature: daydreams and, 65; mythology and, 92
Lowell, Lewisohn on, 149

Macbeth, Lady: wrecked by success,
22-23; mentioned, 24
Macbeth: wrecked by success, 22-23

Macbeth: and the theme of childless-
ness, 23-24; mentioned, 24
Malinowski, Bronislaw, 196
Marx: Freud and, 199
Mastery of reality as gratifying, 99
Mastery through repetition, 96-97
McDougall, 188
Melville: Lewisohn on, 152
Meyer, Conrad Ferdinand: author of
Die Richterin, 21
Mind: as poetry making organ, 235
Motives: Burke and, 183-85
Multiplicity of meaning in dreams
and poems, 40-42
Mythology: and literature, 92

Negative capability, 221
Neurosis: and art, 44
Neurosis, Poe's: according to Krutch,
139-42
Neutralization: sublimation and, 104-
107
Normal: attempted psychoanalytic
definition of, 114-15

Oedipal myth: and psychoanalysis, 35
Oedipus Complex: as universal, 9-10,
21; and childhood, 17; and dreams,
17; and legend of Oedipus, 17; and
guilt, 24; as component of dramatic
impact, 27; mentioned, 47, 92, 196,
228; Shakespeare's, 56-57
Oedipus, legend of: and Oedipus
Complex, 17
Oedipus Rex, of Sophocles: source of
name for Oedipus Complex, 18;
mentioned, 35
Othello: mentioned, 3
Overdetermination, 54, 95

Parricide theme in *Hamlet*, 58
Passivity: creativity and, 109-10
Play: and fantasy, 29, 97-98; effect of,
upon audience, 47; of children, 96;
purpose of, 96; symbolization and
abstraction in, 96-97; functional
pleasure in, 99
Poe: relationship of life to works,
139-40; his neurosis according to
Krutch, 139-42; Lewisohn on, 152-
53, 156

Poetry: and hysterical fantasies, 44
Preconscious mental activity, 99-102
Primary process, 102
Process: primary, 102
Psychic distance: from work of art, 116-19
Psychic energy: shifting of, 71, 99
Psychic equilibrium: maintained by artistic activity, 32
Psychic life: as emotional, 31
Psychic quantities: and beauty, 77-79
Psychoanalysis: and art, 1-2; scope of, 1-2; limitations of, 1-2, 28-29; corroborated by artist's intuitions, 5-7; and aesthetics, 73-76; Lewisohn and, 146-48, 157-60; in Burke's critical scheme, 195-201; and poem as dream, 198-99; Trilling's ambivalence toward, 202-03, 215-16; in literary criticism, 225; and the critic, 237-40
Psychosis: Burke and, 186-87, 189
Psychotics: art of, 114-15

Quantities, psychic: and beauty, 77-79

Rebecca Gamvik: and incest motive for women, 21-22; wrecked by success, 22; mentioned, 24
Religion: and art, 98-99
Repetition compulsion: in play, 85-87; mentioned, 213
Repression: flexibility of, 94, 108, 127
Restitution: art as psychic, 114-15
Richterin, Die: 21, 24
Rosmersholm: and incest motive for women, 21

Sachs's theory: Eros vs. Thanatos in, 74
Schiller: cited, 5
Secondary autonomy in ego functions, 106
Secondary process, 102; as core of creative thinking, 103-04
Self-identity: cathexis and, 221
Sex: and Henry James, 192
Sexuality: and art, 43; and beauty, 77-79

Shakespeare: mentioned, 4, 11, 47-48; theme of childlessness in, 11; *Richard III*, 42; bisexuality, 54; Oedipus Complex of, 56-57; Sonnets, 56, 57
Shelley, 169
Shifting of psychic energy, 71, 99
Social function of art: stressed by psychoanalysis, 44
Social role of fantasy, 66-68
Sophocles: mentioned, 18
Stasis: and beauty, 80-83
Sublimation: in the artist, 43, 62, 127; and neutralization, 104-07
Superego: in aesthetic experience, 87-89

Thanatos, 222-23
Theme of the Three Caskets: analyzed by Freud, 25-26
Thoreau: Lewisohn on, 149-52
Trilling, Lionel: ambivalence toward psychoanalysis, 202-03, 215-16; confusion of scientific and literary ideas, 205; on Freud's attitude toward art, 205-11; on *Hamlet*, 208-12; and Jones, 212; view of the mind as a poetry making organ, 212; on Wilson's wound-and-bow theory, 216-18; on Keats, 220-23
Twain, Mark: pessimism, 120-21; relationship to his mother, 122, 125; Lewisohn on, 156, 170

Unconscious: Brooks's conception of, 125-26, 128-29
Universal experience of beauty, 74-75

Vocational choice: and art, 107-09
Vocational success, 108

Warshow, Robert, 237
Wilson, Edmund: wound-and-bow theory, 161-66; historical approach to literature, 166-67; on Dickens, 167; on Kipling, 167-68; on Henry James, 168; on Samuel Butler, 168; on Hemingway, 168, 177-78, 181-82; on Proust, 168-69; on Byron, 171; on Poe, 171, 176-77; understanding of dreams, 173-76; and the uncon-

scious, 179; and dream theory, 179; on Freud and Marx, 180-82

Wilson, J. Dover: Jones's reliance on, 48; mentioned, 63, 179; reply to Jones, 246, n.35

Wit: condensation in, 40-42; source of psychic pleasure in, 42

Words: in dreams, 175

Works of art: dreams and, 230-33

Wound-and-Bow theory, Wilson's: 168, 170; Trilling on, 216-18

Writer: and play, 32-33; and reality, 33-34, 38-39; and myth, 35

Zweig, Stephan: and psychoanalysis, 8